They Foresaw the Future
The Story of Fulfilled Prophecy

Justine Glass

THEY FORESAW THE FUTURE

The Story of Fulfilled Prophecy

G. P. Putnam's Sons
New York

for
Doreen Valiente, whose help in the
research connected with this book
has been invaluable

FIRST AMERICAN EDITION 1969
Copyright © 1969 by Justine C. Glass

All rights reserved. This book, or parts thereof, must
not be reproduced in any form without permission.

Library of Congress Catalog Card Number: 74-85286

PRINTED IN THE UNITED STATES OF AMERICA

Contents

	Introduction	7
1	Divination in Ancient Egypt	11
2	Augury in Ancient Rome	25
3	The Oracles Speak	39
4	Druid Seers	54
5	Prophecy in the Ancient East and West	68
6	The Saints and the Plowboy	88
7	Prophecies of the French Revolution	103
8	Great Seers of History	112
9	The Brahan Seer and Thomas the Rhymer	130
10	Astrologer Royal and Prophecies About Monarchs	143
11	Witches' Warnings	161
12	Curses Fulfilled	171
13	Dreams: Doorway to the Unconscious	189
14	Modern Seers (I)	212
15	Modern Seers (II)	229
16	What Lies Ahead?	239
	Index	249

Heaven sends down its good or evil symbols,
and wise men act accordingly.

        KUNG FU-TSE (CONFUCIUS, *c.* 551-478 B.C.)

Introduction

Once again prophecy is important. After long years during which its status was reduced from that of a "noble science" to the level of myth or fable, the seal of probity has been set upon it by science, which has "discovered" not only that prevision is a fact, but that its existence affirms the action of nonmaterial agencies, which could be related to spirit—or soul.

The late Dr. Alexis Carrel, great physiologist and biologist and Nobel Prize winner, said, "The facts of prediction of the future lead us to the threshold of an unseen world. They seem to point to the existence of a psychic principle capable of evolving outside the limits of our bodies." Professor J. B. Rhine, the American pioneer parapsychologist, expanded the theme:

> The scientific tests that were initiated by prophetic dreams have already led to the discovery of a new fact about the human mind, a discovery so radical as to call for an eventual revolution in basic human thought. Perhaps the most significant finding that has emerged is that there is known to be present in the personality an aspect that is unbound by the space and time of matter—hence a non-physical or spiritual aspect. Its boundaries and its capacity for growth may well be beyond the limits of our present power to conceive. . . . Is it not then provocative, to say the least, to discover certain capacities of mind that appear to operate beyond the boundaries of space and time within which our sensorial, bodily sys-

tem has to live and move? Here, surely, if ever, "hope sees a star," and the urge toward an inquiry into the question of survival receives valuable impetus and encouragement.

Of this almost unexplored sphere, Sir James Jeans said, "Mind no longer appears as an accidental intruder in the realm of matter. We are beginning to suspect that we ought rather to hail it as the creator and governor of the realm of matter." And Professor Sir Alister C. Hardy, president of the zoological section of the British Association, told a meeting at Newcastle on Tyne that he believed "the communication of one mind with another, other than through the ordinary senses, had been established, and that it had passed scientific tests."

No one knows what mind is, but then no one knows what electricity really is, or energy, or radiation, or how solar systems and nebulae originate. What we do know about mind is that it works independently of time and space and that prophecy, being an activity of mind, is not subject to these limitations either.

Prevision belongs to the spiritual sphere in which we live, as science is demonstrating and proving. Here nothing is old; nothing is new. There is neither past nor future; all things in this world have always existed and will always exist; it is the realm of ideas, of matrices from which the forms of the outer world manifest themselves.

We gain glimpses of this reality beyond appearances through the workings of prophecy; through growing understanding of its nature, we may learn at least enough of this mysterious world to enable us to live in greater harmony than is possible when functioning only on the physical level.

And perhaps of all reasons for its renewed importance the most important, prophecy may offer us a means of knowing —as distinct from hope or blind faith—that immortality is reality.

They Foresaw the Future
The Story of Fulfilled Prophecy

1. Divination in Ancient Egypt

About 6,000 years ago, the Egyptian Empire came into being. From its earliest days it was a center of knowledge, the range of which we may not even now have discovered fully. Its religion Sir Ernest Wallis Budge, the great Egyptologist and keeper of Egyptian antiquities in the British Museum, describes as being of "a lofty spiritual character," to which prophecy, magic (high magic, not sorcery and demonology into which it degenerated and with which it is too often confused in our own times), and the occult arts generally were fundamental. The priesthood was believed to have almost limitless powers; clairvoyance and the art of predicting the future with mathematical exactitude were part of the novice's training.

Egypt was the birthplace of the horoscope. To a Greek nativity scroll in the British Museum is attached a letter in which an astrologer urges his pupil, Hermon, to be "very exact and careful in his application of the laws which the ancient Egyptians, with their laborious devotion to the art, had discovered and had handed down to posterity." India and Persia are believed to have learned astrology from the Egyptians, and even Chaldaea, which later became so famous for skill in the science that the terms "Chaldaean" and "astrologer" were synonymous. But if this is so—and it is a generally accepted opinion—who taught the Egyptians to read the skies?

It is not known, any more than the origin of the Egyptians themselves is known. Even the color of their skins is uncertain. Some authorities believe it was black; others are equally sure it was red. Costaz thinks they were a brownish-complexioned race. Professor François Lenormant puts forward another theory: "The Egyptians painted on the tombs of the first dynasty were yellow." There is even a school of thought which considers that the early Egyptian was white. Painted on the walls of the Edfu temple is the story of Horus and his battles, in which he overthrew Typhon and all his enemies, who were of four different types. The black men were driven out of Egypt to the south; the yellow men to the north; the white men to the west, and the ancient Arabs (a brownish race) to the east. Édouard Naville, writing about the temple in 1870, discusses the possibility that, as in so many cases, tradition (or myth) may be founded on historical fact. If this were so, according to the process of elimination the Egyptians were red-skinned.

There is even more controversy about where the race came from or if it came from anywhere. M. Beauregard says: "The Egyptian civilization, absolutely autochthonous, and certainly the most ancient of all the civilizations of the globe, is consequently the only one whose originality is incontestable." Another theory, which Plato mentions and which might possibly be an explanation of the mystery, is that Egypt was colonized by the inhabitants of the continent often called Atlantis, submerged in the legendary cataclysm believed to have taken place about 800,000 years ago. A picture of this possible mass immigration has been built up from ethnological, botanical, geological, and archeological clues, one of which is the excavation of ships or boats, obviously seagoing, the date of the construction of which is assessed as much earlier than that of any others found in the country. At any rate, it is a theory explaining how there appeared in the Nile Valley, inhabited in the Stone Age by primitive savages, who had no knowledge of science or even a system of writing, a full-blown civilization with a culture of a very high order: art forms, philosophy, an evolved religion, of which the most powerful and integrated system of magic known to the world was a basic part.

To the Egyptians, magic was religion. "Magic was considered as a sacred science, or sacred art, inseparable from religion," says Deveria. So naturally it followed that the priest was also a magician, who could, according to what we call today informed sources, levitate, bear great pressure without harm, walk on air, submerge himself under water for long periods, suffer mutilation without ill effect, handle fire without being burned, dematerialize, travel astrally, read thoughts, read the past from the Akashic records, foretell the future.

The great temple teachers of the magical arts were known as the Rehk-get-Amon; their pupils were not necessarily priests. They might be initiates of the Mysteries, whose innate powers had been developed through training, by long hours of meditation, prayer, and fasting. Joseph was said by Justin Martyr to have reached a high degree of attainment, of which his interpretation of Pharaoh's dream of the fat and lean kine is an example. The Egyptian magical tradition laid down that the practitioner must use some object as focus for the divinatory powers; a special type of cup was the most common. Joseph apparently used this method when making his prophecies. Other means of divination used were arrows without points, trees, birds, clouds, and so on.

Egypt had her oracles, too, which were famous in the ancient world, credited even by the early Christian Fathers. Clement of Alexandria, St. John Chrysostom, Justin Martyr, Origen, St. Jerome, St. Cyprian, Tertullian, Tatian and St. Augustine—all believed in the validity of the predictions made by them. The oracle, the voice of the god, spoke from the adytum of the temple, through specially trained priestesses—probably mediumistic—who made prophecies, displayed clairvoyant or telepathic powers, perhaps talked with spirits.

Spirits were a very real and ever-present threat to men

and women at that time. Spirits could cause distress, could bring ill fortune and could possess a victim. Against their ill will the only defense was magic, by which they could be exorcised or conciliated, according to the formulas used by the priests.

The priests dealt efficiently with the trouble, of mind, body, or estate, which was brought before them. Perhaps they accepted the explanation of the miraculous cause of the cure, perhaps, as seems more likely from Professor Lenormant's judgment of the qualities and level of development of priesthood, they did not. They would have known that it was much easier to let the people go on believing in the agency of gods and spirits than to give them an explanation of a truth which they could not then understand. Professor Lenormant says:

> They were highly educated scientific men. They understood the nature of the loadstone, the virtues of the mineral, and animal magnetism, which, together with the force of psychological impression, constituted a large proportion of their theurgic practice. They perfectly understood the art of reading the inmost secrets of the soul, of impressing the susceptible imagination by enchantment and fascination, of sending their own spirits forth from the body, as clairvoyants, under the action of powerful will—in fact they were masters of the arts now known as mesmerism, clairvoyance, electro-biology, etc. They also realized the nature of magnets, herbs, drugs and fumigations and employed music to admirable effect.

Perhaps we do not yet all know all that they knew. With so many of our modern "discoveries" they had been acquainted for centuries—for example, the fact that rats spread plague. When Thebes was besieged by Sennacherib's armies a large golden image of a rat, upon which the heirophants had worked according to their formulas (among them was probably the ritual known as tying), was set on the city's walls, in full view of the enemy. Very soon afterward, it is recorded, the invaders were decimated by a terrible epidemic of plague.

Magic and mysticism and the exalted doctrines of early Egyptian religion were believed to stem from the founder of Magism, Thoth, whom the Greeks called Hermes Trismegistus, the thrice great. The numerous books he wrote were destroyed in an Egyptian revolution, except for two fragmentary documents. In one of these, the *Poemandre,* he sets down his conception of God as an infinite, omnipotent being, a balance of eternal, active intelligence and absolute wisdom. He said of astrology, "Fortunate is he who knows how to read the signs of the times, for that man shall escape many misfortunes, or at least be prepared to withstand the blow." He might have added—always supposing the warning is not ignored, which happened in the case of one of his few surviving prophecies. Of the fate of his country he said, "O Egypt, a time shall come when instead of a pure religion and an intelligent cult, you shall have nothing left but ridiculous fables that posterity will find incredible, and there shall nothing remain to you but words graven upon stone, almost indecipherable monuments to your ancient piety." The religion and magical arts of Egypt in time were debased, the fate of all cults and traditions, however great. And the world accepted, because there was no one to disclose the truth, that the Egyptians were animal worshipers—and all has come to pass as Thoth foretold.

In the reign of Sesostris II (1906-1887 B.C.), Chechepetresonbu, a priest of Heliopolis of the Hermetic tradition, had a prophetic vision, fulfilled about 1,000 years later. He saw, he said, "the ideal ruler for whose advent he longs—he brings cooling to the flames. It is said he is the shepherd of all men. There is no evil in his heart . . . where is he to-day? . . . Behold his might is not seen."

This was by no means the only prophecy made in Egypt concerning the birth of Christ. Hundreds, even thousands, of years before he was born, predictions current in the land gave evidence that its priests already knew of the purpose of

Christ's coming, of His life and teachings, of the Last Supper and the way in which He was to die.

It was in visions, or dreams, that the will of the gods and their revelations of the future were most often manifested in ancient Egypt. When a priest received a dream message, he could, naturally, interpret it himself; the man or woman in the street called in the services of one of the "official" temple prophets, who were a body distinct from the rest of the priesthood. They were trained in a school of seers from which graduates became first, scond, or third prophet of a god. The top grade, or high priest, was always an *epistalae,* or temple superintendent, in charge of its finances. But every grade of priest who could interpret dreams held high honors because of the Egyptians' unshakable belief in their important role as vehicle for divine guidance and inspiration.

Thutmose IV (about 1420 B.C.) was given a dream message while he was a prince and a little doubtful of his chances as ruler. In a vision the god Harmachis-Chepera Re-Tenu came to him promising him that if he cleared away the sand which had silted up around the Sphinx (the god's image), he would be given sovereignty of the south and north, in fact, all Egypt. The prince put the work in hand at once, and a stele, dated the nineteenth day of the month of Hathor, carrying an edict of King Thutmose IV shows that the promise in the dream was kept.

The success story of Tanuat-Amon, who was co-ruler of Egypt with his uncle Taharka, during the last years of his reign, came about because of guidance in a prophetic dream. When Ashurbanipal of Assyria attacked Egypt, Taharka fled to Nubia, where he died. His nephew felt strongly that he should succeed him, but as Taharka's armies had been destroyed in the struggle with the Assyrians, who by then were masters of Lower Egypt, the problem was whether he would be wise even to try to mount an attack against them and regain power.

While he was still waiting and wondering—and the Assyrians were strengthening their position—Tanuat dreamed one night of two serpents which coiled one on his left and one on his right. The priest-interpreter told him that the serpents, which were symbols of the goddesses Nekhebet and Uachat, whose domain was north and south Egypt respectively, indicated sovereignty over both parts of the country and Nubia as well. In spite of his apparent weakness in resources, he was to go forth, and he would conquer.

Tanuat marched into the countryside, where "Millions, and hundreds of thousands of men" rallied to him. Convinced that the dream was working out, he crossed into Nubia, where he met a similar reception. In the temple of Amon at Napata (Amon of the Holy Mountain) the god acknowledged him as king (he "looked upon the face of the god"). After making a feast in honor of Amon and endowing the sanctuary with thirty oxen, forty gallons of oil and a hundred "shu," he passed on, his way a succession of triumphs. From Aswan (Syene) and Thebes, he went to Memphis, which tried to resist him; he reduced it and reached the delta, where the princes of the north, after a short bout of fighting, submitted to him. And Tanuat-Amon rejoiced, saying, "What the god told me by night hath come to pass by day."

A similar prophecy was made to Nut-Amon (*c.* 670 B.C.); again it was fulfilled. He was told: "All the land of the south is thine, and thou shalt have dominion over the land of the north. The White Crown and the Red Crown shall adorn thine head. The length and breadth of the land shall be given unto thee, and the god Amon, the only god, shall be with thee."

Sometimes on an occasion which was to see the beginning of important events, the gods or goddesses themselves made prophecies in person, as when Isis, Nephthys, and Meskhent went to the house of Re-user. Meskhent helped to deliver his wife, Red-edet, who was in labor, of three boys. As each child was born, Meskhent said, "He shall be a king who shall have dominion over the whole land." The prophecy seemed impossible of fulfillment at that time; since the boys were triplets, its unlikelihood was tripled. But later each of Re-user's sons became a king of the Fifth Dynasty.

The story really begins in the reign of Cheops, about 2580 B.C., when his son, Prince Har-dedef, said to his father, "So far you have only heard old stories of magic. You don't know if they are true or not, but there is one in your own time who is a great magician, a citizen called Dedi, who lives at Ded-Snefru. He is one hundred ten years old, he still eats five hundred loaves, one ox joint a week and drinks ten jugs of beer a day. He can restore a head to the body from which it has been cut off; make a lion follow him; he can raise the dead; he knows the number of the locks of the Sanctuary of Thoth."

This intrigued Cheops, who wanted the locks of Thoth for the pyramid he was building. First he questioned Dedi, whom he had sent for, about his magic. When Dedi had confirmed that he could restore life after decapitation, Cheops ordered that a prisoner condemned to death should be brought in for the magician to demonstrate upon. But Dedi said, "I will not do this thing to a human being. It is forbidden to use one of the noble flock so."

So a goose was given to him, the head of which he cut off, saying, "Put the goose's body on the west side of the hall, and its head on the east side." Then, as Dedi performed his ritual, the goose got up and waddled toward its head, the head approached the body, with which it was united, and the goose went off, cackling. When Dedi had dealt with a duck and then a bull in the same way, Cheops asked him what he knew about Thoth's locks. "I know not the number," Dedi answered, "but I know where they are."

They were hidden, he said, in a flint box in a room called the Revision in a house in Heliopolis. They would be brought to the Pharaoh, he prophesied, by the oldest of three children, "who are in the womb of Red-edet."

Cheops wanted to know who Red-edet was; Dedi told him she was the wife of a priest of Re, Re-user, of Sakhebu (between Memphis and Heliopolis). "All the children will be kings, and the oldest boy will be High Priest of Heliopolis."

Seeing Cheops' downcast look, Dedi said, "Why are you sad? Is it because you fear that if the three children of Red-

Divination in Ancient Egypt 19

edet reign in Egypt, your son will be dispossessed? If so, I tell you that your son, Chephren, and his son (then unborn), Mycerinus, will be kings of the Fourth Dynasty. Then the sons of Red-edet will establish the Fifth Dynasty." And in the Fourth Dynasty—whose rulers were considered impious (because they built pyramids instead of temples) and oppressive—and in the Fifth Dynasty, the prophecies of Meskhent and Dedi came to pass.

Dedi evidently pleased Cheops by his prediction that the Pharaoh's line was secure at any rate down to the third generation. As a sign of royal pleasure, he was given a pension, the first installment of which he took away with him—1,000 loaves, 10 oxen, 100 jugs of beer, and 100 bundles of garlic.

A prophecy recorded personally by one of the pharaohs of the Fourth Dynasty, Snefru (1905-65 B.C.), was made by the lector-priest ("he who carries the ritual") of Bubastis in the eastern half of the delta, from neither a dream nor a vision nor a trance. Nefer-Rohu, seer and magician, initiated into the sacred writing of Bast, was called in by the Pharaoh, who was feeling bored, to beguile his tedium by foretelling the future, from scratch, as it were.

The priest asked the Pharaoh, "Shall I tell you what is past or what is to come?" To which Snefru answered: "Rather of what is to come." Whereupon Nefer-Rohu launched into forecast of coming events which must have been without entertainment value for the Pharaoh. The priest predicted the downfall of the Old Kingdom, struggles and chaos, and eventual establishment of order by Amenemhet, first king of the Twelfth Dynasty. "Foes have come down in the East, and Asiatics have come down into Egypt. The wild beasts of the desert will drink the waters of Egypt. . . . Men will make arrows of metal [metal arrowpoints were first used in the Eleventh Dynasty], beg for the bread of blood, and laugh with the laughter of sickness. . . . The land is diminished, but its administrators are many [a land poorer and smaller always has more bureaucrats and more exacting taxes relatively than a large prosperous country]. . . . I show the land topsy-turvy . . . men salute him who formerly saluted. . . . Then it is that a king will come belonging to the South, Ameni the Triumphant his name. He is the son of a woman in the land of Nubia; he is one born in Upper Egypt. He will take the White Crown; he will take the Red Crown. He will encircle the fields, the oar is in his grasp. [As part of the coronation ceremonies, the Pharaoh, grasping an oar, dedicated a field by running around it four times.] Rejoice, ye people of his time; justice will come into its place, while wrongdoing is driven out."

The prophecy eventually proved to be accurate, but it was scarcely the entertainment for which Snefru had asked. Perhaps its solemnity was a reminder to Snefru that prophecy must not be used as a parlor game. Prophecy was the will of the gods made known to man, whose duty it was to live according to that will. When two courses of action, both moral, opened, the god foretold the future and indicated the right course for the man to take, which his human intelligence could not perceive. "Verily," said Amenemope, the great teacher, "thou knowest not the plans of God, and thou discernest not the morrow."

Divine advice put Thutmose II (about 1500 B.C.) on the road to kingship. While he was still a boy, watching the procession of Amon around the hypostyle hall of his temple, the god noticed him and halted; telling Thutmose, who had prostrated himself, to rise and follow him to the part of the temple called the Station of the Lord, Amon there recognized the boy publicly as king.

Amon's guidance came to Thutmose's sister, Queen Hatshepsut, when she was supplicating at the step of his throne for counsel as to how the country's prosperity could be expanded. She heard the voice of the god in command and prophecy, saying, "The ways to Punt should be searched out and the roads to the myrrh terraces opened." And so she organized her famous expeditions to Punt, still to be seen pictured on the walls of her tomb, through which spices and incense and new plants and trees were brought to Egypt, and a flow of trade which increased the country's wealth.

Very few rulers would initiate a war without reference to a god. When Thutmose IV (about 1420 B.C.) heard while he was in Thebes that a rebellion had broken out in Nubia, he consulted Amon on whether he should open a campaign and on the outcome if he did fight. Amon told him that he should make war in Nubia, and that it would be 100 percent successful—as it was.

Only a very rash man would go against a divine direction, and since the gods were consulted concerning everything of importance, they virtually ruled Egypt at one time. The oracle of Amon-Re at Thebes even chose the next king, when, after the death of the old monarch in the sixth century B.C., there was confusion about which of his sons was the rightful heir. The oracle chose Aspelta, foretelling that he would have a prosperous and successful reign, and that he would rebuild all the temples of Egypt. Aspelta, perhaps taking the latter part of the prediction as a hint from Amon, put the work of reconstruction in hand. He had, as the god foretold, a satisfyingly fortunate reign.

To "sleep on a problem" in ancient Egypt meant that a night was spent in the temple, during which the god sent prophetic dreams or visions and counsel on how difficulties could be overcome. A woman named Mehitousket, who had been married for many years, brought the enigma of her childlessness to the temple of Imouthes (Imhotep), the great healer.

In a dream, Imouthes said to Mehitousket, "Tomorrow go to the fountain of Satni, with your husband. You will find a root of colocasia sprouting there . . . pull it up with its leaves; make a remedy with it, which you will give to your husband. Then you will lie next to him, and you will conceive of him that same night." And Mehitousket, having followed Imouthes' instructions, did conceive, and in due course bore a child.

Thoth, the god of wisdom and magic, came to the rescue of one of his followers, a magician who, in competition with more skillful colleagues, had reached the end of his resources. This man went to Thoth's city, Hermopolis, to pray for the god's help. In a dream Thoth revealed to him the existence of an all-powerful formula, used by Thoth himself. The magician found the formula in the place indicated by the god, copied it as instructed, and returned to triumph over his rivals.

For century upon century, Egypt's history, too, had been a story of triumph, of victory over other nations, which she had outstripped in knowledge and practice of science, the arts and development of an enlightened civilization. She had achieved a greatness as colossal as her monuments, extensive as her cities.

The vast and splendid temple of Karnak was symbolic of the wide sweep of Egyptian vision. So immense were its columns that their shafts could hardly be spanned by six men with arms outstretched, touching fingertip to fingertip, so lofty, that their capitals, carved in the shape of a full-blown lotus, seemed to end among the stars.

No-Amon (the abode of Amon), the Egyptian name of Thebes, the ancient capital, was 1¾ miles in circumference, with walls 24 feet thick and 45 cubits high, according to Diodorus Siculus, who only saw it when it was in ruins, in 50 B.C. It was built in about 2000 B.C. The glory of Thebes passed when Cambyses, invading Egypt in about 525 B.C., sacked and destroyed it. Memphis was made the new capital, and though Thebes sprang up again, it never regained its former greatness. The fate of Thebes had been foretold. In Ezekiel 30:14-16, a prophecy is recorded: "And . . . I will execute judgments in No . . . and I will cut off the multitude of No . . . and No shall be rent asunder." And after it had been restored to something of its former splendor by Ptolemy Lathyrus, it was finally destroyed in 89 B.C., almost leveled to the ground. In 25 B.C. Strabo found all that remained of what once had been a majestic city, divided into separate villages, as are its ruins today . . . "No shall be broken up."

Divination in Ancient Egypt 23

Nebuchadnezzar's invasion of Egypt was predicted, too, in Ezekiel 29-30. Egypt would be held in captivity, said the prophet, the land left desolate for forty years. Then would come a restoration of independence to the country, but not of greatness. "Neither shall it exalt itself any more above the nations . . . her foundations shall be broken down . . . the pride of her power shall come down."

Memphis, which took the place of Thebes as capital of Egypt (Noph was its native name), had been founded by Menes, first king of what is believed to be the First Dynasty of pharaohs. Strabo said it extended a day's journey in every direction. Next to Alexandria in size, it was famous for the beauty of its temple statuary, which was singled out in a prophecy of doom made in Ezekiel 30:13. "I will also destroy the idols, and I will cause their images to cease out of Noph."

Today, a broken colossus of Rameses the Great lies facedown in a muddy pool, submerged with each Nilotic inundation. Near him is a smaller red granite statue, also facedown in the mud. A few sculptured fragments are scattered on the river's bank. Nothing else is left of Memphis' splendor; the pylons, obelisks, avenues of sphinxes—all are gone. The prophecy promised destruction of the "idols" and that the "images should cease out of Noph," and the prophecy has been fulfilled. In Memphis and in no other place in Egypt, "idols" and "images" have been utterly razed and obliterated. No extinction of the race or of the kingdom was predicted. The picture was one of deterioration and decay: "There shall be there a base kingdom." Today Egypt is still a country, inhabited by Egyptians, but the power and the glory which were theirs in the past are lost.

The last of her kings was Nectanebo, a magician, prophet, and skilled astrologer, so skilled in the art that through it, it is said, he was able to circumvent plans made by his ill-wishers to assassinate him.

Whenever he had to make war, Nectanebo would model small replicas in wax of the soldiers of the opposing armies, which he set out on an enormous table. Over them he performed rites to give victory to those representing his own men in battles, the strategy and the outcome of which he mimed. When the engagement was fought, it corresponded in every detail to the blueprint of its course formulated by Nectanebo.

Why he should have left Egypt, as he did, after a long run of success, has never been explained satisfactorily; the only reason given was that the gods would no longer cooperate with him in his magical practices. At any rate he went to Macedonia, where he lived for some time, giving out that he was an incarnation of Amon. He seems to have made a reputation as an astrologer there and to have been consulted by the king and queen of that country. He was in attendance— in his capacity of astrologer—on Olympias when she was in labor. Standing at her side, he calculated from the positions of the stars the most auspicious moment for the birth; on no account, he told Olympias, must she allow the child to be born until that moment arrived. "It was not until he saw a certain splendor in the sky and knew that all the heavenly bodies were in a favorable position that he permitted her to bring forth her child."

As the child was delivered, the earth shook, lightning filled the sky, and thunder rolled as if celestial drums were beating a salute in his honor. "O Queen, how thou hast given birth to a governor of the world," said Nectanebo, as Alexander the Great uttered his first cry.

2. Augury in Ancient Rome

As a race the Romans were hardheaded. They produced some of the keenest intellects of history and some of the most highly trained observers. These facts, I think, we should remember in connection with the records of prophecy which survive from the days of their great empire. Most of these are warnings of disaster, which seem to be a common factor in the prophecies of every era, preceding and succeeding the classic example of the seer Vestricius Spurinna's caveat to Julius Caesar: "Beware the Ides of March."

Some months before Spurinna's pronouncement, a fatal disaster had been foretold for Caesar, according to the historian Suetonius, who says:

> The impending death of Caesar was announced by the most patent of omens. A few months earlier, the colonists of Capua, who had emigrated thither in consequence of the Julian laws, came in the course of their building operations upon prehistoric graves. These they opened with all the more alacrity owing to the fact that they found in them many vessels of ancient craftmanship. In the monument that served as a tomb for Capys, the founder of Capua, they discovered a bronze tablet bearing the inscription in Greek, with the content: "When once the houses of Capys are brought to light, then a branch of the Julian house will be slain by the hand of one of his kindred; his death, however, will soon be avenged by terrible occurrences in Italy."

Cornelius Balbus, Caesar's closest friend, confirmed the discovery of this prophecy. And no doubt some well-wisher had passed on the encouraging news to Caesar himself, so that Spurinna's warning would not have been unexpected. But Caesar having met and overcome many crises in his life, was not disturbed by Spurinna's augury, made during the course of a ritual sacrifice, that Caesar was threatened by a great danger which would be over by the Ides of March.

On the previous night, his wife, Calpurnia, slept badly, dreaming that she saw their home crumbling and her husband stabbed, dying in her arms. Telling Caesar of this dream, she implored him not to go to the Forum that day. Caesar, who was not feeling well, was on the point of agreeing to stay at home, when his friend Decimus Brutus, playing on Caesar's well-known sense of duty, protested that he could not disappoint the great crowd which was awaiting him in the Senate. So just before eleven o'clock, on March 15, 44 B.C., Caesar set out, meeting on the way the seer Spurinna.

"Well, Spurinna," he said, "the Ides of March are come."

"Aye, Caesar," Spurinna answered, "come, but not gone."

Within the hour, the master of Rome was stabbed to death by conspirators in the Forum. All his life he had laughed at auguries and prophecies and ridiculed miracles. He had too much faith in himself to be concerned with the sight of a crow or an owl in inauspicious circumstances or with the outcome of ritual divination by the entrails of a sacrificed beast.

Yet if he had taken seriously, instead of despising, the warnings given to him, among which was a caution from the *sortes Antiatinae* to "beware of Cassius," he would have escaped assassination on the fatal fifteenth and perhaps altogether, as some contemporary opinion held. Cassius, as we know, was one of the leaders of the conspiracy against Caesar, and his dagger was one of the twenty-three which took Caesar's life.

Caesar, although he scoffed at the occult arts, did not despise the Sibylline Books, which were then still treasured in

Augury in Ancient Rome 27

Rome. In one of them was the prediction, echoed from Judaea, Egypt, India, Greece, Gaul, Asia and from the Druids of Britain, that a new king would rise at about this time in the East, who would conquer the world, unite all nations, and reestablish the golden age. Caesar was then at the peak of his power, victorious everywhere, treated as a god in Rome (his bronze statue in the Capitol was inscribed "Jupiter-Julius"), and could not conceive that any man could outstrip his achievements. In ten campaigns he had brought within the Roman Empire vast new territories. The oracles spoke of world conquest; with so much behind him Caesar seems not to have doubted that the oracles were predicting fulfillment of his dream—to outstrip Alexander, conquer India, which had conquered his predecessor, and all Asia, returning by the Caucasus and Scythia, Germany and Gaul and reach the River of Oceanus, Homer's fabulous limit of the world. The "Sons of the She-wolf" mentioned in the prophecy were of course the Romans; the "Sons of the Lamb" could be interpreted as the conquered nations within the fold of Roman rule.

And so Julius Caesar had no doubt about who was cast for the role of divine king. Unfortunately for him he took too much for granted; that was not his destiny. If he had been less confident, he might have paid attention to the warnings which he did not consider could possibly mean downfall to a man of the high destiny he believed was his—if his arrogance had been less, his life might have been longer.

From the moment of the birth of Octavian, Julius Caesar's great-nephew (who later was known as Augustus), prophecies were made concerning the events of his life, according to Dio Cassius, who was a relative of the Cassius who murdered Julius Caesar. Nigidius Figulus, who Cassius says was held to be the greatest astrologer of the era, apparently foretold that the world would be Augustus' empire. The historian tells how Octavius, the father of Augustus, arrived late at the Curia, when the Senate was in session, and explained to

Nigidius Figulus, who asked the reason, that his son had been born that day. Thereupon the astrologer said, "You have given us a master."

Octavius, when he heard this, was neither pleased nor proud. He believed, as did the most upright citizens of Rome, that democracy was the best form of government and that the government was democratic; the idea that he had sired a dictator disturbed him so deeply that he thought it was his duty to have the child killed. Nigidius Figulus, dissuading him, said, "It is impossible that anything of the sort could happen to this child." And so Augustus lived.

When his father, Octavius, was commanding an army in Thrace, he consulted the local oracle about the future of his son. As the ritual libation of wine was poured over the altar, a flame blazed up, leaped to the roof of the temple and into the sky. This was an indication, the oracle's priest said, of outstanding greatness and achievement, adding that only once before had this sign been given, when Alexander the Great was sacrificing.

While Augustus was still a young man, he consulted soothsayers and astrologers, among them Theogenes, all of whom reiterated the promise of the Thracian oracle. Suetonius says that when Augustus told Theogenes the date, the time, and the hour of his birth, the older man knelt at his feet, predicting his rise to imperial power. Augustus seems to have been deeply impressed by Theogenes' forecast of his future. He had the horoscope published, and a silver coin struck, carrying an engraving of the sign of Capricorn, which was his birthsign, on one of its surfaces. And within a few years the prophecy was fulfilled.

After that, Augustus was a regular visitor of oracles, and unlike his great-uncle, he took their advice and profited by it. He recognized and disposed of his adversaries before they could dispose of him. In recognition of and gratitude for his outstanding good fortune, he built a temple of peace and then consulted the Delphic oracle about how long the building and the peace would last. The oracle answered, "Until a virgin gives birth to a child and yet remains a virgin."

Augustus, essentially a practical man, had no doubt that the oracle was predicting eternal peace and duration of his temple, which he dedicated to this consummate end with the inscription *"Templum pacis aeternae"* on its entablature. At the time of the nativity of Christ, without warning or discoverable cause, the magnificent temple collapsed on its foundations.

Before this happened, Augustus consulted the Tiburtine Sibyl, to whom he always submitted all his plans and projects, on whether he should accept the supreme honor which the Senate wished to confer on him: the title of God of the nations. Augustus' faith in himself and in his star of destiny was by this time unshakable, but he was also a realist. He had been content with the modest title of princeps, or "chief among equals," not wishing to upset the long-established Roman constitution; his consent to translation to the rank of emperor had been given because he was shrewd enough to realize that in order to create cohesion between the loosely knit agglomeration of peoples which composed his empire, there must be a central, apparently almighty figure, the incarnation of the power of Rome. In spite of his vaulting pride, Augustus realized that homage was paid not to him as himself, but to this figure as the personification of the genius of the Eternal City; nevertheless, the Tiburtine Sibyl had always made such accommodating replies to his queries that when he asked during that midnight session if a prince greater than he would ever be born, he probably expected her to answer no.

The Sibyl lived on the Palatine Hill, in a temple the doors of which were opened only for the emperor. While she was consulting her sacred books for a ruling on Augustus' problem, the place was lit up by a meteor which flared in the dark sky. The Sibyl put down her books; the answer had been given.

"Look," she said. "It is a sign of the future which is revealed to you. One world is ending and another is beginning." (This referred to the ending of the approximate 2,150-year period of Aries the Ram, and the inception of the sign of Pisces the Fishes, in the precession of the Equinoxes, which had been known since the days of Hermes Trismegistus. Astrologers believed that the entering of the sign of Pisces signaled the birth of a world savior.) "A child has just been born, who is the king of future millennia, the true god of the world. He is of humble birth and of an obscure race. His divinity is unrealized; when he at last makes himself known, he will be persecuted. He will work miracles, he will be accused of trafficking with evil spirits, but I see him victor in the end over death, rising from the place where his murderers entombed him. He will reunite all nations."

Even Augustus could hardly identify himself either physically or allegorically with the subject of this prophecy. It referred to a child born in that hour; he was a mature man, his life and career were progressing along well-worn lines, and there was no new venture or development in them which could be construed as meaning, even in oracular terms, a birth. Whether or not Augustus believed the Sibylline pronouncement, Ludovico Muratori records in his *Antiquitates* that Augustus told the Senate of the vision and that the story, which was placed in the state archives, was read in later years by Constantine, who was a great devotee of astrology.

Most of the rulers of ancient Rome believed that by the stars or some other form of augury the future could be foretold. At one time stargazers were given such titles of respect as *Mathematici, Genethliacs,* as well as *Astrologi, Chaldaci* (a reference to the supposed origin of astrology), or *Babyloni*. Hippolytus mentions that "Under the wisest Emperors, Rome had a School of Astrology, wherein were secretly taught the occult influences of the Sun, Moon, and Saturn." Vitruvius says of astrologers that "their learning deserves the veneration of mankind." For centuries the keeping of a personal astrologer was customary not only in patrician families but in the imperial palace itself. The position of imperial astrologer must have been accepted with mixed feelings; it was an honor, but one which tended to be fleeting.

The astrologer had to know as much about diplomacy as astrology if he wanted to survive. It was a capital offense to foretell the death of an emperor; apart from that, any unpleasant forecast might be the astrologer's last. Or if a catastrophe happened which he had not predicted, the result was the same.

Thrasyllus, who flourished under both Tiberius and Nero, was one of the few who managed to make a success of this double career. His proficiency test in the dual role came when Tiberius invited him to an audience in his castle in Capri, which, built high on a rocky promontory, could be reached only by a steep, narrow flight of steps running along the edge of a sheer precipice which overhung the sea.

It was current knowledge that visitors to this castle were as a rule unsatisfactory in some way to the emperor; either they were implicated in treachery or conspiracy or their bona fides were considered suspect. Romans who received an invitation to the place made their wills and said good-bye to their family and friends; they knew that if a guest was unable to give explanations which Tiberius considered reasonable, at some particularly dangerous point on the return journey the massive Ethiopian slave who acted as guide in ascent and descent pushed the visitor off the edge of the cliff.

Thrasyllus, having climbed this winding Via Dolorosa in the company of the black slave, was received by Tiberius very graciously. For some time the emperor questioned him about astrology and its merits, even confiding to him some of his personal hopes and fears—which must have made Thrasyllus nervous. No man was given an opportunity of betraying an imperial confidence.

The emperor, who seemed to be impressed by Thrasyllus' answers, finally said, "Tell me, Thrasyllus, do you ever read your own stars?" And when Thrasyllus said that he did, Tiberius asked, "What do they promise you in the near future?" After a moment's pause, in which he did some hard thinking, Thrasyllus, apparently very agitated, said, in a despairing voice, "Your Majesty, my planets warn me I am in the gravest danger." Taking his hand, Tiberius told him he was a skilled astrologer and a wise man. "I had intended to have you thrown from the rocks of Capri this very night." Instead, he loaded Thrasyllus with honors, consulted him frequently, became his pupil, reaching a level of proficiency in prophecy. Tiberius predicted events in the life of his successor, Caligula, and foretold that Galba would reign one day.

Ascletarion, astrologer to Domitian, was either not so lucky or not so clever as Thrasyllus. Domitian, who had been horrified by predictions of his doom by the *sortes Praenestinae,* called in Ascletarion to give a second opinion on the situation. Instead of reassuring the emperor, he confirmed that dreadful days were ahead for him. Turning on Ascletarion, Domitian asked him if he knew his own end would come. "I shall be eaten by dogs," was the reply. "I shall prove how wrong you are and how foolish are your predictions," Domitian told him. "I shall have your head cut off, your body burned, and the ashes thrown into the Tiber." The first part of Domitian's plan for Ascletarion's future was carried out immediately and successfully. But no sooner had the pyre on which his body was placed caught alight than a sudden storm of torrential rain put out the flames. The executioners, who had scurried into shelter, came back to find that the corpse of the astrologer had been seized and eaten by a pack of wild dogs, according to his prediction.

Too late to interest Ascletarion, his prophecy concerning Domitian's end was also fulfilled. Domitian was stabbed to death by his wife's servants. As he fell with seven dagger wounds in his body, miles away in Ephesus, Apollonius of Tyana broke off his public oration to cry out, "Strike, strike! The gods command it." Then he said in a loud voice, "Ephesians, it is done. At this moment, the tyrant has fallen, and I see Rome acclaiming its liberty." A few days later the news of Domitian's death reached Ephesus. Dio Cassius verifies this; apparently Domitian was murdered at exactly the time Apollonius told the Ephesians that the emperor was dead.

Apollonius, that remarkable man, famous as a master of occult art and for his prophecies, had a personal reason for disliking Domitian, who had imprisoned him on two accusations—that he had predicted, in the hearing of one of Domitian's spies, the emperor's assassination and the accession of Nerva to his throne. This was a capital crime, which carried the death penalty. Apollonius, brought from prison to trial before Domitian, apparently hypnotized the emperor by a long speech claiming that since he had foretold to Vespasian (Domitian's father) a great destiny and that he would wear the purple, which at that time seemed impossible, Domitian, as his successor, owed a debt of gratitude to Apollonius. He ended by saying that he was not destined to die at Domitian's hands. Domitian had never been spoken to in such a way before; in the stunned silence which followed his speech, Apollonius left the *praetorium,* departing the same day for Greece, before Domitian recovered from the shock.

Probably Apollonius is one of the most outstanding examples of these times of a man gifted with the sixth sense. The legends about him are legion; many of them may owe more to imagination than to fact. But after allowing for embroidery, enough authentic material remains to establish him as a man of outstanding personality gifted with an extraordinarily developed sixth sense. He was born toward the beginning of the Christian Era in Tyana, Asia Minor, of which city his father was a rich and respected citizen, belonging to one of the oldest of its families. Apollonius, having studied the Pythagorean creed, was drawn to the study of mysticism and philosophy. At sixteen years of age he broke away from the pattern of life of his contemporaries, renouncing as a beginning the three things of greatest interest to them—wine, meat, and women. A strip of linen was his only clothing; he wore no shoes and never shaved.

Whether he was a natural healer or whether he learned to become one, he made a great reputation for his skill in curing disease of all kinds, while living in the temple of Aesculapius. From Greece, he traveled to India, Persia, and Egypt, being initiated into the mystery cult of each country by its hierophants. It was a pilgrimage in search of the higher wisdom, the richest source of which he considered he had found in Egypt. The Magi taught that blood sacrifices were an abomination to the Supreme Being; prayer, incense, and the purified, uplifted consciousness were the offerings acceptable to the one God. Renunciation of material values was essential; in return was promised "the opening of the eyes upon the infinite world of immortal essences," the ability to "measure all time with a glance, to embrace all things in one thought," the revelation of divine secrets, power over the forces of nature. "The promises have been kept," said Apollonius. It seems that they must have been; a reputation such as his, as seer and miracle worker, could have endured only if it rested on a solid basis of achievement.

In each case, years before the event he foretold the destiny of the seven emperors who reigned in the twenty-eight years between A.D. 68 and 96. Galba was massacred by disaffected troops; Otho killed himself after a defeat; Vitellius' throat was cut by the mob; Domitian was stabbed by servants. For Vespasian he prophesied a great future, by a means of divination known as the *sortes Praenestinae*. A sanctuary dedicated to this system, which was said to have been taught to the Etruscans by Egyptian seers, was built in Praeneste; it was at one time as famous as the oracle at Delphi. The method of divination was to write each letter of all the names of the consultant on cubes of laurel wood, which were tossed into a silver urn, then taken out one by one by the consultant. Then the magician or seer was inspired by the oracle to construct a sentence of words beginning with each letter chosen by the consultant from the urn. A translation of the prediction made by Apollonius from Vespasian's choice of letters reads: "Thy name, chosen by

Augury in Ancient Rome 35

the sacred Fates of the *sortes Praenestinae,* ascends slowly toward the heights of the future, but at last, become everywhere celebrated, a vanquisher without conquests, thou shalt receive, as sole emperor, the empire of the city."

Long before it seemed possible that Vespasian would wear the purple, the oracle at Carmel told him that he would have "a mighty home, far-reaching borders, multitudes of men." As prediction after prediction concerning events in his life was fulfilled, Vespasian, a hardheaded soldier who needed a great deal of convincing of the reality of prophecy, began to accept it. Later in his life, to consult the stars became a daily ritual; a number of astrologers catered to this imperial whim. The most favored among them probably was Selenus, through whose warnings Vespasian several times escaped from dangerous situations.

Apollonius, who neither asked payment for the exercise of his extraordinary powers nor made their use conditional on sacrifices, incurred the jealousy of the priests of the oracles. There was an occasion on which the hierophant of the Eleusinian mysteries refused to admit Apollonius because he said Apollonius "despised religious ceremonies." Some of his miracles were so spectacular that the clerics of the Christian Church have said he must have been sent to earth by the devil, to surpass the miracles of Christ.

At Nero's court, where astrologer jostled astrologer, was one Barbillius, his most frequently consulted adviser. Barbillius had been established as a leading astrologer for a number of years. The Emperor Claudius (Nero's predecessor, who had married Nero's mother, Agrippina) thought highly of him, although he foretold bad as well as good fortune. He predicted to Claudius that he would die A.D. 54, in the fourteenth year of his reign; Thrasyllus had timed his death to take place when he was sixty-three years, sixty-three days, sixty-three watches, sixty-three hours old, which set the limit of his life at October 13 of that year. On the night of the twelfth, Agrippina, having discovered that Claudius might not ratify his agreement to name Nero his heir, lavishly laced with poison a dish of mushrooms which she prepared for the emperor's supper. On October 13 he died.

And Nero stepped into his shoes, fulfilling Barbillius' prophecy that he would reign as emperor and Agrippina's ambition. Ever since her son's birth, Agrippina had been driven by the desire to make him Emperor of Rome. Barbillius, who cast the child's horoscope at Agrippina's request, confirmed her hopes by telling her that Nero's destiny was to wear the purple. "But," said the astrologer, "if he comes to the throne, he will kill his mother." Unhesitatingly Agrippina answered, "If he but reigns, I do not care. Let him kill me."

When all that Barbillius had predicted had come to pass and Agrippina was dead, the emperor, probably having found matricide exhausting, decided to take a holiday in Greece, where his reception was chilly. Inevitably he consulted the Delphic oracle—no one who was anyone passed through the country without visiting this shrine. The Pythia, the priestess through whom the god spoke, made a prophecy which was not to Nero's taste. "Your presence outrages the god you seek," she shouted at him. "Go back, matricide. The number seventy-three marks the hour of your downfall."

Nero, furious that she should dare accuse him in this way, had her buried alive in the cave of the oracle, with the mutilated bodies of the temple priests, whose hands and feet had been cut off. The prophecy did not disturb him—he understood it to mean that some catastrophe might overtake him when he was seventy-three; he was then thirty. A threat which would not materialize for forty-three years was too far ahead to worry him. The number seventy-three, however, related not to Nero's age, but to the age of Galba, the next emperor, who was seventy-three when he succeeded Nero in 68.

At his accession, Nero went to the Palatine, where he planted a laurel in the grove to which each emperor on enthronement added a tree. In the case of Augustus, Tiberius, Caligula, and Claudius the laurel died at the same time as the emperor who planted it. In the year of Nero's death, the entire copse withered, which, with the decapitation of all the imperial statues and destruction of Augustus' scepter by a thunderbolt, was taken as a token, so Suetonius says, by all Rome that the dynasty of the Caesars would finally become extinct.

Galba reigned only a few months. Otho succeeded him, as prophesied. The Egyptian astrologer Ptolemy had predicted to him, when he was proconsul in Spain, that he would outlive Nero and that one day he would wear the purple.

So many prophecies of disaster had been made and fulfilled in Vitellius' lifetime that he tried to ensure against ominous predictions about his reign by issuing an edict banishing all magicians and seers from Rome. And so they went, but as they went, the seers placarded every street corner with forecasts of Vitellius' impending death. And in a few months he died—massacred by a mob of soldiers.

Banishment from the Eternal City was no novelty for prophets and astrologers. Every so often a reigning emperor would decide that prediction was a two-edged weapon which might be turned against him; edicts would be published exiling the seers or making prophecy illegal. Sometimes all books on the subject were burned by the imperial whim. Two thousand were destroyed by order of Augustus, an irreplaceable loss of learning and knowledge.

Although Hadrian (A.D. 117-38) did not take quite such extreme action, his attitude was antiprophecy, chiefly because he did not want to run the risk of its doing for others what it had done for him. Hadrian was a skilled astrologer and operator of the magic arts. In *Mankind, Their Origin and Destiny,* he is described as assigning "great importance to the influence of the sky and the stars." He "erected a superb building at Jerusalem (which he called Ælia, a name derived from the sun and his own, Ælius), which was called Dodecapylon, or the temple with twelve gates, an evident allusion to the twelve houses of the sun. He also divided the town into seven portions—a division relating to the number of planets and of the planetary spheres. The new Jerusalem of the Apocalypse has also twelve gates, twelve foundations, and twelve angels at each gate. It was astrology which developed the plan of this visionary city, just as it inspired the plan of the new city built by Hadrian."

He wrote a diary of his life, as foreshown in the stars. All the events he predicted happened, including the manner and the time of his death. Early in his career, Hadrian went to Delphi to discover what the future held for him; while there he drank from the "prophetic water," the Castalian stream, through which he learned that his destiny was the imperial throne. Later he had the stream blocked up lest the "prophetic water" gave anyone else the same idea.

This particular source of inspiration remained sealed until the reign of the Emperor Julian (A.D. 361-63) who, believing that everyone should be free to use it, unblocked the spring. He said of the oracles of Apollo that through them the greater part of civilization had come into being because they had revealed the will of the gods in the sphere of politics, as well as religion, which they had regulated wisely for those who accepted their advice. Julian, a deep thinker and a widely read and learned man, was fascinated, according to the historian Ammianus Marcellinus, by all forms of divination. He was also a capable astrologer. Septimius Severus (A.D. 193-211) had his horoscope painted on the roof of his judicial palace, together with his prophecy that he would not come back alive from an expedition to England. He went there and died at York.

Not only the rulers but some of the wisest men of the Roman Empire believed in the possibility of "looking ahead" and in the influence of the stars on men and their affairs. The philosopher Plotinus says, "It is abundantly evident . . . that the motion of the heavens affects things on earth" and, through his knowledge of astrology, saved the life of his friend and pupil Porphyry, who had decided to kill himself. From Porphyry's horoscope, Plotinus realized the danger in time to persuade him to go on living.

3. The Oracles Speak

The three great oracles—Delphi, Dodona, Trophonius—were to ancient Greece as Shakespeare is to Stratford-on-Avon. They were the core of the tourist trade; kings and princes and humble folk came from far and near to one or other of the shrines with the common hope that their problems would be solved and the future foretold. They brought an increase in trade generally, as visitors must, but the shrines received the chief benefits—which probably is true of Shakespeare's birthplace, although the historical places there do not do as well as their ancient predecessors. The wealth and the *objets d'art* amassed at Delphi were fabulous. In its temples and theater were golden and marble statues, whose number grew with the fame and prosperity of the place—carvings, jewels, paintings by Polygnotus, golden cups and platters, everything that symbolized opulence was to be found there.

Although Delphic power was probably at its peak during the sixth century B.C., its importance continued long afterward and had been recognized long before that time. Homer speaks of Pytho's "rocky threshold"; prior to Apollo's takeover, it is supposed to have belonged to Earth and Themis and probably was the shrine of an oracle in Mycenaean days. One of the idols turned up by excavations is a figure seated, as was the Apolline priestess, the Pythia, on a tripod.

For hundreds of years gifts were poured out at this shrine

of Apollo because of a unique reputation for accurate prophecies made there. This wealth, glowingly described by contemporary writers, shows that the reputation was deserved; people will not go on consulting—and paying handsomely for consulting—an oracle which makes too many mistakes. Cicero, skeptic as well as philosopher, says, "Never could the oracle of Delphi have been so overwhelmed with so many important offerings from monarchs and nations if all the ages had not proved the truth of its oracles." Cicero's opinion is confirmed by historical facts, which show that the Delphic oracle kept an unquestioned record for infallibility intact from the time of Croesus all through the testing period of the Persian Wars and, because of this, was accepted as political and spiritual arbiter of the Greek world.

Delphi, the place, is a spectacularly perfect setting for the shrine. As backdrop are the great bare flanks of Mount Parnassus. Towering cliffs form a natural amphitheater, where, as Kyril Demys says in *Wings of Myrahi*, "the luminous mystery of the cleft Phoedriades," the Bright Ones, gleams like a lustral flame in the reflected light of the sun. Below is the profound darkness of the Pleistus gorge; overhead wheel vultures and eagles, whose ancestors' methods of dealing with their prey were translated into omens by the seers.

Apollo's temple dominated Delphi, both before and after the city grew up around it. It stood in the higher part of the town, surrounded by a vast enclosure; at one end of the building, on the pediment of which was an inscription "Let no man enter here unless his hands be pure," was a great golden statue of Apollo. Behind the statue was the entrance to the cave in which the god prophesied through his mouthpiece, the Pythia.

According to the second-century writer Plutarch, this cave was discovered by chance. Some goats, which were grazing among the rocks, suddenly were seized with convulsions, as was the shepherd who was with them. A cleft was discovered from which mephitic gases were escaping; it was found that these had the effect of putting anyone who inhaled them into a trance, during which the subject muttered mysterious, almost unintelligible words. The priests, when they heard of the affair, saw it as a sign that Apollo, the god of eloquence, had decided to transmit his wisdom by the medium of human speech. So the Delphic oracle came into being, prophesying through its priestess, the Pythia. At first she was a young virgin from a noble family chosen for her beauty, but after Delphi had been rocked by the scandal of a Pythia being seduced by a handsome Thessalian, the required age for a priestess was about fifty. Unattractive looks and an obscure family were other qualifications.

At regular intervals—about once a month, most authorities agree—the Pythia, having been ritually purified, possibly in the sacred Castalian stream, was escorted by the priests, or *hosioi*, to the temple. Into an inner room, where stood the omphalos, the holy navel, said to mark the center of the earth, was brought a goat, which was sprinkled with hallowed water. If it shivered in the approved way, it was sacrificed, and the session proceeded. The Pythia, robed, crowned with laurel, a fillet of wool binding her forehead, then descended into the sanctuary, the cavern of the mephitic vapors, where she drank from the waters of the stream Cassotis, which was supposed to stimulate the psychic powers. Bay leaves were given to her to chew; possibly they were believed to have an hallucinogenic effect, as Sophocles hints in a fragment from a lost play, which contains the line "After eating bay, be careful to bite your lip." Bay leaves were also burned to step up the mantic mood. Then, seated on the tripod, the Pythia awaited the message of the god.

Meanwhile, her client, after offering a ritual cake, which served as fee, had sacrificed a sheep or a goat on the holy hearth, in the presence of sponsors or priests, who claimed the skin and various parts of the animal as their perquisite. Then the seeker was allowed into the sanctuary, or probably a screened-off part of it so that the Pythia should not be disturbed by the presence of a stranger.

Apollonius of Tyana has given an account of his visit to the Delphic oracle, with his disciple Damis. After the ceremony of purification with holy water and the animal sacrifice—in this case a bull, as well as a goat—they were taken into the temple, crowned with laurel, and given a laurel bough twined with a band of white wool. Holding these, they passed on into a sanctuary where, says Apollonius, "one suddenly smelled a wonderfully sweet perfume." From there, they came into the adytum, "whose walls are decorated with the rich offerings which attest the truth of the oracles and the gratitude of those consultants who have been favored by fate. At first we had difficulty in seeing anything, the burning incense and other perfumes filled the place with dense smoke. Behind the statue of the god is the crypt, into which one descends by a gradual slope, but the servants of the temple keep the consultants far enough away from the Pythia to make their presence unnoticeable."

Apollonius describes a change which took place in the physical appearance of the Pythia. Her chest swelled; first she flushed, then paled; her limbs trembled convulsively and more and more violently. Her eyes seemed to flash fire; she foamed at the mouth; her hair stood on end. Then she tore off her fillet, and as she threw it on the ground, she uttered a few words, which the priests at her side noted down. The handing of this message to Apollonius signified the end of the session.

He had asked whether his name would go down to posterity; his disciple, without mentioning his intention to Apollonius, had asked the same thing. The Pythia's answer was that his name would be known in centuries to come, but that the reason it would be remembered would be the calumnies attached to it. Apollonius' reaction to this unflattering prediction was hardly what one would expect of a philosopher or a great man. "I tore up the paper, as I was leaving the temple," he says. "That is what all consultants do whose pride has not been satisfied." But whether or not he liked the

Pythia's forecast, she was right. During his lifetime, Apollonius was given respect and homage; after his death, he was denigrated by the Fathers of the Christian Church. He is remembered chiefly because of their vilification of him.

The priests apparently kept records of all of the Pythia's predictions, as did the attendants in the other shrines of auguries made there. For 2,000 years at least these collections of prophecies existed; when the Turks took Constantinople, they disappeared, except for the chance survival of a few fragments.

One of the best known of all such pronouncements probably is the story of the Delphic oracle's dealings with Croesus, King of Lydia, in about 550 B.C. Croesus had a problem on which, since he felt it was too vital for the human mind to resolve, he decided to ask an oracle for guidance. The difficulty was to know which, if any, of the oracles could be relied on. They all claimed, of course, 100 percent accuracy, but Croesus dared take no risk of being given faulty advice. He had to know in advance the chances of success of an attack which he was all but committed to launch against the Persians, whose increasing power was a danger on his very doorstep. The wrong decision could cost his kingdom and his life.

He decided to choose his oracle by test. He sent a personal ambassador to the shrines of prophecy at Didyma, near Miletus, Abae and Delphi in Phocis, of Amphiaraus and Trophonius in Boeotia, of Zeus at Dodona in Epirus, and Zeus-Amon in Libya. At each shrine, the ambassador was to ask its priestess what the king was doing at home in Sardis, his capital, on the hundredth day after the mission had left him. One after another, the oracles' answers to the king's question, written on papyrus rolls which the ambassadors brought to him, proved wide of the mark. On the last of all, he read:

"I know the number of the sand, and all the measures of the sea. I understand the dumb, and hear the voice that speaketh not. A savor has assailed my nostrils of a strong-shelled tortoise boiled with lamb's flesh in bronze, both laid beneath and set above."

This was the answer sent from Delphi, and as Croesus alone knew, it was the right one. One hundred days after his ambassadors had set off, Croesus occupied himself in one of the most unlikely ways he could think of. An Oriental monarch, who normally would not have lifted a finger to do the smallest thing for himself, he played chef in secret. He cut up a lamb and a tortoise, boiling their flesh in a brazen urn with a brazen lid, so that it was impossible to see inside the vessel.

No one but he could have known what he had done; no one could have guessed at it. Croesus was convinced that the Delphic oracle was genuine; he would consult the Pythia.

First, he commanded a sacrifice on a colossal scale to Apollo. Three hundred cattle were slaughtered and burned together with fine furniture, jewels, robes, gold and silver cups. The metal was cast in bricks afterward and sent to Delphi, where they were heaped in a gleaming pile, with a golden lion atop. With this offering went four silver jars, silver bowls, two lustral vases of gold and silver, a golden statue of a woman, four and a half feet tall (known as Croesus' pastry cook), and two enormous bowls for wine mixing, one of gold and one of silver. Herodotus says that the gold bowl weighed about a quarter of a ton, it could hold more than 5,000 gallons.

Having paved the way for consultation, Croesus sent his ambassador to Delphi, with the crucial question: Should he attack Persia? And ought he first to find an ally? The Pythia answered, "After crossing the Halys [a river of Asia Minor], Croesus will destroy a great empire." He should, she said, find out which was the most powerful of the Greek nations and ally himself with it.

His other question was whether he would have a long reign. The Pythia said, "Nay, when a mule becometh king of the Medes, flee, soft-soled Lydian, by pebbly Hermus, and stay not, nor feel shame to be a coward."

Croesus had a son who had been dumb from birth. Was there hope, he asked the oracle, on another occasion, that the boy would ever be cured? The Pythia's answer, foretelling that he would speak, was also a warning.

"Son of Lydia, ruler of men, Croesus, thou prince of fools, desire not to hear in thy halls the voice long prayed for of a son speaking. 'Twould be better for that to be far from thee. He will speak first on a day that is not propitious."

Perhaps he did not take this last prediction seriously. At any rate Croesus seems to have felt that, on the whole, he had got value for money since the auguries for the main queries he believed to be favorable. He took them at their face value; he forgot that predictions sometimes were double-edged.

All of the Pythia's prophecies were fulfilled, but not all according to his interpretation. His alliance with Sparta, undertaken according to her advice, went well. And then he crossed the Halys, attacked and was defeated by the Persians. A great empire was destroyed—but it was not theirs, as Croesus had thought; it was his own. The Pythia's warning that his reign would end when a mule was King of the Medes, Croesus had interpreted to mean that he would keep his throne indefinitely; a mule could not be a monarch. He might have realized, if he had considered the prophecy more carefully, that Cyrus, the man who conquered him, was a "mule," a child of mixed parentage, Mede and Persian.

The victorious Persians, having routed Croesus' army, swept down on his capital, Sardis, which fell to them after a short siege. They forced their way into the palace, where Croesus' son saw one of the soldiers advancing on his father. He cried out, "Wretch, wouldst thou slay Croesus?" And so the last prophecy of the oracle to the king was fulfilled.

The behavior of the oracle was unpredictable. As in Croesus' case, some questions were answered directly, some obliquely, some not at all. When the Siphnians, for instance, who had become fabulously wealthy through the working of the gold and silver mines on their small island, sent to Delphi for reassurance that their prosperity would continue, the reply was: "But whenever in Siphnos the city hall becometh white, the marketplace white-browed, then the wise men ought to beware of an ambush of wood and a herald all red." The descriptions "white" and "white-browed" referred to the gilding of the buildings mentioned, with gold and silver. A few days after the prophecy was received in Siphnos, the island was attacked by Samian pirates, who came in ships with red prows, an "ambush of wood and a herald all red," which resulted in the capture of some of the islanders, for whose ransom 100 talents had to be paid.

Not a word was said by the Pythia about the mines, which were, in fact, destroyed by a sudden inundation of the sea. Perhaps the god ignored the Siphnians' question on the ground that, disaster being unavoidable, it was pointless to distress them by foretelling it; but they might gather from his silence, if they were able to interpret it, that their prospects were not too good. This was one of the times when, as Heraclitus said, "The god of Delphi neither revealeth, nor concealeth, but hinteth."

Thucydides, called by Macaulay the greatest historian who ever lived, although a skeptic himself, never admitting the psychic character of a factor unless it could not possibly be explained on any other grounds, records a verified prophecy by the Delphic oracle. In his history of the Peloponnesian War, he mentions a prediction which had been current for many years that a Doric War would break out and that with it would come pestilence. "There was a difference of opinion," he says, "as to whether the ancients in this verse had meant 'loimos' or 'limos'; that is, whether 'pestilence' or 'famine' were meant. . . . Some of the people of that time knew that when the Lacedaemonians asked Apollo whether to begin the war, the answer he gave was: 'If you press the war with energy, then victory will be on your side,' and he promised to assist them. They proved the facts to be in consonance with this oracle. The pestilence began as soon as the Peloponnesians invaded Attica and a remarkable circumstance was that the Peloponnesus remained wholly free of it. Its most virulent effects took place in Athens and in other places belonging to different peoples."

Historical records confirm that the pestilence, whatever it was, broke out directly the Spartans crossed into Athenian territory; it has been established that they did not bring it with them and the Peloponnesus was free of it. Apollo, the god of pestilence, had promised aid and had kept his word; he had promised victory to the Spartans, and they were the conquerors. There was also famine, so that whichever word was used originally, the prophecy was fulfilled. All its details were confirmed by contemporary documents.

Plutarch had a high opinion of the oracle's accuracy; he says that valuable predictions and advice were given not only to public figures, but also to ordinary men and women. No record of these remains; only here and there can be found a few instances when such prophecies were concerned with events of more than personal importance. The augury given by the oracle to Battus was one of these. He came to Delphi merely to ask for a cure for stammering; whether or not it was given to him there is no clue. But he went away with Apollo's assurance that he was to be an empire builder; the god told him to found Cyrene, which he did.

Apollo's advice to the Greeks on expansion and colonization was wise and sound, judged by its results; it was also just. He counseled Archias to inaugurate Syracuse, the Cretans to colonize Sicily, dispatched the Boeotians to Heraclea in Pontus, and commanded the foundation of Byzantium. The Spartans were directed to found a colony at Heraclea in Thessaly, but when they petitioned the god to give his blessing to an attack on Arcadia, his answer was: "Thou askest of me Arcadia. I will not give it thee." And there was no reason, except political greed, for their wanting it.

Apollo often gave Solomon-like replies to his questioners. Asked "How best are we to worship the gods?" he said, "After the custom of your nation." If there was more than one custom, he advised: "Choose the highest." When Polycrates, famous as the greatest tyrant of those times, refounded the festival in honor of Apollo on the island of Delos, his legendary birthplace, he asked the god whether it should be known by its ancient name, Delian, or whether he would prefer it to be called Pythian. Apollo's answer was: "It will not matter to you what it is called." Soon afterward, Polycrates, whose court on the enchanting island of Samos was a magnet for the literati of the day, was carried off by a Persian commander and crucified.

In times when bloodshed and violence were even more common than they are today, the Pythian oracle recommended moderation and restraint in all things. Apollo warned the Greeks to beware of allowing superstition to be an excuse for cruelty; sculptured over his temple portico at Delphi were reliefs picturing the "victory of an ideal humanity over the monstrous deities which are the offspring of savage fear." The god's maxims and the teachings of great sages—such as Solon; Chilon, the Spartan ephor; Thales, the first philosopher—were so much in accord that many of them consulted his oracle and all of them praised it.

The wisest of the Greeks—many of them skeptical intellectuals—believed that the Delphic shrine had been for centuries a channel through which lofty ideals and ideas, counsel, and prevision had been given to their nation. No one could remember its beginning; no one could imagine that it would ever end, except the oracle itself. This was the prophecy foretelling the close of Delphi's long day:

> Aye, if you hear it, if you endure to know
> That Delphi's self with all things gone must go.
> . . . And thus, even thus, on some long destined day

> Shall Delphi's beauty shrivel, burn away;
> Shall Delphi's fame and fane from earth expire
> At that bright bidding of celestial fire.

The other two great Greek oracles, neither of which ever reached Delphi's eminence and fame, were at Dodona and in Boeotia. Dodona was situated at the foot of Mount Tomaros, at the southern end of Epirus. Temple, shrine, and town were dedicated to the worship of Zeus; the sanctuary of the oracle, which was probably as ancient as that of Delphi, was in an oak forest. One of these oaks, which stood alone in a clearing, was known as the prophetic oak, through which came the predictions. According to tradition, the oracle originated when two black doves dedicated to Isis had left Thebes in Egypt. One had flown to Libya and one to Dodona, where it perched on the prophetic tree. Each dove declared that its resting place was beloved by the gods, where "they would reveal the future to worthy men." The story is supposed to be an allegory of the Egyptian account of the divinely ordained pilgrimage of two Theban priestesses, whose mission was to travel as far as their strength would carry them, teaching knowledge of the gods. One went west, reaching Libya; the other came to rest in Dodona. The link between allegory and history is that in the old language of Epirus the same word means both dove and old woman.

The priestess of the Dodona shrine had a much easier life than her opposite number at Delphi. She was not required to go into a trance or to be subjected to hallucinogenic vapors. When the oracle was to be consulted, she went with her attendant priests to the prophetic oak, which stood on the bank of a stream. This stream mysteriously dried up each day at noon and began to flow again at midnight. The prophetess, standing under the tree, listened to the sound made by the leaves or the boughs and by the stream, which rose from a spring near the oak; each sonant variation had its meaning, listed in an ancient book of ritual. This method of interpreting the message of the oracle was also used by the priestess when the god spoke through the medium of seven copper bowls, which were hung so closely together on the inner walls of the sanctuary that if one was struck, all the others vibrated in sympathy.

The third oracle of Greece, in Boeotia, was named Trophonius, after the architect Trophonius, who, with his brother Agamedes, had built the temple at Delphi. Its site was on the slopes of a mountain, from which rises the Hercynos River, making its way in numberless cascades past the town of Lebadea. Why the oracle was named after Trophonius, no one seems to know; the legends connected with the shrine seem to indicate that Apollo looked on him with no favor at all. One version says that he and his brother used to sneak into the temple by night, to steal the votive offerings left there by day. Agamedes having been caught in a trap set for thieves, Trophonius cut off his head so that he would not be recognized; soon afterward Trophonius was killed by a landslide. According to another legend, when the temple was finished, the brothers asked for a reward from Apollo, who told them they would receive it in seven days. A week afterward, they both died in their sleep.

The shrine of the oracle was a near copy of Delphi's, but it was much more awe—even terror—inspiring than its counterpart. Visitors had to climb down a ladder, then negotiate, feet foremost, a long narrow tunnel, at the bottom of which was a device which carried the would-be consultant downward at breakneck speed. Even if it were possible to find the springs which controlled the apparatus, the consultant, who had to hold, on pain of death, a honey cake in each hand, would not have been able to touch them.

The pilgrimage could be made only at night, the culmination of long preparations and examination. When Tersidas the Theban came to consult the oracle, Pausanias says that he was shut up for three days and nights in the temple of Fortuna and made to fast. Before he was allowed into the sanctuary, he had to drink two cups of water; the first, drawn from the spring called Lethe, blotted out all past memories; the second, from the stream Mnemosyne, enabled him to remember all that he would see and hear in the shrine. Then, robed in a linen alb, he was taken by torchlight into the cavern. The next morning he had to be helped out by the priests. His face was white; his eyes were glazed and staring; apparently he was only half-conscious. In that condition he was taken back to the temple of Fortuna, where he gradually recovered from his experiences.

Tersidas was luckier than Timarchus, whose story Plato, to whom he told it, has recorded. Timarchus asked the oracle "what he should think of the *daimon* or familiar spirit by which Socrates believed himself to be inspired." After a long time in the darkness and silence of the cavern, Timarchus says he heard distant music. Then he had a vision of different-colored islands that floated on a lake of fire. A voice called, "Timarchus," and said, "The radiant isles that float on the lake of fire are the sacred regions, inhabited by pure souls. . . . Those who have kept their original purity amid the ordeals of their first experience are clothed in divine radiance by crossing the lake of fire, source of eternal life, and go on to find among the islands of the blest the dwelling-place inhabited by the virtue whose most perfect image they have realized. The soul of Socrates was one of these; always superior to his mortal body, his soul had become worthy of entering into communion with the invisible worlds and his familiar spirit, a deputy from them, taught him a wisdom that men did not appreciate and therefore killed. You cannot yet understand this mystery; in three months it will be revealed to you."

When the voice stopped speaking, Timarchus became unconscious, recovering to find himself outside the temple. His experience seems to have left him only half-alive; he went about like a man in a dream, dwelling always on what he had seen and heard in the sanctuary. At the end of three months, as prophesied by the oracle, he died "babbling," so

Plutarch says, "of luminous islands and lakes of fire, and holding out his hands to the image of Socrates, which he said was coming towards him."

As a medium for divination, in Greek estimation astrology came next to the oracles, which of course, being direct channels of the god, were in a class by themselves. Astrology is said to have been brought to Greece by Thales, the first philosopher of that country, from the East. Plato is the first extant writer to mention astrology; his own horoscope is a blueprint of the great philosopher's physical appearance, mental qualities, tastes and abilities and of his life-span.

The horoscope's main features are described by the astrologer. "If the Ascendant shall be Aquarius, Mars, Mercury and Venus therein posited, and if Jupiter then be placed in the seventh, having Leo for his sign, and in the second the Sun in Pisces and the Moon in the fifth House, beholding the Ascendant with a trine aspect, and Saturn in the ninth from the Ascendant in Libra; this Geniture renders a Man Interpreter of Divine and heavenly Institutions, who, endued with instructive speech, and the power of Divine Wit, and formed in a manner by celestial Institution, by true License of disputations shall arrive at all the secrets of Divinity."

The sun in Pisces indicated that Plato should be heavy and broad. His father, Ariston, apparently nicknamed him Plato because of his large frame and broad shoulders. Neanthes says he had a broad forehead; he was known as Serapis because of his majestic appearance and his dignity, qualities given by Jupiter, ruler of Pisces, when powerful. Plato's life was keyed to a search for truth; Aquarius is called the sign of the truth seeker. The high-level Aquarian nature is serene, firm of purpose, humane, and rational; the sign gives ability to classify and synthesize, all of which characteristics Plato displayed.

Venus, Mercury, and Mars were in his first house. Venus in that position gives power as an orator—the "large eloquence" mentioned by several writers—and good looks; contemporary writers comment that "there was not any imperfection throughout his person." Love of and skill in the arts are also gifts of Venus; Plato painted and wrote poetry. Mercury is the planet of the writer, the speaker and the arguer, and the inventor. Plato was master of all these activities. Stanley says that he "added much to learning and languages by many inventions, as well of things as of words"; he created many terms now used in rhetoric, grammar, and geometry. Mars gives bodily strength; Plato, a champion wrestler, competed in the Pythian games, where it was said that at least once he fought "best of all the soldiers." Courage, moral and physical, is a Martian attribute shown by Plato who defended his ideas brilliantly and fearlessly.

Finally, Plato fulfilled the prophecy of his horoscope that he would live into old age. He was found dead, with his head pillowed on the books of Sophron, "having completed the most perfect number of years, namely, nine multiplied by itself."

4. Druid Seers

For centuries before the beginning of the Christian Era, Druids had been famous as seers. Druidism was the core of a great mystery tradition, which was held to equal or rival that of Egypt or Chaldaea. Pliny says there is evidence that the Persians learned their magic from the Druids. The great sixth-century mystic Pythagoras—whose name every schoolchild learning geometry knows only too well—who taught the doctrine of dualism and the concept that in principle the substance of the universe is unlimited, received his training in esoteric philosophy from the Druids, not they from him, according to Hippolytus, Diodorus Siculus, Timagenes, and Clement of Alexandria.

In the *Bardic Triads* is a passage indicating that Druidism was the second-oldest religion of Britain: "There are three special doctrines that have been obtained by the nation of the Cymry; the first, from the ages of ages was that of the Gwyddonaid, prior to the time of Prydan (from which the word Britain is said to derive), son of Aedd the Great, the second was Bardism, as taught by the Bards, after they had been instituted. . . ." The *Triads* are part of the sixteenth collection of Bardic (or Druidic) literature, compiled by Llewellyn Sion of Glamorgan.

The power of the priesthood, which was a force to be reckoned with in those early times, did not rest on superstition, but on the scientific ability and general scholarship of the

Druids, as well as on their arcane knowledge. According to Pomponius Mela, they knew the size and shape of the earth; they had medical skill and were adept herbalists. They are credited with inventing Ogham, a system of writing named after Ogmios, Celtic god of learning, although they never used it for transcription of inner rituals or secret doctrines. Deeper mysteries, they believed, in common with all esoteric cults, must be transmitted only by word of mouth or by symbolism, which is the shorthand of psychic vision.

The ancient world was impressed, not only by the majesty of conception and imaginative sweep of the Druids' philosophical, mystical system, but by their power as prophets. The first-century Roman historian Pompeius Trogus was one of the many who claimed that the Celts "excel all others in the skill of augury." According to Joseph Déchelette, they had perfected a method of numerology long before Pythagoras, who is usually credited with having originated the science, developed his system.

Since the beginnings of their history, the Celts and their priests (the Druids) have been celebrated for *an-da-shealladh*, the two sights. In the Celts, prevision is a racial characteristic which crops up as persistently as, say, red hair north of the border (between England and Scotland) or dark eyes in Italy. It was—and is—as natural a feature as they. No artificial aids, such as hallucinogenic drugs (about which a great deal was known in early times) or narcotic drafts, were used to produce it. Contemporary writers mention this fact almost in surprise, probably because in many forms of Eastern magic "euphrosy and rue" were used to heighten perception and stimulate the visual nerve.

Among the Druids, prophecy was not a hit-and-miss affair, to be uttered when a member of the priesthood felt so inclined. It was a clearly defined function reserved—in theory at any rate, according to Strabo—for the *vates,* or ovates, one of the three degrees of the hierarchy, of which the other two were bards and Druids. They were supposed to be equal in importance but different in function: Ovates were guardians of the sacred rituals, and practiced divination; bards were poets and warriors; the Druids formed a pontifical college. They taught the secret knowledge; they sat in judgment; they could declare war or make peace.

The chosen chief, or Arch-Druid, was elected to their head; he also was the virtual ruler of the Gallic people. Egypt had much the same form of government when her priest-kings were in control.

Initiation rites which were similar to those of the Egyptian Mysteries followed a novitiate of twenty years, during which the ovates learned the many forms of divination used by the Druids. Diodorus Siculus, the Sicilian-Greek contemporary of Julius Caesar, mentions that one of these forms was the flight of birds. Or the Druid (all three degrees were often, without specification, called Druids) might sing self-composed verses over the person or object concerning whom or which he wished to obtain clairvoyant knowledge, after placing on the object his magical staff, made of yew, hawthorn, or, more usually, rowan wood. Bone divining (known as scapulimancy) was another method. For this they used the right shoulder blade of an animal, which had been boiled clean of flesh. Sometimes the future was read from the shapes of clouds, or tree roots, or sticks. Taliesin, Druid and bard, says:

> I am Taliesin,
> Chief of the Bards of the West,
> I am acquainted with every sprig
> In the cave of the Arch-diviner.

When war was threatened or was being waged, augury from sacrifice might be made. It would take place at the great assembly of Druids, which was held in the spring in a sacred forest and which took the form of a court of justice, combined with political deliberations.

First came the rite of the cutting of the mistletoe, with a golden sickle, from oaks which were thirty years old. The sprigs were gathered in a white veil and distributed among the heads of families present. To the Druids the mistletoe was the emblem of the secret of life, the divine life substance, of protoplasm. Pearls or bosses on ritual caldrons are believed to symbolize the sacred berries.

Then came the sacrifice: two white bulls when the land was at peace; when there was war or the threat of war, men. The victims were either criminals who had been sentenced to death or prisoners captured from the enemy; they were packed, like fish in a creel, into gigantic wickerwork figures, which were carried on the shoulders of the *eubages,* the priests of the sacrifice, to a vast bonfire, to which each tribe had contributed fagots. When the fire, the wickerwork figures, and their contents were burning well, the priests took their auguries from the shrieks and the crackling of the flames.

If it happened that no regulation human fuel was available for this form of divination, the alternative was an old man. A volunteer was asked for; if none was forthcoming, an arbitrary choice was made from the crowd. The victim was dragged to a stone slab, in the hollowed center of which stood an iron bowl, in readiness to collect his blood, and his throat was slit with the sacred knife by a priestess. Steam rising from the hot blood was studied for signs by the diviners.

Whether or not the priestesses were known as ovates, they certainly functioned as diviners. Boadicea may have been one of them; she is known to have discharged priestly functions. Lampridius and Vopiscus said that women diviners were also *dryades* (which denoted Druidesses). Forms of the word are often varied by contemporary writers for male as well as female Druids; opinions on its origin also differ. Some authorities say "Druid" is the nominative plural of *drui,* the Irish equivalent of the Gallic *druidae* of Caesar's description. Later forms and meanings were *drai* and *draoi,* denoting magician, wizard, and diviner. Other pundits claim that it derives from the Celtic substantive *deru,* meaning oak—a tree which is a dominant feature of the rituals of the cult.

However their name came into being, the priestesses

were called Druidesses because they were the daughters of Druids. They were initiated in adolescence into the cult, and the wreaths of sacred verbena with which they were crowned were insignia of their rank and of the perpetual virginity to which they were dedicated.

They were supposed to have the power of making themselves invisible, of changing their physical shape into any other that they fancied and of controlling the elements—and, of course, of prophecy. Diocletian was told by a Druidess while he was still a soldier in Gaul, that he would be Emperor of Rome. "You shall be so," she said with not unusual obscurity, "when you have slain a boar." For some time Diocletian hunted and killed every discoverable boar, without getting any nearer to the purple, until he realized that *aper*, the Latin word for boar, was the name of Numerian's father-in-law. The prophecy was fulfilled after Diocletian had had Aper put to death. He was chosen emperor.

Before setting out on his last campaign, Severus Alexander consulted a Druidess on its outcome. All she would say to him was: "Go, my lord—but beware of your soldiers." Perhaps he did not realize what she meant; perhaps he did not take the warning seriously. At any rate, during the campaign he was assassinated by his own men.

It was a Druidess whom Vercingetorix, the Gallic general who probably gave Caesar and the Roman legions more trouble than any other of their adversaries at that time, consulted when he wanted to discover whether he would succeed in his attempt to make Alesia a stronghold of Gallic resistance. Often before, he had been given encouragement by the Druid seers, so he was full of hope when the nine priestesses in charge of the adytum went down to the beach to invoke Tarunn, the god of the thunderbolt, in order to learn from him the fate of Alesia.

On the granite altar, the sacred fires were lit; when they had been sprinkled with the herbs and perfumes dedicated to the spirit of storms, the head priestess, with Vercingetorix, put off in a small boat, she, upright in the prow, intoning a chant. While her voice still echoed around the little bay, black clouds crowded over the clear sky. A squall whipped the sea into tumult; lightning struck three times to the left of the boat and broke off the top half of the lighthouse standing on the cliff.

Tarunn had answered. "Alesia will be struck, even as that lighthouse," the Druidess prophesied. "Son of Gaul, you know the war-cry of our ancestors—Woe to the conquered. Your two-bladed axe you will wield only once more. The eagles with the golden claws [the Romans] will eat the brains of our people; the sun shall go down in blood, and the virgins of the land of oaks will be left to weep for the dead."

At first Vercingetorix of the many victories could not believe that his achievements were to be scattered to the winds by defeat. At last after Alesia had fallen and Gaul's resistance crumbled, realizing the bitter truth of the Druidess' prophecy, he offered his surrender to Caesar, in exchange for quarter for the remnants of his armies. He went alone to Caesar, who was seated on the throne of military justice, among his legions. At his feet Vercingetorix threw down his helmet and his sword. And Julius Caesar, who had called Vercingetorix the "noblest and most tenacious" of his opponents, had him sent to Rome in chains, to be dragged like any petty prisoner behind his triumphant procession and then executed by the ax.

Vortigern, another great leader, but of Britain, not Gaul, had happier auguries when he consulted the *vates* on his personal safety, after most of the British nobility had been massacred at Stonehenge in a Saxon conspiracy. He was told that he would survive if he built a tower on Mount Eryri (Snowdon). The foundations were laid, but as soon as the walls were raised, they fell down again because of earth tremors. It was a case which could be dealt with only by sacrifice, the *vates* decided, telling Vortigern that the victim must be a fatherless boy. Eventually a lad was found who was the son of the King of Demetia by a nun. Fortunately for him, in the meantime, Merlin had diagnosed the cause of the disturbances as the fighting underground of elementals, or dragons, after the exorcism of which the building was able to be completed. As the *vates* foretold, Vortigern lived there in safety.

In the time of Tacitus (about A.D. 70), the Roman Capitol was destroyed by fire. The Druids, when they got news of this, interpreted it as an omen of the fall of the Roman Empire. "The sovereignty of the world," they said, "will pass to a people beyond the Alps."

A Druid foretold to Herod Agrippa his rise to power, and its ending. Herod, later King of Israel, who had been taken prisoner by the Emperor Tiberius, was standing under an oak tree when, from a branch above him, an owl's dropping fell on his shoulder. Herod, preoccupied with his gloomy foreboding that Tiberius meant to have him executed, did not notice what had happened until a fellow prisoner, a German chieftain who was also a Druid seer, told him it was a good omen. The Druid, who was well known as an augur in his own country, said that the owl's dropping and its appearance in broad daylight without hooting meant that he would soon be released, that he would achieve great powers and dignity. He added a warning to Herod: "When you see an owl again in daylight, and if it settles near you and hoots, then, although this may happen when you are at the peak of your prosperity, your happiness and success are over. The number of times the owl hoots will be the number of days left to you."

Soon afterward Tiberius' death brought release for Herod, followed by his installation as King of Bashan by the new emperor, Caligula. The first part of the prophecy had been fulfilled; the second was accomplished in the course of the years, during which Herod's power and dominions had grown to a fabulous extent. On the point of founding, as he believed, an empire of the East, with himself as emperor, he arranged a great festival (supposedly in honor of the emperor Claudius' birthday), at Caesarea. The kings of neighboring countries gathered under white awnings in the amphitheater, where Herod, robed in silver tissue, crowned with a diamond-set golden diadem, sat on a silver-studded throne, under purple silk awnings, a silver sword in his hand. While Tyrian and Sidonian leaders groveled at his feet, he raised his hand to order the ram's horn should be blown, to signal the opening of the proceedings—raised his hand and let it fall.

In the arena he had seen an owl fluttering to and fro. It flew toward him: it perched on a guide rope of the awnings sheltering him. Then it hooted five times.

Within a few hours Herod was taken so ill that he had to be carried into the palace. "That was the same owl," he told his wife, Cypros, "which I saw in the prison yard at Misenum." He died five days later.

An early saint, Columba, was taught by a Druid who forecast the pattern of Columba's mission.

St. Columba was a very small boy when the clerk who was in charge of him went to the Chief Druid to ask his advice on when the child ought to begin to read. The *Faidh* (or Druid), having looked at the sky—perhaps divining the answer by clouds—said, "Write an alphabet for him now."

The clerk wrote the letters on a piece of cake, which Columba ate, half to the east and half to the west of a nearby stretch of water. The prophet, watching him, said, "So shall this child's territory be—half to the east of the sea, half to the west of the sea."

In this phrase he pictured Columba's future work, in Iona and among the Picts—half in Ireland and half in Scotland.

St. Bridget's future was predicted before she was born by Maithgen, a Druid who was famous for the "sight." Bridget's father, Dubthach, an Irish chieftain, was driving his chariot near the wizard's house, when Maithgen came out and signaled to him to stop.

"Whose is the woman hiding in your chariot?" Maithgen wanted to know. Dubthach answered that she belonged to him.

"Is she pregnant?" was the next question, and when Dubthach said that she was, Maithgen exclaimed, "Marvelous will be the child that is in her womb."

He was being pressed by his wife to sell the bondswoman, Dubthach told Maithgen, who protested that this must not be. "Your wife's children will serve the bondswoman's daughter, who will shine like a star among the stars of heaven."

About A.D. 125, a Druid made a prophecy to a King of Ireland, Modha Nuagat, which paralleled Joseph's prediction for Pharaoh. Seven years of plenty, he said, would be followed by seven years of famine. Modha Nuagat listened to the seer's advice; during the period of abundance, provision was made for the lean times, enabling him and his people to survive them.

Another Irish King (or god-king) of Ireland, Balor, was warned by a Druid that he would be killed by his grandson. Balor who had only one child, his daughter, Ethnea, decided to prevent the fulfillment of the prophecy by keeping her shut away in a tower on the summit of an almost inaccessible rock on the east coast of Tory Island, with a guard of twelve matrons for additional security.

The story of Balor's treatment of Ethnea spread around until it reached the ears of the hero chieftain Mackineely. With the help of a Druid he broke into Ethnea's tower, and in course of time she produced three sons. Balor had them drowned, as he thought, in a whirlpool, from which one of them escaped—and returned to kill him.

The gift of prophecy probably came to Eachtach through Druid blood. She herself could not have been a Druidess; she was no virgin, being the favorite of Art, son of Conn of the Hundred Battles. One night she had a dream in which she saw her head slashed from her shoulders and a tree growing out of her neck, whose branches overshadowed all Ireland. Then came a great storm, and the sea destroyed the tree. Then she saw a second tree, which the wind shattered.

The dream was interpreted to mean that Art would be killed in an impending battle, that the son of Art and Eachtach (then unborn) would be King of Ireland, that he would choke to death when a fishbone lodged in his throat, that his son would die in a battle with the Fianna Evisonn (militia of Ireland symbolized by the western wind, or tempest), which would rise against him.

And all these things came to pass, as foretold.

The Chief Druid of Barra was a guest at the festivities which celebrated the completion of the castle built by the MacNeils. "Tell us the fate of this place," the head of the house said to the Druid, perhaps regretting the question when the seer answered, "It will be an abode of thrushes when the Rattle Stone [which had disappeared some time before] is found; when people work at gathering seaweed in a village far from the sea; and when deer swim from Barra to Uist."

In the years that followed, all these things happened—and then as foretold, the great castle of the MacNeils was deserted, except by nesting thrushes.

The web of Druid predictions covers Scotland, as well as the other countries of the British Isles. The early settlement of the land north of the border between England and Scotland owes something at least to the famous Druid seer Calcer, who, when the Caledonians were expelled from Scythia, advised them to sail to a western isle, where they should, would—and did—make their home.

But Scotland, England, and Ireland probably cannot compare numerically in Druid predictions with Wales, last stronghold of the priestly cult. Their prophecies are recorded in her ancient national literature. *The Black Book of Carmarthen* tells of a prediction concerning war in Prydyn, the old name for the Welsh counties of Flint and Denbigh, which ran: "The Cymry [Welsh nation] will defend their coast against the men of Dublin. Seven ships will sail over the broad waters." Even to the number of ships, it seems, the presage proved true.

And then there was perhaps the greatest of the Druid seers, Merlin, who was magician, wizard, and prophet. For many years, particularly in the dark age of nineteenth-century materialism, he was rated as a myth, a fairy-story figure without historical reality, as was King Arthur, until the clearer view of modern science and scholarship uncovered evidence of substance behind the shadows.

The date on which Merlin was born is uncertain, but it was about 415, give or take a few years. At any rate, King Vortigern, the usurper who succeeded Constantine (407-411) was on the throne when Merlin made his first recorded appearance. According to Geoffrey of Monmouth, his mother was living in a nunnery and was the daughter of the King of Demetia; his paternity is uncertain.

While still a child, he was brought to the notice of King Vortigern, in whose court he remained for some years. He had already begun his career as a prophet; a number of predictions made by him during this time are recorded. In one of these, he foretold the Saxon invasion, the struggle of the Red Dragon of Wales (*ddraig goch*) with the White Dragon of the Saxons. Rivers would flow with blood, he said; then "out of Cornwall will come a Boar, who shall tread upon the neck of the White Dragon"—King Arthur, who defeated the Saxons.

Merlin stayed at Vortigern's court until, not wishing to be involved in the king's downfall which he foresaw was imminent, he thought the time had come to leave. After a good deal of difficulty he finally persuaded Vortigern to let him go, but before he went, Merlin left a written message in the king's closet, telling him to flee from the approaching disaster. The exiled sons of Constantine were on the way to avenge his murder.

Merlin's prophecies range over almost as many centuries as those of Nostradamus. Among those relating to times near to his own was his prediction of the civil war which broke out in Britain in the reign of Cadwallo, of famine and desolation when Cadwallader (circa 686), son of Cadwallo, was king, of the first Danish invasion, in the third and last year of his reign.

The Danes came again, as Merlin had said they would, in

the reign of Ethelred. He being too cowardly to fight them, Merlin foretold, would be forced to pay geld. The Danes exacted first £10,000, later £40,000, from Ethelred.

Merlin foresaw the elevation of a "man of humble birth, Edricus [Edric]" (whom he called the Snake), to high honors and a great position. Edric, who was made Duke of Mercia, was described in contemporary chronicles as "false of tongue, subtle of brain, perfidious and eloquent in speech."

The death of Hardicanute, the son of Canute and Emma of Normandy, was predicted by Merlin. Hardicanute, after drinking to excess, was unconscious for eight days before he died. Merlin had said:

And Helluo [Hardicanute] then with open jaws shall yawne,
Devouring even until midnight from the dawne.

Merlin foresaw the strange way in which Earl Godwin, father of King Harold, would die, and that his lands in Kent would disappear under the sea, leaving only the quicksands which still bear his name. The earl, it seems, was dining with King Edward the Confessor, who remarked that his brother Alfred would still be alive and "sustaining him" were it not for Earl Godwin. Hoping to convince Edward of his innocence, Godwin cried out: "May this bread choke me if I am guilty." Almost as he spoke, it did choke him, and he died.

Merlin's version of the incident and of the inundation of his lands is that:

Burst shall he after gordg'd with human blood [Alfred's murder]
And leave his name in part of the sea flood.

Of the sons of William the Conqueror, Merlin said:

One aims at but attains not his desire
By envious dart the other shall expire.

Robert Curthose, William's heir, was neither Duke of Normandy nor King of England. William Rufus was wounded fatally by an arrow on August 3, in the thirteenth year of his reign, when he was forty-four years old.

Merlin said of Richard I:

> The Lionheart will 'gainst the Saracen rise,
> And purchase from him many a glorious prize . . .
> But whilst abroad these great acts shall be done,
> All things at home shall to disorder run.
> Coop'ed up and cag'd the Lion then shall be,
> But after suffrance ransom'ed and set free.
> . . . Last by a poisonous shaft, the Lion die.

Seven centuries or so later, the man whom Merlin had foreseen would be known as Lion-Heart fought against the Saracens and during another campaign was captured and escaped. His end came three days after being hit with a poisoned arrow shot by archer Bertrand Genedow, from the battlements of a castle near Limoges. Richard captured the castle before he died.

In one of his prophecies, Merlin said that one day England would be again called Britain, a prediction fulfilled when the English and Scottish crowns were united under James I. Merlin had foretold his coming:

> O'er Boreas' [north wind] wings then hither shall be borne
> Through Reek [Berwick] o'er Tweed, a princely unicorn . . .
> Joining by Fate's unchangeable dispose
> The Northern thistle to the English Rose.

And of the Gunpowder Plot:

> . . . Yet from the old lupanar shall wolves be sent
> To undermine both Crown and Government.
> Striving in Hell to register their names,
> By blowing up the State in powder flames.

Merlin predicted the Crusades, Henry VIII's break with Rome, the reigns of his three children—Edward, Mary, and

Elizabeth—and many later monarchs, and the French Revolution. By the twelfth century his fame had spread all over Europe; one of the French kings, Louis the Fat, it is said, formulated the policies of his kingdom on Merlin's prophecies.

His forecast for his own nation, the Welsh, has a Thoth-like ring. "You will keep your language and your race," he said, "but of your old kingdom, nothing will remain but Gwalia's [Wales'] rugged mountains."

5. Prophecy in the Ancient East and West

Not so long ago the only wheels to be seen or heard in Tibet were prayer wheels—brass cylinders—clacking and creaking as they turned in endless petition. "When wheels come into the country, peace goes out," the ancient prophecy said, so for centuries, wheeled vehicles were forbidden. But men's rulings cannot affect nature's laws of growth and change; eventually wheels rolled over the frontiers and into Tibet. And as the prophecy foretold, with their coming, peace went.

Prophecy has always played an important part in Tibetan religious and everyday life; since early in the eleventh century, astrology has guided the making of political decisions. Before 1850, the British invasion of Tibet in 1904 was foretold. A translation of the prediction reads: "In the Year of the Wood Dragon [1904]. The first part of the year protects the Dalai Lama, after that, fighting and quarreling, robbers come forward. There are many enemies, troublous grief by weapons will arise, and the people will fight. At the end of the year, a conciliatory speaker will end the war." During the Wood Dragon War, as it was called, Colonel Francis Younghusband, who commanded the British forces, saw the prediction at Lhasa; in 1902 it was shown to L. A. Waddell, then serving with the British Army. Sir Charles Bell, who

Prophecy in the Ancient East and West   69

went later to Lhasa, was able to examine this prophecy and a number of others, all of which were fulfilled.

Among these were predictions of the Chinese invasion of Tibet in 1910; of the Chinese Revolution and rise of the national government in 1911; of the expulsion of the Chinese from Tibet at the end of 1911; of war between England and Germany in 1914; of the death of the Dalai Lama in 1933 and the appearance in 1935 of another incarnation. For 1950, there was a warning: "Evil forces will invade Tibet." In that year, the Chinese again crossed its frontiers.

Tibet has its oracles, as famous in the East as were those of Greece in the West. When the Dalai Lama dies, the key to discovery of his new incarnation is given by an oracle.

Buddha's vice-regents have been incarnating in Tibet since the early stages of its history; the first Grand Lama to be known as Dalai Lama was given the name by the famous conqueror Altan Khan when the lama visited him in Mongolia. Altan, who knew that the lama's predecessor had also been known as Gyatso, thought it must be a family name; he addressed him as Dalai Lama, *dalai* being the Mongolian equivalent of the Tibetan word *gyatso*. Since that time, all incarnations have been called Dalai Lama; the first was Gedun-gyatso, born in 1412. According to tradition there were to be twelve incarnations, then no more. The twelfth of the series is thought to be the present Dalai Lama.

After the death of a Grand Lama, the ritual procedure for discovering his successor was to write down the names of children in whom he was said to be reincarnated on tablets or paper and to shake them in a gold jar. The name which fell out of the jar three times, together with a pellet inscribed with "yes," was accepted as the choice of the oracle, subject to tests, such as picking out from a number of similar objects the rosary, rings, cup, and miter of the dead lama. The oracle would then indicate the birthplace of the incarnation, around which confirmatory signs would be found, such as the blossoming of fruit trees months before their season.

In 1875, after the death of Tinle-gyatso, the oracle declared that the incarnation must be discovered by a monk pure in thought, word and deed, indicating that a gelong (monk) named Shar-tse-Khampo, of the monastery of Gaden, with a reputation of saintliness and profound knowledge, should undertake the mission.

The oracle told the monk the incarnation would be found near a place called Kong-po. The Khampo meditated for seven days before setting out; at the end of that time, a vision was given to him. He saw the Grand Lama in his mother's arms, while his father fondled him. The house, the furniture, the surroundings of the place—all were shown him.

On his way to Kong-po the gelong stopped to ask his way at a house in Tag-po. It was the house of his vision; he recognized the people living in it as the parents he had seen in his vision and their child as the incarnation of the Grand Lama.

One of the great oracles of the century, Lhamo Sung-Chyongma, consulted at the end of the nineteenth century by the government of Lhasa, foretold invasion of and great calamities for Tibet in the twentieth century. Lhasa itself has two leading oracles, Nachung and Karmashar, each of which has a long list of fulfilled prophecies. The Nachung shrine is attached to the principal monastery, Drepung, the high priest of which has a retinue of a hundred yellow-hatted (high-ranking) monks; its towering roof is golden.

The temple is at the head of a flight of broad stairs, flanked by two great Chinese types of lion. Inside, it is hung with silk banners, *kakemono* scrolls, and armor; massive red pillars support the roof.

At the far end of the temple, between two great altars, around which stand six colossal figures, a brass gateway leads into the oracle chamber, a small dark room, in a recess of which can be seen, by the light of the sacred fire burning on a table altar, the priest of the shrine. Robed in silk, hung with necklaces of jewels, wearing a breastplate, with a massive sword on his left, in front of him a great brass cup inlaid with gold, he sits on a chair covered with silk cushions, surrounded by an aura of dignity and power. He is arbiter of the ritual of the incarnations, indicator of the sacred place in which the new Grand Lama is to be found.

The Karmashar oracle, which is consulted chiefly by the rank and file, makes auguries for the current year. Its prophecies included a prediction made at the end of the nineteenth century of war in the Sheep Year, 1907: "Great slaughter, many dead bodies, encampments around and in Tibet. Plentiful crops." In fact, it was in 1904 that there was "great slaughter" in Tibet, bloody battles in which thousands were killed, armies camped in the country and around its frontiers. The British reached Lhasa on August 3, 1904.

The Karmashar oracle's shrine is a dark inner room of a small temple, hung with devil masks and a large drum. The seer sits in the shrine, on a cushioned chair, wearing a heavy conical hat, a breastplate, robes covered with jewels, long Chinese boots, and a sword.

L. A. Waddell, an authority on Tibet, consulted this oracle when he was a lieutenant in the Indian Medical Service. When the seer asked his age and Waddell gave it, the priest said, "No, you are one year more." And then Waddell remembered that he had just had a birthday.

Tibet is a country of mysticism and mystics, many of whom are said to have developed fabulous psychic powers by hours of meditation, fasting, self-discipline, and mind control. Many of these men, lamas (teachers, not necessarily monks) or gelongs (monks), consider much of the séance-room phenomena produced in the West so childish as to be unworthy of serious attention. When the Lama Tashil-hunpo was told of cases of apports, such as letters dropped from the ceiling or out of the air, and that some people believed it possible to make contact with spirits by such means, he said, "And these are the men who conquered India. . . ."

Time out of mind, prophecies have been made and recorded in Tibet. One of these, dating from about 1290, concerns Pu-ton Rimpoche, who was born in that year. He was such an ugly child that his mother, ashamed of him, hid him from the neighbors. One day, in spite of her precautions, a distinguished lama saw him. This child, he predicted, would have a great future, high honors, and great learning. The Boy Who Was Shown, as he was called after this experience, later achieved the eminence foretold by the lama; the name Rimpoche became a household word for scholarship.

Prophetic vision, being an everyday occurrence among lamas and gelongs, is thought remarkable only if the event foreseen does not materialize.

Alexandra David-Neel, in her book *Journey to Lhasa*, says that when she was staying in Jakyendo, before the First World War, she was told by an old bard of a prophecy that the Tashi Lama would leave Tibet and go northward. (The Tashi Lama is the political leader, the Dalai Lama the spiritual head of Tibet.) It seemed so inconceivable that the mystic lord of Tashi Lumpo should go from Tibet into the northern latitudes that Mme. David-Neel could not take the prophecy seriously. "How many centuries ahead will this happen?" she asked the bard, jokingly. "You yourself will see the fulfillment of the prophecy," he told her. "The Tashi Lama will leave Shigatse before two and a half years are gone." Two years and one month after this prediction was made the Panchen Rimpoche took refuge in China during political disruptions in Tibet, escaping from Shigatse just in time to avoid arrest and possible execution.

When the Lama Tspia psychically saw his fellow (or *gyud*) lama from the college of magic ritual saying good-bye to a young *trapa* (or novice) with a pack on his back as if beginning a journey and watched the lama send the boy off in a direction leading to his (Tspia's) house, he knew that he would be having a visitor before long and thought as much of his precognition as he would of receiving information by letter. He had noticed in his vision a large tear in the *trapa's* robe; when a few weeks later the novice presented himself to the lama, Tspia saw that his robe was torn.

Mme. David-Neel, who lived for some years among the Tibetans and who was at one time the only white woman to have entered Lhasa, constantly met with examples of the telepathic and precognitive powers or clairvoyance of the lamas and priests. One day she and her Tibetan companion Youngden, having spent a night in a ditch without food, water or fuel, saw a lama finishing his midday meal with three *trapas*. Four horses were grazing near them. The lama, as Mme. David-Neel and Youngden came up to him, muttered: "*Ning Je* [How sad—Poor things]." He gave them tea and tsamba (the staple food of Tibet—barley flour, moistened with tea), and then he sat silent. Lamas do not believe in speaking unless there is something which must be said.

Mme. David-Neel, who had noticed an empty curd pot, whispered to Youngden, "You can get some curd from the farm [which they could see nearby] when the lama is gone." The lama could not have heard the whisper, but apparently sensed what had been said. "Poor things," he repeated, then turned his head in the direction of one of the disciples who had gone to retrieve a straying horse. The man, who was leading the horse toward the lama, suddenly stopped, tied up the horse, and went off to the farm. Soon he came back, carrying a full curd bowl, which he gave to Mme. David-Neel.

Passing through the primeval forest area between the Tagan and Kunka Pass, she met a party of six travelers, one of whom was a monk en route to join his master; he was going to work with him in a rite to exorcise a powerful demon. This was something Mme. David-Neel had always wanted to see; she first asked, and then implored the *ngaspa* to take her with him. "Impossible," he said. All the same, she decided that she would follow him; she and members of her party took it in turns to watch him so that he could not leave them unnoticed, but so tactfully, she thought, that he would not realize what they were doing. One day he said to her, "Do not be afraid that I shall run away. There is no need; I do not have to go ahead to warn my master of your coming. He knows already. *Ngais lung gi teng la len tang tsar* [I have sent a message on the wind]."

Soon afterward the monk's veto was reinforced by a troop of horsemen dispatched by the lama-exorcist. They told Mme. David-Neel politely but unbendingly that she must give up the idea of visiting him. Only initiated disciples could be allowed in his secret sanctuary.

To send a message on the wind (telepathy) is to a Tibetan as unremarkable a procedure as the dispatch of a telegram would be to us. And it costs nothing in terms of money. All that is necessary is what the Tibetans call "one-pointedness of thought," intense concentration, ability to receive and transmit mental orders and messages accurately; the long strenuous training necessary to reach these goals makes even the price of our telegrams seem cheap by comparison.

Mind control is the basis of Tibetan psychospiritual teaching, as it must be of any such system; development of telepathy is one of its by-products. *Tum-mo,* ability to generate body heat through thought, is another. If at last he masters the art, while sitting naked in the snow, the initiate is able to dry off wet sheets draped around him; the more he can dry, the greater his powers are estimated to be. I have heard that forty dried sheets in one night are considered a respectable score.

Tum-mo, more than anything else, was the feat Milarepa, the great Tibetan mystic and prophet, who has been called one of the world's greatest yogis, longed to be able to perform. Apparently he could fly, make a month's journey in three days, manifest himself in two places at the same time, alter his pulse rate, stop his heartbeat, arrest a hemorrhage after a deep (self-inflicted) cut, heal the wound almost immediately, suspend physical animation, and see into the future, but he took so long to master *tum-mo* that he almost despaired of achieving it.

The great Jetsun Milarepa was born in Kyanga-Tsa on August 5 in the year of the Male Water Dragon, 1052. His father, a wealthy man, owning a fine house, died when Jetsun was seven and his sister, Peta, three years old. The uncle and aunt whom the father, Mila Sharao, appointed as guardians of the estate behaved monstrously to the widow, Karmo Kyen (White Garland), whose money and jewelry they stole, and to the two children, whom they forced to work in the fields. Karmo Kyen, who retired to the small holding she owned, eventually raised enough money to send her son to a lama of repute to study black magic, so that he could deal with their enemies. Milarepa may or may not have wanted to learn the black arts—probably not, since his mother had to put pressure on him by threatening to kill herself if he did not go to the lama.

In the end he went. For some years he studied under two teachers; then, as he had foreseen during his studies, a day came when celebrations were held in the house which had been his father's, for the wedding of his uncle's son. All the guests, Milarepa knew, were people who had helped his uncle and aunt dispossess his mother. He set to work, according to the formulas he had learned. Evidently he had been a good pupil; the house collapsed. Afterward he was told that thirty-five of the people who had worked against his family had been killed.

It was an encouraging beginning, but in spite of it, Milarepa soon lost any enthusiasm he had had for the "black" path. For years he underwent almost incredible hardships and sufferings to purge himself of its influences; in the end he attained a degree of psychic power and enlightenment beyond the range of most human beings. Disciples crowded to him; he accepted only those whom he was shown in a vision, in which he was also told where to find them. Some were shepherds; some were women. Milarepa taught all sorts and conditions of people; his fame grew with the number of his pupils.

He was not only the greatest occultist and miracle worker in the country, people said, but also the wisest and the most saintly man. Some of the other lamas found this very hard to bear; one of them, Tsaphuwa, decided that the sooner Milarepa was disposed of, the better for his colleagues.

Tsaphuwa promised his mistress a fine turquoise if she

took a bowl of poisoned curds to Milarepa, who had already prophesied that this would happen. Milarepa told the woman to take the curds away; then, knowing that he *must* die soon, he called her back. "Bring the curds again and I will eat them."

The woman told her lover that she would not go again to Milarepa with the poisoned food. It took a great deal of argument and the promise of marriage, as well as of the turquoise, from Tsaphuwa, to make her change her mind. When finally she gave the curds to Milarepa, he said, "So you got the turquoise for doing this." Weeping, she begged him to give back the bowl to her, so that she could eat the curds and die instead of him. He refused, adding a warning not to rely on Tsaphuwa's promise to marry her and that both of them would suffer because of the wrong they had done him.

The poisoned curds seemed to have no effect on Milarepa for some time. When he became ill, he would not take any remedies or allow anything to be done to help him to recover. If he had wanted to be cured, he could have healed himself, he told his disciples. "But," he said, "the time has come when the body that is mind-evolved only must become merged into the realm of light, and no rites are necessary for this . . . there is no means by which anyone can postpone the decreed day of his death."

In Milarepa's case it came during the last month of the Wood Hare Year, January, 1135.

The mystical tradition of Tibet, which produced seers and prophets such as Milarepa, had as complement a system of astrology, which was consulted before any decision was made and was used to predict events in this world and the future of the soul in the next.

The father of Tibetan astrology, Padmasambhava, known as the Lotus-Born, or the Precious Guru, brought the science from India, where he was a professor at the great Buddhist University of Nalanda, to Tibet about A.D. 749. But although Tibetan astrology was based on the Indian system

Prophecy in the Ancient East and West

and shows the influence of its next-door neighbor, China, it is not a mere hodgepodge of two schools of thought. Its practitioners—who calculate from fixed cycles, not from planetary positions, and do not use an ephemeris—evolved a method of procedure of their own, producing results which compare favorably in their accuracy with the Brahmanic and Ptolemaic systems and even with the Chaldaean, although Chaldaean astrologers were the acknowledged masters of the science in the ancient world.

At one time, because of this, "Chaldaean" and "astrologer" were almost interchangeable terms. Among the notable members of what must have been a rather overcrowded profession in that country one man stands out, Berosus, initiated priest of Baal, first and greatest of Chaldaea's astrologers and historians.

His name means son of the physician; his early years were spent in Babylon, and he was contemporary with Ptolemy Philadelphus, who reigned in Egypt for thirty-eight years. When Alexander the Great conquered Babylon, Berosus, who was Greek-speaking, went to Cos, where he established an observatory and opened a school of astronomy and astrology, then synonymous terms. Vitruvius said he was the forerunner of a long line of astrologers "of genius and great acuteness." As a seer, the Athenians thought so highly of him, his learning, his wisdom and prophetic gifts, that they put up a statue to him which had a gilded tongue, symbol of the truth of his predictions. "Nearly all his prophecies were fulfilled," a contemporary record comments.

Almost every prophet and seer, ancient and modern, has foreseen a global catastrophe and a great deluge. Berosus said the great year (that is, the period of disaster which will destroy this planet) will come "according to the course of the stars." When all the planets coincide in the sign of Cancer, "and are so placed that a straight line would pass directly through all their orbs, all things terrestrial will be consumed." When the same conjunction takes place in Capricorn, the great deluge will be at hand. Seneca, mentioning this prophecy, points out that Cancer is a sign belonging to the summer months, Capricorn to the winter. According to this reckoning, in the January of some as yet unknown year, the "waters will cover the earth"; on a July day "the great conflagration," which will consume it, will break out. Berosus gives no clue to when these fatalities fall due, though it seems that he could have used the vast reservoir of knowledge and data at his disposal to predict their dates. Cicero, in his first book of divination, says that the Chaldaeans had records of the stars, which covered 370,000 years; Diodorus Siculus gives the period of their observations as 472,000 years; Critodemes, Epigenes, and Berosus himself put it at between 490,000 and 720,000 years. And also, for many thousands of years, the Babylonians kept the horoscopes of all children born in the country, from which vast mass of data they calculated the influence of the planets and zodiacal signs on human beings and their affairs.

"The Sumerians and the Babylonians [Chaldaeans] believed," says Sir Ernest Wallis Budge, "that the will of the gods in respect to man and his affairs could be learned by watching the motions of the stars and planets, and that skilled star-gazers could obtain, from their motions and varying aspects of the heavenly bodies, indications of future prosperity and calamity . . . these observations and their comments on them and interpretations of them have formed the foundations of astrology in use in the world for the last 5,000 years . . . we are bound to believe that the period during which observations of the heavens were made on the plains of Babylon comprised many thousands of years."

Abraham, the Biblical patriarch, who was called the Chaldaean, was a skilled interpreter of the lore of the stars. A reference to him in the *Jewish Encyclopaedia* reads: "Abraham the Chaldean, bore upon his breast a large astrological tablet on which the fate of every man might be read; for which reason—according to the Haggadist—all the kings of the East and of the West congregated every morning before his door in order to seek advice."

Prophecy in the Ancient East and West 79

Brahman seers told Alexander the Great that he would die at Babylon. So many prophecies had been fulfilled in his life that when astrologers warned him: "Flee from this town where the fatal star reigns," he withdrew his armies, although they had already reached the walls of Babylon. Later he entered the city . . . and died there.

Persia, too, had her stargazers, one of whom told Cambyses that he would die at Ecbatana. Cambyses, taking it for granted that the prophecy referred to the Median city of that name, did everything he could to defeat fate by taking no risks in any fighting in that area, and thus he avoided even a scratch. He died in the city of Ecbatana in Syria.

One of Persia's most notable prophets was Al Hakim, whose name means "the wise one." He was court astrologer to the Emperor Darius, who is supposed never to have taken a decision without first consulting him. Al Hakim wrote a number of books, in one of which he recorded predictions of the coming of Christ, the birth of Mohammed, the end of the Magi, and many others.

Babylon figured in a prophecy made by Avicenna (Ibn Sina) of the Tartar invasion. "When Mars arises from the land of Babylon," he said, "and the two unlucky planets [Mars and Saturn] are in conjunction, then Beware: Beware: there must needs happen great things, and needs must the Tartars come to your country." Avicenna, who was born in August, 980, and died in 1037, was a great poet, as well as a prophet, a combination of gifts not uncommon around this period. The great Persian poet Anwari foretold the arising of a "great tempest" on September 16, 1188, because of the conjunction of five planets in the sign of the Balance (Libra) on that date. The day and the night were exceptionally calm; everyone who had heard the prophecy believed Anwari had blundered badly.

But Anwari's prediction did not refer to the weather. That night a great tempest did arise; Genghis Khan, the Mogol who devastated and conquered half the world, was born. His father is said to have died before his birth; the boy had a sketchy education, but these circumstances could not prevent the consummation of his destiny or the unfolding of his genius, which was prefigured by the extraordinary conjunction of five planets. An old astrologer, Sujujin, predicted to his father that Genghis Khan would be a great soldier and conqueror. His rule would extend to the distant corners of the earth; he would be the Khan of all Tartary.

Years afterward, when all these prophecies had been fulfilled, the khan, whose title then was the Emperor of All Men, knowing something of astrology, foresaw in an unfavorable conjunction of planets disaster for himself. He turned back to the west, but when he reached the Si Kiang River in Kansu, his health gave way. After a short illness, he died in the camp in the province of Shansi, at the age of sixty-five. The great empire he had founded, which was named the Wise Government or Government of Wisdom, passed eventually to his grandson, Kublai Khan.

Genghis Khan's astrologer in chief, Ye-lü Ch'u-ts'ai, was constantly at his side during his triumphal progresses. His nation, the Chinese, in the ancient world, were famous for their skill in this science and for the system of star study they had evolved in the days when China was virtually cut off from the rest of the world.

According to Richard H. Allen, who says that China is a "Country never Backward in Claiming the Invention of Almost Everything," in the *Annals of China,* the formation of constellations is represented as being discovered by Tajao, Prime Minister of Huang-ti, 2037 B.C. Great parade is made, he says, of an observation of the Pleiades from an observatory "Said to Have Been Erected 2608 B.C." Allen does not seem to have thought too much of these claims, but the opinion of the honorary secretary of the Royal Astronomical Society is that "China was one of the leading nations of antiquity in astronomical study . . . the Chinese zodiac is quite independent of that in use in the west."

And in *The Horoscope,* A. J. Pearce says:

Astrology was firmly established among the learned Chinese from the earliest periods in the history of their remarkable country. From the days of Fohi, about 2752 B.C., for nearly 2,500 years, Sir David Brewster said, astronomy was studied in China solely for the purposes of astrology, and it was held in the highest veneration—emperors being chosen on account of their knowledge of astronomy and astrology. This was expressly the case with Chueni, who, in the year 2513 B.C., himself computed an ephemeris of the motions of five planets, "a great conjunction which is thought to have been observed by him, as it took place in the year 2449 B.C." Marco Polo evidently was impressed by Chinese astrologers, who were, he said: ". . . very skilful in their business, and often their words come to pass, so the people have great faith in them."

The Chinese court had its official astrologer, an office which at one time was hereditary. In the middle of the third millennium B.C. it was held jointly by the princes Hi and Ho, whose ancestors had been appointed to observe and interpret the behavior of the stars, under the Emperor Yao. Their career ended when a solar eclipse, which they had not predicted, occurred. This was considered neglect of their hereditary duties; they were charged with "having done violence to the five fundamental forces and having idly abandoned the three fundamental regulations," offenses for which the penalty was death. Sentence was carried out by the majordomo, Yin.

Along with astrologers, seers who foresaw the future by clairvoyance were in demand; among them were women, as well as men. One of these prophesied that seventy-six states would submit to the house of Shang, later the Yin Dynasty, which came to pass. A member of this house, Wu Ting, according to contemporary records, was himself a gifted psychic.

He was looking for an assistant but could not discover anyone suitable for the post. One night, in a dream, he was shown a man, and told that he would be the ideal adjutant, with whose help he would do great things for his empire. Wu

Ting remembered the face of this man so clearly that next day he was able to have a picture made from his description of the vision. Armed with this, his agents scoured the country searching for its original, finding him, at last, among the feudal bondsmen. The prophetic message of the dream was fulfilled by Fu Yue, who, as Wu Ting's right-hand man, was instrumental in bringing about a period of great prosperity to the empire.

There was augury by oracle, too, in ancient China. One of the methods used was divination by tortoise. The bones were scraped smooth, then notched on the back with a red-hot stick, by which cracks were produced. The shape and number of these were interpreted as the oracular pronouncement; this was scratched on the bones, which were buried. From the ancient ruined capital of Yin, bones have been recovered which probably had been buried there after the oracle had been consulted.

King Li of the house of Chou—*c.* 841 B.C.—employed seers to divine by tortoise and also by the sixty-four hexagrams of the *I Ching,* the Book of Changes, to discover every person in the kingdom who was against his government. The divination was successful, but its results were not; a rebellion against the plan broke out. Li lost his throne.

Astrologers or seers since the earliest days of Chinese history held the important post of scribe, or script magician. Part of their duty was to record events, so that China's past could be traced back to very ancient times in their chronicles. They, being astrologers as well as historians, were responsible for handing on celestial and terrestrial knowledge and wisdom, in the form of the written word; they were regarded as sages whose opinion was final on any issue about which they were consulted. In the days of Huang-ti, before 2200 B.C., perhaps *c.* 3000 B.C., they existed; among the names mentioned of the early script magicians is that of Lao-tse.

Unfortunately an emperor of a later period, the tyrant Ch'in Shih Huang-ti, decided that in order to persuade posterity he was the superman he considered himself to be, history must appear to begin with his reign. He ordered all the ancient books which contradicted his claim to be burned. And so the accumulated wisdom and knowledge of centuries went up in the smoke of a holocaust like that at Alexandria, on the excuse that the ancient classics might be misunderstood by the undiscriminating and thereby the welfare of the state be endangered.

Astrological works were not touched under Huang-ti's edict, they being regarded as the reference books of a science considered essential to the smooth running of the state. And at least two of the ancient chronicles survived the burning of the books: the *Annals of the Bamboo Books,* dug up from the grave of one of the rulers of Wei, and *Spring and Autumn Annals* of the Lu state, on which Confucius based historical judgments.

A vision of astrological symbols heralded the birth of Confucius. In it five ancient sages appeared leading a lionlike creature, scaled like a dragon, with a horn in the middle of its forehead. According to astrologic interpretation, the dragon-lion of China signified, as did the phoenix of Egypt and Arabia, a certain period of time; at the end of each of these cycles, a "superior man" manifests. The five ancient sages represented the five planets, conjunction of which indicated (or "led in") the sacred animal, the superman, which Confucius proved himself to be.

He believed that the future can be foreseen; the method of divination he used was the *I Ching,* the Book of Changes. Confucius—and C. G. Jung, the great psychologist, many years later—wrote a zealous commentary to the *I Ching,* said to be one of the most mysterious documents in the world. It is older than the Vedas of India, "more curious than the cuneiform inscriptions of Babylon"; interpretations of combinations of its sixty-four hexagrams foretell what lies ahead.

Confucius studied astrology, to which he refers in his writings. "Without recognizing the ordinances of heaven," he says, "it is impossible to be a superior man," and "In order to know men, he may not dispense with a knowledge of heaven."

At the other side of the world, in Mexico, astrological knowledge and techniques were at least as developed as those of Eastern countries at the same period; the soothsayers of the far West were as famous as Oriental sages for their powers of divination. They had a deeper insight into astronomy than any nation except possibly the Chaldaeans; the Maya, having made observations of the stars for 4,000 years, had a calendar developed to a point where any given day could be distinguished without duplication for 370,000 years.

Astrology was taught to the ancient Americans by Quetzalcoatl, the first and greatest of their philosophers. He is an avatar figure; like many of the others, including Christ, he was born of a virgin, Xochiquetzal. His story follows the familiar pattern: He was the son of the Universal Creator; an annunciation of his coming was made by a heavenly being (a messenger from the god of the Milky Way), whose purpose was to discover a "blessed virgin" worthy to become the mother of the divine incarnation. Quetzalcoatl was always known as "he who was born of the virgin" to mark his miraculous origin, and since he established a school of sacerdotal initiates, to whom he passed on his teachings, as "priest-prophet-king."

The sacred astrological calendar of the old Mexico, the tonalmatl, was the work of Quetzalcoatl, although he is supposed to have had the divinities Oxomoco and Cipactonal as collaborators. The Book of the Good and Bad Days, or the Book of Fate, was a calendar of favorable and unfavorable periods, which was always consulted as to the outcome of any undertaking, the beginning of a journey, the prospects of a newborn child. But since in those days in Mexico it was thought important to have as complete as possible a blueprint of the new citizen's future, an astrologer-prophet was called in as soon as the child was born, and it was his duty to discover in detail the child's destiny.

The two astrologers in Mexican history who are considered to rank in knowledge and skill next to Quetzalcoatl—whose divine origin perhaps gave him a natural advantage—were

Nezahualcoyotl (Nazahualpilli) and Montezuma. Both were kings; astrology was a profession in those days which attracted to it men of the highest position and great learning. Nezahualcoyotl was King of Tezcoco; Juan de Torquemada mentions him in *Indian Monarchy:*

> They say that he was a great astrologer, and prided himself much on his knowledge of the motions of celestial bodies, and being attached to this study, that he caused inquiries to be made throughout the entire of his dominions, for all such persons as were at all conversant with it, whom he had brought to his court, and imparted to them whatever he knew, and ascending by night on the terraced roof of his palace, he thence considered the stars, and disputed with them on all difficult questions concerned with them. I at least can affirm that I have seen a place on the outside of the roof of the palace, enclosed within four walls only a yard in height and just of sufficient breadth for a man to lie down in; in each angle of which was a hole of perforation . . . and on inquiring the use of the square place, a grandson of his, who was showing me the palace, replied that it was for King Nazahualpilli, when he went by night, attended by his astrologers to contemplate the heavens and the stars; whence I inferred that what was reported of him is true.

When Montezuma, as a young man, became King of Mexico, Nezahualcoyotl congratulated the nation in a speech at the coronation, on the election of a ruler "whose deep knowledge of heavenly things insured to his subjects his comprehension of those of an earthly nature."

Later, some years before the Spanish invasion of the country, he warned Montezuma of the coming catastrophe. He prophesied that the sands were running out for the Mexican Empire and that with the destruction of Montezuma's cities and the slaughter of his people, the old civilization of the country would disappear. Phenomena and evil omens, he said, would occur during the coming years to confirm that the time of the fulfillment of his predictions was at hand.

The signs and portents he foretold began to manifest in

1505, when there was a famine. At the beginning of the new cycle, 1507, inaugurated by the symbolic "lighting of the new fire" by Montezuma, an eclipse occurred, a disastrous augury, according to the astrologers. An earthquake followed it. Each succeeding year, according to Hubert H. Bancroft's *History of the Pacific States of America,* contributed its quota of "one or more signs of occurrence of an ominous nature." Soon after the earthquake, a comet with three heads was seen traveling rapidly eastward, sparks seeming to spurt from its tail. It was interpreted as a bad omen, as was a "pyramidal light, which scattered sparks on all sides, rose at midnight from the eastern horizon till the apex reached the zenith, where it faded at dawn," a phenomenon which appeared regularly for forty days. It was a presage, the seers said, of "wars, famine, pestilence, mortality among the lords."

Nezahualcoyotl, whom Montezuma called into consultation, agreed with the other astrologers' findings. Having cast his horoscope, he realized that neither he nor his kingdom could escape the cataclysm which would destroy Montezuma.

The last of the evil omens appeared in 1519, the year of the Spanish invasion. For several days a comet hung over Mexico City; it was, the astrologers predicted, a sign that ruin and devastation of their country were imminent.

For at least four generations before the Spaniards came to Mexico, prophecies were current that one day the country would be invaded by bearded men from across the sea who would wear strange garments and "caskets" on their heads. They would be armed with sharp swords; they would overrun Mexico and destroy it and the Aztec gods.

Montezuma himself had foreseen the cataclysm that would end his rule. The last king of the Indians had been called the outstanding organizing genius of the Aztec race; he conquered forty-four cities and turned a monarchy into an empire, throughout which he was respected for the wisdom and justice of his rule. He was a great statesman, lawgiver, and prince; he was also famous as an occultist and astrologer. In 1508, an ashen-hued cranelike bird was taken to Montezuma, who was in the Tlillancalmecatl (place of heavenly learning). This was in the second of the two divisions of the day recognized by the Aztecs, the afternoon. In a mirror-shaped crest on the bird's head, Montezuma saw reflected the heavens and the stars and the fire sticks, used to generate flame—an evil omen. The picture changed to show a concourse of people advancing, massed, as conquerors, in battle array. They were riding what, no Aztec having seen a horse, he described as deer. This was in 1508.

About the same time, Montezuma's sister, Paranazin, fell into a cataleptic trance, diagnosed by her doctors as death. As her funeral procession made its way to the tomb, Paranazin recovered. While in trance, she said, she had had a vision, in which she had seen great ships from a far country, bringing to Mexico men in foreign dress, armed, wearing metal casques on their heads, carrying banners. They would become masters of the Aztec lands.

In 1520 the catastrophes foretold, in visions and by prophecies, materialized. And Montezuma, who was described in *Collection of Mexico* as "by nature wise, an astrologer and philosopher, and skilled and generally versed in all the arts, both in those of the military, as well as those of a civil nature," died in his fifty-third year.

6. The Saints and the Plowboy

All the stars of Maelmaedhog ua Morgair—otherwise Malachy O'Morgain—whom Eire canonized and considers her greatest prophet, must have been in the most propitious positions and conjunctions when he was born in 1094 or 1095.

He began life with everything in his favor. His father was wealthy, of high rank, and, what in those days was rare even among the nobility, a man of great culture and learning. A lay professor, he was described as "chief Lector of Armagh and of all the west of Europe." In those days, teaching in Ireland was a profession so highly thought of that kings were proud to belong to it. The King of Munster in the ninth century and his successor, Cormac MacCuilenon in the tenth, both were college professors.

Malachy's mother came from a powerful and wealthy family in Bangor, County Down; she is described as a woman of great mental attainments and fine character; she must also have had strength, to judge from the way in which she met the loss of her husband when Malachy was about eight years old and coped efficiently with the problems of financial affairs and of bringing up single-handed a young family (Malachy had a brother and a sister).

Malachy's childhood seems to have been happy and, since nothing else is recorded of it, uneventful. At a very early age he had shown religious and mystic leanings; when he was in his teens, he became the disciple of Ivor O'Hagan, a monk widely considered to be a saint, who lived as a recluse in a cell adjoining the great church of Armagh.

Soon after he joined O'Hagan, Malachy decided that the path of austerity and self-denial was the way of life for him, too. He broke all ties with the worldly life, much to the disapproval of his friends and the disgust of his sister. Everyone in his circle felt that it was madness to give up the possibilities of a brilliant and useful career for the living death of an anchorite's cell. His sister used every argument she could think of to make him change his mind, without effect. And in about 1117, Archbishop Celsus (a great friend of Ivor O'Hagan's), conferred on Malachy the order of diaconate, the canonical age for receiving which is twenty-five, when he was only twenty-three.

A few years later, he was appointed abbot of the restored Bangor Monastery, where he performed his first miracles: healing a woman of an apparently mortal ax wound, restoring a dying man, and curing a fellow cleric at death's door with dysentery.

When Celsus died, he appointed Malachy as his successor. After reluctantly taking the appointment, for he felt it was not in keeping with the simple life to which he was vowed, he held it until 1137, when he resigned.

On a visit to England, as he neared York, he met a priest called Sycarus, who, knowing nothing of him, said, "This is the man of whom it was told to me in vision: from Ireland shall come a holy bishop who can read the thoughts of men's minds." He predicted to Malachy that very few of his disciples would return with him to Ireland, which was misinterpreted as a prophecy that many of them would die on their travels. In fact, most of the members of Malachy's entourage remained abroad at one monastery or another for training in Cistercian observance.

On his way home after visiting Pope Innocent in Rome, Malachy, passing through Scotland, was sent for by King David, whose only son, Henry, was dying.

"Pray for him, my lord bishop," the king implored Malachy, who blessed some water, sprinkled the youth with it, and said, "Be of good cheer, son. You shall not die this time." The next day the boy was as well as ever.

Once more in Ireland, Malachy journeyed all over the country, on foot, founding monasteries and convents, reviving useful laws, restoring order. Wherever he went, he performed miracles of healing, even raising the dead. At Clonmel, he saw a youth in the crowd who, as he told the monks in the monastery where he was lodged, would seek him out and ask his help in being admitted to the community. The next day, as he had foretold, the young man came to him, and Malachy presented him to the Abbot Congan. "And from this," says St. Bernard, "the brethren knew that Malachy had the spirit of prophecy."

Soon afterward Malachy made another prediction. He had begun to build an oratory of stone, instead of the usual wood or lath and plaster, which roused a great deal of opposition. The people in the neighborhood were conservative; the introduction of a stone construction which they considered a foreign fashion offended them so much that violence was threatened to prevent the building from being continued. The ringleader—incidentally, a man to whom Malachy had been generous in the past—coming up to him as he watched the walls of the oratory rising on the foundations, tried to terrorize Malachy by threats into stopping the work immediately.

Malachy answered, "Wretched man, the building you have seen begun shall most certainly be completed, but its completion you shall not see."

The building of the oratory was finished not long afterward. Before the last stone was in place, Malachy's persecutor was dead.

Malachy foretold the place and date of his own death. He said it would take place at Clairvaux, on All Souls' Day, but when in 1148 he set out on his last journey to Rome via

Clairvaux, he only gave one indication (which at the time was not taken as such) that he knew he would not return.

When he embarked for the cross-Channel voyage—probably at Bangor—a monk named Catholicus (who had been for six years an epileptic, subject to frequent fits, sometimes several in one day) said to him in tears, "Alas, my father, are you then going to leave us? And although well aware to what almost daily afflictions you are abandoning me, you have no compassion on my misery?"

Malachy, taking the monk in his arms, comforted him. "Rest assured, my child. You shall not be troubled again until my return." From that moment, the monk was cured, nor did he ever suffer another attack. The return of which Malachy was speaking was not that of his physical body.

A few days after he arrived in Clairvaux, on October 18, Malachy became feverish and had to stay in bed. The illness did not seem to be dangerous, but to the monks who nursed him assiduously, he said, "You are troubling yourselves to no purpose. Nevertheless, I will do as you bid me." And when his Irish disciples assured him he would soon recover, he told them, "It is necessary that Malachy's soul should leave his body this year."

On All Saints' Day, he went without assistance from his bedroom to the church to receive extreme unction. Neither St. Bernard nor any of the monks present could see any signs of illness, let alone approaching death. Nevertheless, on the next day, November 2, just before midnight, Malachy, bishop and legate of the Holy See, died at the time and place he had predicted, in his fifty-fourth year, and in the arms of his closest friend, St. Bernard of Clairvaux.

It has been suggested that Malachy wrote his famous papal prophecies, which described each Pope from 1143 up to and beyond our own times, while on his first visit to St. Bernard in 1139. Possibly this was so, but there is no evidence either way. At intervals after his death, historians and critics, Catholic and non-Catholic, either attacked the authenticity of the prophecies or showed that they were genuine. At the beginning of this century, an eminent scholar, Abbé Joseph Maître, published two intensively documented books which, defeating dissentient arguments, established the validity of the prophecies and their authorship, more or less with finality.

The really heated controversy on the subject has centered not on who wrote the prophecies or when they were written, but on the fact that they apparently foretell the end of the Papacy, which would seem to mean the end of the Catholic Church in its present form. According to the list made by St. Malachy 800 years ago, there will be four more Popes. The fourth and last Pontiff will be Peter of Rome, who "during the last persecution of the Holy Roman Church . . . shall feed the sheep amid great tribulations, and when these are passed, the City of the Seven Hills shall be utterly destroyed and the awful Judge . . . will judge the people."

Many Catholics—and non-Catholics—do not believe in the imminent ending of Roman Catholicism. Others think it is incredible that a high-ranking prelate should predict the downfall of his own church—but prophecies of such a nature are not unusual. Thoth foretold the downfall of his country's greatness; the Delphic oracle, its own ending; prophets of Israel announced the scattering of their nation and Jerusalem's destruction.

The objection of the municipality of Toulouse to Malachy's prophecy was that if it were accepted, it would "paralyze human activity and slow up the march of human progress." Whether or not it could have such an effect, and apart from all the arguments about it, that list of recognizable descriptions of 111 Popes must rank among the world's great prophecies.

Fifth on that list is Adrian IV (1153-59), who is specified as *De Ruro Albo*—he was an Englishman, born at St. Albans. *Signum Ostiense* is the phrase which refers to the twentieth Pope, Alexander IV (1254-61), who was Cardinal of Ostia before his election to the papacy. Clement XIII, ninety-fourth Pope, had been governor in Umbria, before his accession to the Papal See. The symbol of Umbria is a rose; Clement is designated as *Rosa Umbriae*. Next comes *Ursus Velox* (swift bear); a running bear was the coat of arms of Lorenzo Ganganelli (Clement XIV, 1769-74).

Pius VII (1800-23) was Pope in Napoleon's time. His designation is *Aquila Rapax* (rapacious eagle), which he certainly was not. Since Napoleon, who had often been called the Eagle, dispossessed Pius of the papal territories, imprisoned him in Savona, Italy, and then in Fontainebleau, France, *Aquila Rapax* could well refer to the emperor's victimization of the Pope.

Malachy described the ninety-ninth Pontiff, Mauro Cappellari, who took the name of Gregory XVI (1831-46), as *De Balneis Etruria* (from Balnea in Etruria). When he was elected Pope, he was living as a member of the Camaldolese order, in a monastery at Balnea, near Florence, in Etruria. One of his chief interests was archeological research; after his accession he founded a museum of Etruscan antiquities.

Lumen in Coelo (a light in the firmament) is said to delineate the character of Leo XIII (1878-1903) as accurately as it pinpoints the coat of arms of his family, the Pecci—which means a comet. Although skepticism was at peak during his years at the Vatican, even hardened nonbelievers were impressed by his profound spirituality. It surrounded him, so people who met him say, with a visible aura of light.

The reign of the Pope who held office during the First World War (Benedict XV, 1914-22), Malachy describes as *Religio Depopulata* (Christianity laid waste), a prediction fulfilled by the death of millions of members of all churches in Flanders and many other parts of the world.

Pius XII (1939-58) was hailed by Malachy as *Pastor Angelicus*. This Pope was known as an ardent follower and student of the teachings of St. Thomas Aquinas—the Angelic Doctor, as he was called.

Next on the list is *Pastor et Nauta*—shepherd and navigator (Pope John XXIII, 1958-63). Malachy's prophecy suggests that this Pontiff would be outstanding for his guidance of affairs of the Papacy and of the Catholic Church generally, navigator as well as shepherd, a prophecy which Pope John fulfilled by initiating new policies and promoting new ideas, from which stemmed radical forms of progress in many directions. Immensely more liberal conditions were brought into being by him through the Ecumenical Council which he convened, the first since 1869—at which there was the widest ever representation. The convention agreed to mass being said in the vernacular—the first time in history this had happened in Britain. In Rome there was an increased influx of visitors to the Vatican from foreign countries and a rapprochement with other Orthodox churches. And last, the badge of the Ecumenical Council was a cross and a ship—symbolical of *Pastor et Nauta.*

In 1963, Paul VI was crowned Pope. Malachy called him Flower of flowers; his coat of arms is a floral design. After him come *De Medietate Lunae* (from the half-moon), *De Labore Solis* (from the toil of the sun), *Gloria Olivae* (the glory of the olive), and finally, *Petrus Romanus* (Peter of Rome).

Another prophet of papal succession came on the scene in the eighteenth century, the Monk of Padua. His predictions concern the last twenty Popes; printed in 1890, they were in manuscript form at least by 1740, while Clement XII or Benedict XIV was in the Vatican. They follow the Malachy pattern in many respects, but go into greater detail, in many cases giving correctly the actual name of the Pope to whom the prophecy refers.

De Medietate Lunae (from the half-moon), the Monk of Padua says, will be a Pope sent to Rome by "the Divine Doctor." His reign will be marked by persecutions of the Catholic Church; he is destined to fall victim to his enemies. For the last Pope but one, Leo XIV, according to the monk, whose designation is *Gloria Olivae,* he foresees a glorious reign. Leo XIV will unite humanity in the Christian faith,

The Saints and the Plowboy

says the seer, adding, "Oh, what a messenger of peace, of the glory of the olive tree, of the Lord."

The "glory of the olive" apparently will be the last brilliant flare-up which so often occurs before a fire or the life of an individual or corporate body burns out. Malachy's prediction that the Papacy would pass with "Peter of Rome," and the city itself be destroyed, squares with the Monk of Padua's forecast of the burning of Rome when the last Pontiff sits on the papal throne of the Vatican. The term for fulfillment of both prophecies is roughly the same: the end of this century or the beginning of the next. Allowing an average of ten years per Pope, the last reign would end in 2013.

This is the period which many seers have set as the time of devastation by war, fire, flood, and earthquake of life as we know it today. The Pyramid prophecies do not go beyond 2001. Nostradamus sees the debacle come to pass in 1999—but after that he allows another 6,000 years before the final call comes to this earth's inhabitants.

Three hundred years or so after Malachy's death, Joan of Arc, also a saint and a prophet, was born. He is remembered chiefly as a prophet, she as the liberator of France. Her gift of divination was as remarkable as her other great achievements, although it seems to have been overshadowed by them and, more often than not, forgotten.

On January 6 (under Capricorn), Joan was born in Domrémy, France. The year is thought to have been 1412, but although the date of her birth seems to have been uncertain, it was not unheralded. Prophecies foreshadowing her appearance and her work had been current for some centuries beforehand. One of them, attributed to Merlin, was to the effect that in France a "marvellous Maid will come from the *Nemus Canutum* for the healing of the nations." The house in which Joan was born was almost on the edge of the Bois Chenu, an oak grove. At the end of the fourteenth century, Marie d'Avignon, a famous prophetess of the day, dreamed of arms and armor, which were not for her, she was told, but for "a maid who should restore France."

When Joan was eleven years old—two years before her mission began—her father dreamed that he saw her going away from home with a company of men-at-arms. At thirteen, she first heard the voices and saw the visions which were to be a constant experience during her short, spectacular life. Perceval de Boulain-Villiers describes how this manifestation came to Joan, in his letter to the Duke of Milan. He says that Joan, who was running races with other girls in a common meadow, while watching the family sheep, was told by a boy that her mother needed her. She hurried home, to find that her mother had sent no message. As she was leaving the house to go back to the sheep, a bright cloud appeared before her; from it a voice spoke telling her "she was to do marvellous deeds. She had been chosen to aid the King of France, she must wear man's dress, take up arms, all would be ordered by her advice. She was to be a captain in war." Joan apparently was stupefied by the vision and incredulous of its message, but she was not allowed to forget it. The vision, about which she told no one but the curé, continued day and night for almost five years.

She was seventeen when, as in her father's dream, she set out in the company of men-at-arms to fulfill her mission of turning the tide of the English victories in France. Before this mission could be begun, she had to win other victories, over the skepticism of tough soldiers, among them Robert de Baudricourt, the captain who was holding the town of Vaucouleurs for the dauphin, whom she first approached with the story of the work she had been charged to do; over the incredulity of the dauphin himself and of the learned doctors of Poitiers, whom he appointed to test her bona fides.

One of her first recorded prophecies was made when, as she neared the castle of Chinon, she met (as her confessor Jean Pasquerel confirms) a man on horseback, who insulted and swore at her. "In God's name," Joan said to him, "do you swear, and you so near your death?" Within the hour, the man fell into the castle moat and was drowned.

During the siege of the Tourelles (bridgehead forts on the

The Saints and the Plowboy 97

Loire), Joan predicted that on May 7 she would be wounded by an arrow, but not fatally. On May 6, she repeated the prophecy, saying, "Keep close by me because tomorrow I will have much to do, more than ever I had, and blood will flow from my body, above my heart." Pasquerel confirms this; an Orléans lawyer gives evidence that she predicted the capture of the Tourelles and her return by the bridge, although several of its arches were broken, when she would be wounded by an arrow.

While Joan was at Chinon, or shortly after she left there, instructed by her voices, she sent to Fierbois to ask for an old sword, which she said was in the church there. At her trial the question of how she came by this sword was raised; the account she gave of it to her judges is one of the most intriguing instances of her remarkable clairvoyant powers, supported as it is by other statements.

Joan said, "While I was at Tours or Chinon I sent to seek for a sword in the church of St. Catherine at Fierbois behind the altar and presently it was found, all rusty." She was asked how she knew it was there. She replied: "It was a rusty sword in the earth with five crosses on it, and I knew of it through my Voices. . . . I wrote to the churchmen of Fierbois and asked them to let me have it and they sent it. It was not deep in the earth, it was behind the altar as I think, but am not sure whether it was behind the altar or in front of it. I think I wrote that it was behind it. When it was found the clergy rubbed it and the rust readily fell off . . . the clergy of Fierbois gave me a sheath; the people of Tours gave me two, one of red velvet, one of cloth of gold, but I had a strong leather sheath made for it."

According to the clerk of La Rochelle, the sword was in a coffer within the great altar of the church of Fierbois. None of the clerics nor the townspeople knew of its existence. After receiving Joan's request, a search was made; the sword was found in the coffer, which had not been opened for twenty years—before Joan of Arc was born.

One prophecy which she constantly repeated was of the

length of time allotted to her mission. The Duc d'Alençon said that she was always impatient of delays, urging that time should not be wasted in long councils. "I have so little time," she would say, "one year and a little more." In fact, she had thirteen months.

At the height of her triumph, during Easter Week (April 17 to 23), when she had freed the passage of the Seine and opened brilliantly the campaign of the Oise, on the ramparts of Melun, which had been taken by the French, her voices warned her that time had run out for her. "St. Catherine and St. Margaret warned me I should be captured before Midsummer Day . . . and I prayed that when I was taken I might die in that hour without the wretchedness of long captivity but the voices said so it must be. Often I asked the hour but they told me not; had I known the hour, I would not have gone into battle."

During her trial, she made several notable prophecies. On March 1, 1431, she said, "I know that before seven years are passed the English will lose a greater stake than they did at Orléans [referring to the loss of Paris in 1436], and that they will lose all they hold in France. They will have sorer loss than ever before through a great victory given by God to the French. I know by revelations that this will be in seven years."

The Battle of Formigny, by which the English lost Normandy, took place in 1439, about one year later than the limit set in her prophecy.

On March 17, she predicted: "The French will soon win a great matter, which God will send them; it will put almost the whole kingdom in motion. And this I say, that, when the event comes to pass, my words may be held in memory." This prophecy referred to the Treaty of Arras, in 1435, by which France and Burgundy were reconciled, a treaty which gave the *coup de grâce* to English rule in the country and to the Duke of Bedford.

Joan's voices seem to have failed her during the last weeks of imprisonment, when her need of their inspiration was greatest. Or perhaps she could not—or would not—interpret admonitions such as "Take all things peacefully, heed not thine affliction. Thence thou shalt come at last into the kingdom of paradise" as a warning of her death. She could not believe that her mission would end so.

In a sense she was right. The flames in the marketplace of Rouen on June 7, 1431, consummated but could not consume it, or prevent its ultimate victory.

As regards range and accuracy of prediction, Robert Nixon, the fifteenth-century plowboy-prophet, is on equal terms with St. Joan and St. Malachy. And although he did not attain the status of a saint, he can claim distinction of another kind. As a person, Robert Nixon presents an enigma which has never been solved.

He seems to have been so stupid that he could be called witless, according to Woodman of Copnal, an old man who knew him well. He had not even compensatory good looks; old Woodman described him as "a short, squat fellow" with a large head and goggle eyes, who dribbled when he spoke. He was surly, disliking especially children, who called out rude remarks about his appearance as he passed them. Son of a farmworker, he became a plowboy on Farmer Crowton's farm at Swanlow, where he seems to have done very little except make a nuisance of himself. He would work only when he felt inclined; whatever anyone said to him, he either did not speak or grunted or simply answered Yes or No. Neither Farmer Crowton nor any of his men could do anything with Robert unless they beat him or docked his food. Food seemed to be the only thing that interested him. He had a phenomenal appetite and capacity for eating; he would think nothing of getting through a whole shoulder of mutton at a meal (if he were allowed to), following it by hunks of bread and cheese.

Yet unpromising material though Robert Nixon appeared to be, he was the vehicle for a remarkable gift of prophecy. One day at Swanlow, he made a prediction about one of Farmer Crowton's oxen which was fulfilled—one of the first times he had been heard to speak coherently. The incident was told to Mr. Cholmondeley, of Vale Royal house in the forest of Delamere, who, becoming interested in Robert, employed him at his house. Mr. Cholmondeley had hopes, it seems, of improving Robert and educating him. At least, he could be taught to read, so Mr. Cholmondeley thought.

But book learning of any kind was quite beyond Robert's powers, as was proved by the failure on the part of local schoolmasters to teach him anything at all. So Robert went back to his plow. One day, dropping his goad, he stood still, looking up at the sky. After a time, some of the other plowmen spoke to him. He took no notice. The overseer told him to get on with his work; when Robert did not obey, he beat him. For an hour Robert stayed without moving in the field; then he picked up his goad and went on with his work as if nothing had happened.

When the other plowmen asked him why he had behaved in this way, he answered lucidly, instead of with his customary grunts. "I have seen things I cannot tell you, and which man never saw before." Later, for two hours, he spoke to them. Clearly and without hesitation, he foretold the English Civil War, the manner of Charles I's death, the restoration of Charles II, the abdication of King James II, the accession of William of Orange and the way in which he died, the French Revolution and war with France, and subsequent prosperity for England. He predicted when there would be periods of bad weather and times of scarcity of food. Finally, he said, "I shall be sent for by the king and starved to death."

His numerous predictions of local events were accurately fulfilled. Luddington Mill was removed by Sir John Crewe, as he had foretold, Ridley Pool was drained, and so on. And he said that an heir would be born to the Cholmondeleys on a cold snowy day, when an eagle perched on top of the house in Vale Royal, which, before it came into the possession of the Cholmondeleys' ancestors, had been an abbey founded by Edward I.

Later the ancient family of Cholmondeley was threatened by extinction. The heir had married Anne St. John, who was of an age when it was doubtful that she would bear a child. However, she did become pregnant, and Charles, son of Thomas Cholmondeley, was born on January 12, 1684. Cold and snowy, as Robert had said it would be, on that day and for three days before it, an eagle hovered around the house, perching intermittently on the rooftop, as was confirmed by a number of people, including the sister and brother of Mrs. Cholmondeley.

"When a raven shall build in a stone lion's mouth on top of a church in Cheshire, a King of England shall be driven out of his kingdom and return nevermore. . . . As token of the truth of this, a wall of Mr. Cholmondeley's shall fall. . . ." So ran another of Robert's predictions. Shortly before the abdication of King James II, a raven did build a nest in the mouth of a lion carved on the steeple of Over church in the forest of Delamere. And the wall at Vale Royal indicated by Robert did fall down, the day after Mr. Cholmondeley, having examined it, said to his bailiff, "Nixon was out here. That wall will never fall down." No reason for its collapse could be found.

By the time Robert's prediction that a three-thumbed boy would be born in the parish of Balderton had been fulfilled, his fame as a prophet had spread beyond his native country. When it reached the court, Henry VII, whose victory at Bosworth Robert had foretold, was so much intrigued by reports about his powers that he summoned him to the royal residence.

Months before the king's messengers brought the royal command to Robert, he had said that Henry would send for him, that he would go to court, and never come home again. He would starve to death. No one in his home village of Over believed him . . . until a company of men-at-arms came to escort him to the palace.

Henry, who seems to have been skeptical at first of Robert's psychic gifts, tested him by hiding a ring, which he told the boy had been lost, ordering him to discover where it was. When Robert's answer, given unhesitatingly, "He who hides can find," had demonstrated the reality of his clairvoyant powers, he seems to have become a favorite of the king's, who gave him the run of the palace and ordered the staff to look after him and provide him with everything he wanted.

The cooks of the royal kitchens did not share Henry's high opinion of Robert. He was forever getting in their way, picking at food, eating what was not meant for him. So, when the king went off on a hunting trip, they locked Robert in an unused room where he could not bother them . . . and forgot about him.

So, as he foretold, he starved to death. With him ended one of the most curious stories in the history of prophecy: the story of a near moron, illiterate, incapable of stringing so much as a coherent sentence together at most times, without even the wish to communicate, apparently, who yet could predict with authority, lucidity, and accuracy, in well-turned phrases, events in circumstances and conditions far beyond his limited range of experience. If Robert Nixon had made his prophecies while in a trance state, they would have been remarkable but not unique. The gift of tongues has descended at various times in many ages on men or women who were as unlikely vessels for its manifestation as he. The case of the plowboy-prophet is outstanding because his divinations were made *after* the passing of a near-cataleptic state, while he was apparently functioning normally in his ordinary consciousness.

7. Prophecies of the French Revolution

The sound of tumbrels on their way to the guillotine had been heard for centuries before they rumbled through the streets of Paris, by prophets who foresaw the terror, the cruelty and bloodlust of the French Revolution—and warned against its outbreak. The Bishop of Cambrai, Pierre d'Ailly, foretold it in the 1300's. In 1531 an astrologer, Turrel, described a "marvellous conjunction, heralded . . . for the year of our Lord 1789 . . . which will bring prodigious changes and alterations in the world, even in its sects and laws." Nineteen years later, Richard Rousset confirmed Turrel's interpretation of the conjunction with which he said all astrologers of that time were in agreement. Nostradamus, predicting the Revolution, had traced as part of its pattern the royal family's futile attempt to escape and its sequel.

In 1788, at a dinner party given by the Duchesse de Gramont in Paris, Jacques Cazotte, poet, author, and clairvoyant, made a prophecy concerning the Revolution which is probably one of the most interesting of its kind. It was written down verbatim by one of his fellow guests, Jean de La Harpe, fanatical atheist and skeptic, so that later he could use the record to show the absurdity of taking prophecy seriously. These notes of La Harpe's proved valuable, not in the way he had intended, but as authentication of the prediction, every detail of which was fulfilled within five years of its utterance.

At the end of dinner, when wine was circulating to a brilliant company of the greatest courtiers, writers, lawyers, and wits of France, a toast was given by Chrétien Guillaume de Lamoignon de Malesherbes, one of Louis XVI's ministers and his confidant: "Here's to the day when reason will be triumphant in the affairs of men—a day which I shall never live to see."

Only one of the guests did not join in the laughter which greeted the toast. Rising as if to respond to it, Jacques Cazotte said, "Sir, you are wrong. You will live to see that day. It will come within six years."

He went on to say that the Revolution, of which there had been a good deal of talk, was not far ahead. "You know that I am something of a prophet." Somebody objected that one could reach that conclusion without being a prophet; Cazotte agreed. "But," he added, "the lives of everyone in this room will be affected by the Revolution, and to know in what way they will be affected, insight is necessary, you will admit."

All the guests clamored to know what was in store for them. Turning first to the Marquis de Condorcet, Cazotte told him: "You will die on the stone floor of a prison cell, having taken poison to cheat the executioner." Condorcet wanted to know what a prison cell, poison, and an executioner had to do with the reign of reason—liberty, humanity, and philosophy. Cazotte answered that Condorcet would come to his end under that so-called reign of reason; at that time the only temples in France would be temples dedicated to "reason."

Another guest, Sébastien Roch Nicolas Chamfort, one of the king's favorites, commented that Cazotte would not qualify as one of the priests of those temples. Cazotte answered him: "You will be one . . . you will cut your veins twenty-two times with a razor, but still you will not die—until some months later."

"You," he said to another of the guests, Dr. Félix Vicq d'Azyr, "will not open your veins yourself. At your own request, someone will open them for you, six times in one day, and you will expire during the night."

He told a famous astronomer, Jean Sylvain Bailly, that "in spite of your good deeds and great learning, there lies ahead only death by execution at the hands of the mob."

M. Nicolai and Jean Antoine Roucher would die on the scaffold; M. de Malesherbes would share their fate. When Cazotte had predicted a terrible death for the male guests, the Duchesse de Gramont remarked that it seemed the women would escape the attentions of the executioner. Cazotte took both her hands in his. "Alas," he said, "you will be treated, all of you, exactly like the men." He predicted that she, and many other ladies, would be taken to the scaffold in the executioner's cart, hands tied behind their backs. Even greater ladies than they would end in that way. Of all the victims of the Revolution, Cazotte said only one would be allowed, as a great favor, a confessor before he died. And this favored man would be the present King of France.

To most of his fellow guests this was the ultimate absurdity in a fantastic farrago, not even in good taste. La Harpe, who did not believe a word of the prophecies and despised Cazotte—a feeling which was mutual—decided to give the *coup de grâce* to a ridiculous performance, by asking: "What of me? Have I no part in all this? Am I not to be allowed to hiss at the mob in the company of my friends? Surely you can grant me this favor."

La Harpe's satire was wasted on Cazotte, who answered equably that he would have been delighted to oblige the philosopher but that the fates denied him the pleasure by reserving for him a more fitting destiny; he would become a Christian.

When the laughter at what all the guests agreed was the most exquisite jest, considering La Harpe's bigoted atheism, died down, Cazotte was asked what lay ahead for himself. Instead of giving a direct reply, he repeated the story of the man who, during the siege of Jerusalem, walked around the ramparts for seven successive days, crying out, "Woe to Jerusalem! Woe to myself!" At the last moment of his last round, a huge stone from a Roman catapult hit and killed him.

Within six years of that summer night, Cazotte's prophecies were all fulfilled in every detail. Chamfort, threatened with arrest, opened his veins, but this was not the direct cause of his death. He died as the result of subsequent wrong medical treatment. Condorcet poisoned himself; he was found dead on the floor of his cell in 1794. Some months before Condorcet's death, Bailly, astronomer and ex-mayor of Paris, had been guillotined, as were Roucher and Malesherbes, the noted lawyer who defended Louis XVI at his trial, the Duchesse de Gramont and other ladies who had been guests at the party at which Cazotte made his prophecy. The King and Queen of France died on the scaffold. Jean de La Harpe entered a monastery and became an ardent Catholic.

When La Harpe died in 1803, the records of the Cazotte prophecy were found among his papers, but these are not the only evidence of its authenticity. Jacques Cazotte's must be among the most verified predictions ever made. Dr. Walter Borman, well-known parapsychologist at the turn of the century, who investigated the case, found confirmatory evidence from many sources. A letter from the Comtesse de Genlis, who had been nurse to the children of the Duc d'Orléans, written in 1825 to a Dr. Deleuze, came to light, in which she said: "A hundred times before the Revolution, I heard M. de La Harpe tell it [Cazotte's prophecy], and always almost exactly as it had been printed, as he himself had it printed." Several witnesses testified that the famous Dr. Vicq d'Azyr, who was one of the guests on the momentous evening, heard Cazotte's predictions, which very much disturbed him, although he was notoriously skeptical. The Baronne Henriette Louise d'Oberkirch, who was about thirty-five years old when the prophecy was made, mentioned it in her memoirs, which cover her experiences up to the year 1789 (when the Bastille was stormed). Her son, Comte Montbrison, published them, but not until 1852.

"Heaven avert from us the dreadful omens," writes the baronne. In the last chapter of the book she tells of "many persons who heard the Cazotte prophecies, whose actuality cannot be doubted"; she says that she herself had read La Harpe's account of them.

The problem of how the baronne could have seen in 1789 a record which was not published until after 1803 (the year of La Harpe's death) was solved by the discovery that the manuscript had been sent to her from Russia by one of her great friends, the Grand Duchess Maria Feodorovna. The duchess followed the custom of many great ladies at European courts of employing some eminent man of letters at the French capital to keep them *au fait* with what was happening there. Gossip and scandal, as well as events, were retailed in these newsletters; their writers were the eighteenth-century forerunners of today's foreign correspondents. La Harpe had sent to the grand duchess the details of Cazotte's prophecy, which the grand duchess forwarded to the Baronne d'Oberkirch.

Cazotte's prediction of his own end was as accurate as his other prophecies. For some time in public and in private he had spoken against the Revolution; at last, on August 10, 1792, he was arrested, perhaps because the men in power were afraid too many people might agree with him. His friends were delighted when he was released after only a short time in the Abbaye Prison; Cazotte himself did not share their cheerfulness. To M. Saint-Charles, who had come to congratulate him on his freedom, he said, "It will not last long. Just before you came I had a vision; it was of a gendarme, who brought a summons to me to appear before Pétion, the Mayor of Paris. Pétion ordered me to be taken to the Conciergerie, and from there to the Tribunal of the Revolution. This time there is no release for me, except through the guillotine."

On September 11 a gendarme came to Cazotte, as he had

predicted, with an order signed by Mayor Jérôme Pétion de Villeneuve, to appear before him at the *mairie*. Afterward Pétion had Cazotte taken to the *conciergerie*. The next step was examination by the Revolutionary Tribunal, by which, after twenty-seven hours of unceasing questioning, he was condemned to death. On September 25, he was guillotined. He was seventy-two.

Cazotte's predictions and Cazotte in person figured in two other prophecies of the Revolution. One of these was recorded by the Baronne d'Oberkirch, who, as I have mentioned, had been sent a copy of the Cazotte predictions by the Grand Duchess Maria Feodorovna. The baronne describes an experiment at which she was present, arranged by the Marquis de Puységur, the discoverer of somnambulism, in Strasbourg.

While the sitting was in progress, the Marshal de Stannville joined the group. At that time, everyone was talking about the Cazotte prophecies, though most people did not take them seriously. The old soldier had decided to ask the medium—a girl from the Black Forest—about them: Would they be fulfilled; what was the future of France and of the queen?

Before he could put the questions, the girl told him their subject.

"Tell me whether the prophecies I have heard will be fulfilled, and whether I can believe them."

Unhesitatingly the medium answered that he could believe them all; all "and still more" would come to pass, within a few years.

Asked what was then happening in France, she said, "There is a conspiracy in progress, and the chief conspirator will be the victim of his own wickedness eventually."

Violent death would come to those for whom Cazotte had foretold it. The marshal asked if he would share in the disasters predicted for his family. The girl said he would not; she did not answer when he pressed her to tell him what lay ahead. "My friends are to be beheaded; perhaps there is worse in store for me. To be hanged would be an unworthy fate for a soldier."

Finally, since the medium was still silent, the Marquis de Puységur insisted on her answering the marshal. In a whisper, she said, "Poor man—why does he ask me what in a few months he will know himself?" The marshal died within the time limit the girl had set.

The second prophecy concerning the French Revolution with which Cazotte was associated was made by the celebrated Cagliostro (whose title of Count was probably self-conferred) at a Masonic gathering held in Paris under the aegis of Antoine Comte de Gebelin, the learned Orientalist. Alessandro di Cagliostro, born in Sicily in 1743, was then at the peak of his fame as an occultist. He had studied alchemy under the Grand Master of the Knights of Malta, who introduced him to Roman and Neapolitan society; he had traveled in many countries, learning, according to himself, esoteric secrets from great teachers who had incarnated with the purpose of helping mankind to progress.

Cagliostro demonstrated to the assembly the possibility of divining a person's fate through a form of numerology; indications of the future of the consultant were arrived at by totaling the digits allotted to each letter of the alphabet in the consultant's name. The value of the letters, he said, had been fixed by the Magi. "It is from the history of France that I shall take my proofs," Cagliostro went on, producing a chart on which the alphabet was arranged in a circle.

Having demonstrated how the system worked by applying it to the names of great figures of the past, such as Catherine de Médicis, Henri III, and Henri IV, and having pictured by numerology the events of their lives, Cagliostro said, "Let us hasten to confront the future by the same means. Do not be afraid to take as your subject your king, Louis XVI, and the unfolding of his destiny."

The readings Cagliostro obtained from various combinations of the letters of Louis' full name and titles warned: "Let Louis XVI, supposed king, cast down from the ruined throne of his ancestors, beware of dying on the scaffold towards the thirty-ninth year of his life . . . fall, affliction, violent death. . . . Lie low, sixteenth king . . . delivered to a fatal executioner." Louis having been born in 1754 would die, Cagliostro said, before August 23, 1793. The final delineation specified: "He is condemned to lose his head, for being guilty of war." Cagliostro was not certain if this phrase meant foreign or civil war; his interpretation of it was that the king would be accused of inciting armed combat, which would be one of the most serious charges brought against him.

The oracle of numbers foretold for Marie Antoinette that she would be "unfortunate, unhappy in France, a queen without a throne or money, wrinkled prematurely through grief, kept on a meagre diet, imprisoned, beheaded."

And the Princesse de Lamballe? Cagliostro was asked. As Marie Antoinette's constant companion, she could not hope to escape imprisonment and the guillotine. She would be imprisoned, then released, said the count. "She will not be condemned to death; she will not be guillotined, but she will not escape her destiny. Her numbers signify that her fate is to be beautiful, great, unhappy, alone, massacred in Paris. Thwarted, recaptured, she is massacred at the corner of the Rue des Ballets," Cagliostro went on. "Is there a street of that name in Paris?" He was told that there was. "That will be the murder scene."

All of Cagliostro's predictions about the Revolution were fulfilled; this, the most detailed of them, happened exactly as he had foreseen. The Princesse de Lamballe was arrested with the royal family and then imprisoned. She was set free, it was said on payment by the Duc de Penthièvre, her father-in-law, of a huge bribe to Pierre Louis Manuel, an attorney of the Paris Commune. Truchon, one of the revolutionaries, was ordered to take her to a place of safety; not an easy assignment. The sight of heaped corpses in the streets, blood running in the gutters, reduced the princess to a fainting condition. Truchon succeeded in leading her along the Rue des Ballets, the last house of which they were passing as four men

—Grison, Chariot, Mamin, and Rodi—turned into the street. Grison knocked the Princesse de Lamballe down; the others set on her, cutting her in pieces; Chariot, a wigmaker, decapitated her. For some time, he exhibited her head in the streets; finally it was thrown on a rubbish heap, to be burned with other debris.

What would be the end of the Revolution? Cagliostro was asked. He told his audience that "an elected Corsican would finish it. . . . I conclude from this," he said, "that after the destruction of the Royal family, a man from Corsica, elected by vote, will assume under a new title the powers of kingship wrested from Louis XVI."

A tall white-haired old man rose from his seat to question Cagliostro about the name of the Bourbons' successor. It was Jacques Cazotte, to whom Cagliostro bowed, saying, "Your question is in itself a prophecy. The numerical total of the letters of its words predicts that his name will be Napoleon Bonaparte. He will be elected to the throne of victory, then ruined soon by an adverse destiny. The final reading describes 'a victorious general, who dominates thrones, in the end pacing the circle of a melancholy island.' "

8. Great Seers of History

Between the beginning of the sixteenth and the end of the seventeenth century, some of the most notable prophecies of history were pronounced. Nostradamus was making his long-term predictions. William Lilly was among the seers who foresaw the Fire of London and the Great Plague it followed.

Lilly, who has been called the "greatest of English astrologers," was born on May 1, 1602, of farming stock, in Diseworth, about seven miles south of Derby. His schooling seems to have begun in earnest when, at the age of eleven, he was sent to the school of one John Brinsley in Ashby-de-la-Zouch, who taught him Latin, Greek, and Hebrew. While William was still in his teens, the fortunes of the Lilly family took a turn for the worse. Lilly senior was imprisoned for debt; his son set off on Monday, April 3, 1620, to try his luck in the city of London. He arrived, having walked most of the way, with 7s. 6d. in his pocket.

William seems to have fallen on his feet from the first. He got work as a footboy with a couple, both of whom became fond of him. The wife left him £5 *"in old gold"* in her will when she died a few years afterward, and when her widower married again, in 1626, he settled £20 for life on William.

Soon afterward his master died. Without much loss of time, William married his master's widow, who inherited the estate; she died in October, 1633, thereby adding considerably to William's already adequate assets.

His interest in astrology was awakened by a meeting with a "practitioner of the abstruse sciences," Dr. Simon Forman, in 1632, after which he began to study astrology under a Welshman named Evans. He worked, he said, twelve, fifteen or eighteen hours, during day and night, first to discover if there was anything in it, then, having decided that there was, to master the science. In this he seems to have succeeded; he soon built up a practice in horary astrology and took pupils as well. One John Humphreys paid him £40 to learn the art.

In his own life, at any rate at this time, his knowledge was not of much use to him—he either did not use it to guide his decisions or, like many others before and after him, ignored its leadings. He married on November 18, 1634, a wife with whom he got a dowry of £500—but no happiness. She "was of the nature of Mars," he says—bad-tempered and belligerent.

His marriage may have been unsatisfactory; in other ways his affairs were prospering. After passing through a brief phase of interest in magic, William Lilly began to write about as well as practice astrology. In April, 1644, his first book of prophecies, *Merlinus Anglicus Junior,* was published, followed in the same year by *A Prophecy of the White King and Dreadfull Deadman Explained,* which sold 1,800 copies in three days.

By this time his status as a fashionable astrologer was established. In 1647 General Fairfax consulted him; Charles I in the same year asked his advice on a safe place to hide. Charles, Lilly says, did not follow the indications given in his horoscope, nor did he, on a second visit to Lilly in 1648, when the astrologer told him safety lay in going to London with the commissioners. If he had done so, according to Lilly, Charles would not have been captured and executed.

Lilly had finished in 1647 his third book of Nativities, while unable to go out of his house because of the plague, of which two of his maidservants died. In 1648 his prophecies of the Great Plague and Fire of London were published in his *Astrological Predictions*. "In the year 1665," he says, "the Aphelium of Mars, who is the general signification of England, will be in Virgo, which is assuredly the ascendant of the English monarchy, but Aries of the Kingdom. When the absis therefore of Mars, shall appear in Virgo, who shall expect less than a strange catastrophe of human affairs in the common wealth, monarchy and Kingdom of England. There will then, either in or about these times, or near that year, or within ten years, more or less of that time, appear in this Kingdom so strange a revolution of fate, so grand a catastrophe and great mutation unto this monarchy and government as never yet appeared of which as the times now stand, I have no liberty or encouragement to deliver my opinion—only, it will be ominous to London, unto her merchants at sea, to her traffique on land, to her poor, to all sorts of people, inhabiting in her or to her liberties, by reason of sundry fires and a consuming plague." In 1651 his *Monarchy and No Monarchy* followed, in which he had drawn up a hieroglyphic symbolizing "a great sickness and mortality; wherein you may see the representation of people in their winding-sheets, persons digging graves and sepultures, coffins, etc." On the next page there is a hieroglyphic representation of "a great city all in flames of fire."

In this year, 1651, Lilly predicted that "parliament stood upon a tottering foundation, and that the commonalty and soldiery would join together against them," which was fulfilled when Cromwell turned its members out of the House. And he foretold that the Commonwealth would last eleven and a quarter years.

The Great Fire of London broke out so much according to the pattern of Lilly's prophecy that members of the commission set up to inquire into its causes, believing he might have been involved in a conspiracy to destroy London, had him brought before them at the House of Commons on Friday, October 25, 1666. They asked him what he knew about its outbreak and "whether there might be any design therein." He satisfied the commission that the only knowledge he had of the fire was through his astrological calculations, whereupon he was "dismissed with great civility."

Later, in 1670, having studied medicine, he became a licensed physician and used astrology to help him in diagnosis and treatment, with remarkable results. Most of his patients he treated without fee, until his own health and eyesight began to fail. He went blind after an attack of flux in 1681, and on June 9 of that year he died, "without any shew of trouble or pangs." He is buried in the chancel of Walton Church.

About 111 years before Lilly's prediction of London's Great Plague and Fire, the French prophet Nostradamus (Michel de Notredame), probably the most celebrated seer of all time, foretold by what he called "Astronomical Affections" that *"Le sang du juste à Londres fera faute, Bruslez par feu, de vingt et trois, les six."* Or, in English: "The blood of the just requires London to be burned with fire in sixty-six."

Some of his innumerable prophecies, which cover the seven centuries following the sixteenth, at the beginning of which he was born (on December 14, 1503), are less clearly worded than the forecast of London's fate. It has been said that many of them are so obscure that they could mean anything—or nothing. But it has been found that when carefully studied, they do mean something; there are facts and indications in them which relate unmistakably to the events they foreshadow. And, of course, obscurity was fashionable—of necessity, for seers, when forecasts of disaster could often mean disaster for themselves. Even Nostradamus dared not be too outspoken too often; when he felt it advisable, he wrapped up his meanings in symbolism. And so, unlike many gifted but less diplomatic prophets, he died in his bed, of natural causes, on July 2, 1566.

Nostradamus was of Jewish blood, but his parents having become Roman Catholics, he was baptized into that faith, to which all his life he professed, perhaps overemphatically, his deep attachment. When he was a small boy, he went to live with his mother's father, Jean de St. Remy, a learned and scientifically minded man, who taught Michel Greek, Latin, and Hebrew and the use of the astrolabe. A skilled herbalist and physician, the old man trained him in the preparation of medicines, and unguents, and the virtues of herbs. Even then Michel was more interested in the study of the stars than in anything else; no doubt, since in those days medicine and magic were so closely related, he would learn how to calculate the right astrologic moment for herb gathering.

Michel was sent to the University of Avignon as soon as he was old enough—at about the age when boys today go to a preparatory school. From there, he went on to Montpellier, which then had the best school of medicine in France, and perhaps in Europe. Michel wished to become a doctor. He took his final medical degree on October 23, 1529, having already made a great reputation through his treatment and successful cure of the plague which ravaged Provence for four years.

Even his enemies admitted that he was a great doctor, but all his skill could not save his wife and their two sons. Within a few years of the marriage in the small town of Agen, she and the little boys died in an outbreak of plague.

For eight years after his loss, Nostradamus, unable to settle in one place, wandered through France, through Italy and Corsica. And as if his sorrow were a catalyst of his inner development, now his clairvoyant gifts began to show themselves. In spite of himself, since he did not wish to incur the adverse attention which he would risk if he became known as a prophet, he could not help making predictions. And as these were fulfilled, more and more people believed him to have the gift of foretelling the future.

They did not include the Seigneur de Florinville, at whose castle of Fains Nostradamus stayed when passing through Lorraine. To prove the foolishness of such belief, the seigneur pointed out to Nostradamus in the farmyard a black and a white sucking pig. "Foretell their future," he said. "You will eat the black one; a wolf will eat the white one," Nostradamus answered.

To make sure the prophecy was not fulfilled, the seigneur presently told his cook to kill and serve the white pig for supper that night. The piglet having been killed, it was cooked and left on the table ready for dressing. While the cook was out of the kitchen, a wolf cub which some of the seigneur's servants were trying to tame got in and ate the pig.

All roasted pigs being the same color, the cook killed the black one and served it at supper that night. The seigneur no doubt took some pleasure in telling his guest that they were eating the white pig. When Nostradamus insisted that it was the black pig, the cook was sent for, to prove Nostradamus wrong. He confessed that the white pig had made, as the seer had predicted, the wolf cub's meal; the pork they had been eating had been the black pig, which was substituted for its white brother.

While Nostradamus was in Italy, he saw a young monk walking along the road toward him. Nostradamus knelt in the dust before the startled young man, Felice Peretti, who, born of poor parents in a nearby village, had worked as a swineherd before he entered the church. Nostradamus' explanation—"I kneel before his Holiness"—was treated, under the circumstances, as a joke by those who heard it. It was remembered, not with laughter, when after Peretti had been made Cardinal of Montalto, he was elevated to the Papacy in 1585 as Sixtus V.

Back in his native country, Nostradamus was told of a search which had been organized for a treasure known to be hidden in a mountain. "It will never be found," said he, "until excavations for another purpose are made." Some time later, when the ruins of a Roman temple were being dug up, the treasure was discovered.

In 1547 he settled in Salon, practicing as a physician, but giving more time to astrology and metaphysics than to medicine. It was a year which was a milestone in his life; on November 11 he married again and began to compose his prophecies, which when completed covered seven millennia. The first edition was published in 1555; its title, *Centuries,* was bald and simple, but the contents were neither. In the preface, Nostradamus says he had decided to "show by abstruse and twisted sentences . . . so as not to scandalize their [the public's] fragile hearing and write down everything under a figure cloudy rather than plainly prophetic." Whatever else he may have been called, Nostradamus has never been written off as a fool. He very well knew the occupational hazards of a prophet's life in his day; he therefore produced his predictions in a form which would yield little or nothing to cursory reading. The long and careful study necessary for their decoding protected their meaning from discovery except by the understanding few.

He gives dates—which proved correct—for some of the events he foretells. He claims that he could give exact years in all his quatrains, but if he had done so, he would have been accused of being in league with the devil, which would have produced unpleasant repercussions for him. One of the dates given in the second edition of *Centuries* is 1792, the great persecution of the church, which he said would follow the French Revolution. This he foretold, giving the names of some of the principal characters in it, calling it the "Vulgar Advent," or accession of the people to power.

After publication of the second edition of *Centuries,* Nostradamus was summoned to court by King Henri II, almost certainly because the prophet's fame had reached Queen Catherine. She, who had what has been called "a mania for occultism," would not have been satisfied until she had seen the man of whose predictions all France was talking. She may also have wanted to compare his forecasts with those of Gauric, called "the most famous astrologer of his time," who had drawn up the horoscope of Catherine and of her father, Lorenzo II.

Gauric had said in 1493 that Giovanni de' Medici, then a fourteen-year-old cardinal, would be Pope; this happened in 1513, when he acceded to the Papacy as Leo X. Gauric's medical skill and prophetic gifts made him sought after in many countries; while he was in Scotland, he was called in to treat the Archbishop of St. Andrews for a complaint, which he cured —only to tell his pateint that he would die on the scaffold, as he did.

Gauric prophesied the exact date of the death of Pope Paul III—November 29, 1549—some years before it happened. When Catherine de Médicis was still only Dauphine of France, he said that the accession of her husband would be marked by a sensational duel and that a later duel would cause his death. The first duel, between Guy Chabot de Jarnac and François de Vivonne de la Châtaignerie, took place on July 10, 1547; the young king saw Châtaignerie killed. As for the second duel, Gauric warned Henri he must avoid "single combat in an enclosed place, especially near his forty-first year." There would be great danger then of being wounded in the head, a wound which might blind him or result in death.

Catherine's purpose in sending for Nostradamus in 1556 may have been partly to get a second opinion on this prediction of disaster for Henri. She also asked him to forecast the future of her children.

He arrived on August 15, having taken more than a month on the way. A striking figure, in his long gown and square cap—the uniform of a doctor—and bearded, he seems to have made a deep impression on Catherine. He was given the current VIP treatment at court, but the 130 ecus he received—100 from Henri and 30 from Catherine—he apparently thought incredibly paltry. His journey had cost him 100 ecus.

However, in one way and another he did quite well out of his trip. Courtiers and their wives and daughters flocked to him. They paid handsomely for his advice, horoscopes, cosmetic recipes (a specialty of his), and prescriptions for gout and stones. He was the talk of the town; a widely publicized incident was a late-night visit to him of a page from the Beauveau family, who woke the neighborhood by his noisy assault on Nostradamus' door. The boy was in despair at having lost a favorite—and very valuable—dog. Nostradamus, not even asking why he had come, called out: "You are making a great deal of fuss about a lost dog. Go and look on the road to Orléans. You will find him there, on a lead." The page rushed off; the dog was found as and where Nostradamus had predicted.

Dealing with Catherine was a very different matter. She had asked him to tell her what was ahead for her children; he had to find some formula which would satisfy her that he had told her the whole truth about them, although in fact he dared not do so. Already in his *Centuries*, he had obliquely but accurately told their stories; François, the thirteen-year-old boy, would be married to Mary Stuart, live with little happiness, and die after reigning for one year; his eleven-year-old sister, who would be the child wife of old King Philip of Spain, would also die young. The girl, then nine, would marry the Duc de Lorraine, and live only into her twenties. The six-year-old Charles would be the ninth French king of his name; his reign would be darkened by the terrors of the Huguenot massacres. Two crowns waited for his five-year-old brother, who in both kingdoms would be unhappy; his end would be assassination. The youngest girl, Marguerite, would be the wife of Henri of Navarre until he discarded her because of her adulteries. The baby of the family, two-year-old François, as Duc d'Anjou and titular ruler of the Netherlands, would be treated as a figure of fun in every European court, Elizabeth of England's "little frog," whom she allowed to consider himself her suitor for reasons of statecraft.

How could Nostradamus pass on his foreknowledge of wholesale tragedy to Catherine? Out of humanity, he could not; out of expediency, he dared not. But there was one element in the future of her sons about which he could speak without causing grief to Catherine or danger to himself. He said, "They will all be kings."

Nostradamus prophesied the death of Henri II in much the same terms as Gauric used. The quatrain relating to it in his *Centuries* translates:

> The young lion shall overcome the old
> In war-like field in single fight
> In a golden cage he will pierce the eye.
> Two wounds one, then die a cruel death.

In the summer of 1559 a three-day tournament was held in Paris, celebrating a double wedding in the royal family, Henri's daughter Elizabeth marrying (by proxy) Philip II of Spain; Marguerite, the Duke of Saxony. The lists had been set up near the Palais des Tournelles, and there, on June 30, Henri rode against the captain of his Scottish Guard, Comte Gabriel de Montgomery. In the third encounter, the jagged point of Montgomery's splintered lance pierced the king's visor (which was gilded and, as was the fashion for jousting helms, shaped like a cage) and entered his eye. Apparently a splinter also injured his throat—"Two wounds one."

Ten days later Henri died. Nostradamus foretold the results to France of his death in a quatrain which promised that in the year a one-eyed king reigned (there had never been a one-eyed King of France) "the Court will enter upon very serious difficulties . . . the Kingdom, put in tribulation, will be split." Troubles and disturbances came thick and fast after Henri's accident and death. There were the St. Bartholomew's Day massacre and the near civil war between Royalists and Legitimists, and Henri III was assassinated when he attempted to surround Paris, which was in revolt in 1589.

Meanwhile, after Henri II's death, although he had ordered that no harm should come to the man who had without intention caused it, Montgomery wisely left France for Britain. But Nostradamus had written of him in the *Centuries*: "He who fights on martial field, and shall have carried off the prize from one greater than he, shall be surprized by six men at night, naked, without armour, suddenly."

And so fifteen years later Nemesis caught up with Montgomery. He returned to France to fight with the Huguenots and was captured at Domfront; the terms of surrender were that his life was to be spared. On Thursday, May 27, 1574, he was arrested by six noblemen of the royal Army while in bed (naked, as was customary then), by express order of Queen Catherine, and delivered to her vengeance at Caen.

Nostradamus foresaw the conspiracy of 1560, by which Lyons was to be handed over to the Huguenots. He says that the "Grand Bailiff" (the chief magistrate) of Orléans "will be condemned to death, but his bonds on hands and feet shall not succeed in keeping him captive." The death penalty was passed on Jérôme Grasdot, the chief bailiff of Orléans, for having attempted to hand over Orléans to the Prince de Condé. He was bound hand and foot but managed to break his bonds and escaped.

After the death of François II (prophesied by Nostradamus), his mother, Catherine, and his successor, the fourteen-year-old Charles IX, while on a goodwill progress through France, visited Salon, the hometown of Nostradamus, in 1564. On a dais, draped with white and purple damask, the chief men of the town, among whom was Nostradamus, received the royal visitors. The chief magistrate read an oration to the king; Charles, not yet having learned statecraft, replied: "I came to see Nostradamus."

That evening Nostradamus was commanded to the royal apartments to cast the horoscope of the young brother of the king, Henri, then the Duc d'Anjou. One day he would be King of France, the astrologer said. To ten-year-old Henri of Navarre, who was in the royal entourage, Nostradamus foretold that one day he would "have the whole inheritance."

As if it were a spool of film, the future unrolled before Nostradamus. He foresaw and predicted almost every major historical event in France and crises in many other countries through the centuries between his own and the year 3797. Whatever his powers were, they operated independently of space and time.

That milestone in his nation's development, the Revolution, is the theme of a number of quatrains, naturally enough, since he must have recognized its immense implications. He referred to it as *"le Commun Advenement"* (Advent of Commons, or Rise of the Third Estate) in his epistle to his son Caesar. He listed among its results that the "topography of France would be arbitrarily altered," as it was when the ancient provincial division of France was changed into departments with new names; that the tombs of the French kings would be desecrated, which also came to pass. And philosophy would replace religion—he was experiencing precognitively the days when the teachings of Voltaire would supersede those of Christ.

Two hundred and thirty years before it happened, Nostradamus foretold the disastrous flight of Louis XVI from Paris. Louis, the first King of France to hold the title not only by divine right, but also by mandate of a constituent assembly, who was by temperament monkish, as was well known, fled through the night of June 29, 1792, to Varennes dressed in gray. It was dark in the little town when the royal party arrived; all its members were captured there, taken back to Paris, and later executed.

Nostradamus had said that:

> At night will come through the Forest of Reines
> A married couple, by a devious route,
> Herne, the white stone, the monk in gray, into Varennes,
> The elected Capet—the result will be tempest, fire,
>   blood—and cutting off.

As there is not and never has been a Forest of Reines, some commentators think that probably the word Nostradamus used was not "forest" but *fores,* Latin for door, referring to the queen's door through which the escape was made. "Herne" is an anagram of *reine,* or queen. (Nostradamus was devoted to anagrams, and the rules of making them permitted change or suppression of a letter. "Rapis" is his favorite transliteration of Paris.) "The white stone" was a poetical description of Marie Antoinette, who was dressed all in white—and by the time she arrived back in Paris her hair had turned white, *"blanchis,"* as she said herself, *"par la dou-*

leur." Some historians think that Nostradamus may also have had in mind when he spoke of *"la pierre blanche"* the famous diamond necklace which made the queen so unpopular. "The monk in gray . . . the elected Capet" could refer only to Louis himself.

The ending of the affair was as Nostradamus had described it—destruction, disaster, chaos, then blood and "cutting off" by the guillotine. *Tranche* was the word he used, meaning a cut, a slice.

In another quatrain, he said that the mob would return to the Tuileries, 500 strong, after their first invasion of June 20, 1792. It is a matter of record that this happened. And at the time this prediction was made and published, the royal residences were Fontainebleau or the older palace of the Louvre. The Tuileries palace did not exist. Catherine de Médicis began to build it in 1564 on the site of a tileworks (Tuileries).

Nostradamus covered the full course of the Revolution in his quatrains, predicting, concerning the execution of Louis XVI on January 21, that his body (after death) would be covered "with a powder that burns." The king's corpse was taken in a wicker basket to the Madeleine, where it was thrown in a deep pit. Over it was spread a thick pall of quicklime.

The victories of Suleiman the Magnificent, the disasters which followed them, and the treaty between Persia and Turkey of which he gave the correct date (October, 1727) were among the events outside France foretold by Nostradamus. Of England, he said that the "senate [Parliament] of London will put their King to death." The Scots, he added, would basely sell this king to Parliament. His usurper (*le bastard*) would be *almost* received as king (Cromwell never achieved a title higher than that of Lord Protector).

Nostradamus found nothing praiseworthy in the dictator. "More like a butcher than an English King," he says of him, "Born in an obscure place, by force he will take his empire. Coward without faith or law, he will cause the earth to bleed.

The time approaches so closely that I sigh." Cromwell was born in 1599; Charles I was executed in 1649; to a man whose vision ranged over five centuries and more, England's Civil War and the events leading to it must have seemed to be only just over the threshold of another day.

In his time, Britain was not a major European power; the ordinary man could have seen no reason why she ever should be. Nostradamus, looking down the years, saw her unchallenged ascendancy. "The great empire will be held by England. It will be all-powerful for more than three hundred years. Great armies will go by sea and land. The Portuguese will not be pleased." The reference to Portuguese vexation is taken to mean that because the growth of England's overseas trade and her control of India virtually closed to Portugal many markets for her exports, she was "not pleased."

The "more than three hundred years" of England's imperial power is thought by some authorities to begin with the passing of the Navigation Act of 1651, which, by ruling that imports could be brought to Britain only in ships of the nation which produced the merchandise, resulted in a rapid expansion in Britain's trading fleet. It laid the foundations of a general growth of economy.

Three hundred years—and a little more—have passed since then and, in their passing, verified Nostradamus' prophecy. Armies, some of them millions strong, went from Britain, by sea and land. Great power came and went, within the time limit he foresaw.

When he gave dates, Nostradamus was usually exact, which is surprising, considering that the time dimension is meaningless to the clairvoyant. Of Elizabeth I, he said, while her sister was still alive:

> The rejected one shall accede to the throne
> Her enemies shall be found to be conspirators,
> Her time shall triumph as never before,
> At seventy she shall surely die, in the third year of the century.

On September 7, 1533, the queen was born. When she died, she was sixty-nine years and six months, in her seventieth year. The date was March 24, 1603.

He foretold indirectly the union of the English and Scottish crowns, by saying that "Great Britain, comprising England," would "suffer a great inundation [flood]." In January, 1607, the dikes in Somerset were broken down by the sea; a stretch of country 30 miles long and 6 miles wide was underwater. The Norfolk coast suffered in the same way, but not so extensively. England had become Great Britain in March, 1603, when James I (VI of Scotland) in his person united the crowns of the two kingdoms as successor to Elizabeth, less than four years earlier.

The Great Plague and the Fire of London could not escape Nostradamus' keen psychic eye. Being an ardent royalist, he seems to have considered both in the nature of a judgment on the city—and perhaps the country generally—for having consented to the execution of its king, whom he always spoke of as "the just."

Of the plague he said:

The great plague of the maritime city
Shall not cease till death is avenged
For the blood of the just taken and condemned though innocent,
And the great dame outraged by feigning saints.

And of the fire:

The blood of the just shall be required of London
Burned by fire in thrice twenty and six:
The old dame shall fall from her high place
And many edifices of the same sect shall be destroyed.

("Dame" is Nostradamus' term for a cathedral or Mother Church and obviously refers to St. Paul's.)

Looking on into the eighteenth century, Nostradamus foresaw the rise of Napoleon, whose birthplace and many other details about him are described in the quatrains. What seems to have most impressed Nostradamus about Napoleon's appearance was his short hair, which, in those days of long-haired males, would have seemed unusual. *"Teste raze,"* he calls the emperor, saying, "The man with short hair will assume absolute power for fourteen years." After the *coup d'état* of 1799, Napoleon was in supreme control of France until his abdication in 1814.

Nostradamus calls him "an Emperor [of France] born near Italy.... His alliances will be much talked about and he will be more of a butcher than a prince.... From a private soldier, he will become Emperor, valiant in arms but to the Church most tiresome."

His victories and defeats, his escape from Elba, and his landing made near Nice are forecast. Napoleon in fact landed at Golfe-Juan a few miles from Nice.

His exile on St. Helena, Nostradamus describes as "the general who led infinite hosts, ending his life far above his native land among people of strange customs and language on a chalky island in the sea."

On to the twentieth century and the eruption of another dictator. "A leader of the Great Germanies will come to give help which is only its counterfeit, or will cause to yield by offering 'protection.' This man will stretch the borders of Great Germanie to include Brabant and Flanders, Bruges and Boulogne. France will be divided into two parts." Hitler and Mussolini (and the place of their first meeting, Venice), the chaos of armies retreating from France, are clearly described; the first impact of the German forces, the streams of refugees—all are set out in the quatrains, one of which pictures a bombing raid as vividly as if Nostradamus had been on the spot while it was going on:

> Living fire and death hidden in globes will be loosed, horrible, terrible,
> By night enemy forces will reduce the city to powder,
> That it is already on fire [incendiaries?] will be favorable to the enemy.

Nineteen hundred and ninety-nine years and seven months is the date he sets for the coming of the third Antichrist (Napoleon and Hitler, according to Nostradamus, filled this role each in his own time), the "King of Terror." His reign will last twenty-seven years; heretics will die, be taken captive, or exiled. The period will be one of "blood, human corpses, reddened water, hell on earth." He predicts that "a yellow race" will sweep across Europe and that Paris will be destroyed by an aerial attack before the tide of invasion is turned.

This prediction reads almost as if it were Nostradamus' version of the end of the world, the great Armageddon, the final debacle which will destroy the human race and which has been predicted regularly every so often since the history of prophecy began. In many centuries there seems to have been a widespread conviction that the world could not last much longer; perhaps the belief is a shadow in race memory cast by major cataclysms of the past, such as the engulfing of continents in floods, stretching to cataclysms which no doubt must occur in the future. The poles of the globe tilt; the land and water masses shift; mighty stresses and strains build up; vast upheavals occur. Some scientists think we are doing our puny bit to hurry such conditions along by extracting gas from the land (as in parts of Russia) and from the sea (the North Sea gas project), which apparently causes subsidences of the earth's crust.

The physical end of the world in 1999 seems unlikely, but prophets often speak in allegories. The end of the world as we know it—the present civilization—is a different matter; it could be that, as some psychics think, a great cycle of evolution has almost completed its span; another is due to begin.

Perhaps that is what Nostradamus saw, clairvoyantly. His predictions were not purely astronomical. Chauvigny, his disciple and biographer, says that Nostradamus' prophecies were made when he was in a state of ecstasy or trance, as it seems they must have been. Horoscopes cannot be set up for the unborn; their names and futures cannot be forecast by astrology.

But according to Nostradamus, the catastrophes and terrors of 1999 are as a dress rehearsal for those of the year 7000. Looking ahead, not a few hundred years, but 6,000, he says that the Gobi Desert will become once more a sea when the land is devastated, and the geography of the world changed by a deluge vaster than that of which the Bible tells.

Nostradamus foretold the date of his own death and its manner. "On returning from an embassy [he went to Arles, as representative of Salon], the King's gift safely replaced, I shall do no more, I shall have gone to God. By my relations, friends and brothers I shall be found dead, near my bed and the bench."

In June, 1566, ill with gout and with dropsy, he said, "My end is near." On July 1 he sent for a priest to hear his confession, saying afterward, "You will not see me alive at sunrise." On the morning of July 2 he was found dead as he had predicted in the quatrain quoted, between the bench he had had made to help him lever his body, cumbersome with dropsy, in and out of bed and the bed itself.

He is almost always referred to at this period of his life, as an "old man," as if he were an octogenarian at least, but he was not old when he died, at least by our standards. His age was sixty-two years, six months, and seven days. He may have looked like a patriarch and had the solemnity attributed to one, but he could sometimes show a puckish sense of humor, of which his last joke was typical.

Nearly fifty years after his death the authorities of Salon decided to remove his coffin to a place of greater importance in the church. In the hope that other predictions might have been buried with him, the casket was opened and there, on his breastbone, was a small metal plate, engraved with the date of the exhumation. He had foreseen even that.

9. The Brahan Seer and Thomas the Rhymer

More than 300 years ago—no one seems to know the exact date—one of the most curious chapters in the history of prophecy began with the birth at Baile-na-Cille in the parish of Uig, island of Lewis, of Coinneach (Kenneth) Odhar Fiossaiche, later known as the Brahan Seer. Among the Highland Scots, as with the gypsies, the "sight" is more remarkable when absent than when present. It is—or was—so much taken for granted that the fame and respect which Coinneach earned, unlike most prophets, in his own country, meant that his gift was recognized even among a psychic people as outstanding.

There are several versions of how it came to him. According to one of them, his mother, who was tending her sheep near the burial ground of Baile-na-Cille, saw the graves in the churchyard opening and their tenants hurrying out and off in all directions. Within about an hour they were all back, except one. The shepherdess put her distaff across this grave, so that she would know when its occupant returned. Presently a fair woman appeared; seeing the distaff, she spoke to Coinneach's mother, telling her that she was the daughter of the King of Norway, who had been drowned while bathing. Her body had been washed up on the beach of Uig and had been buried there. She asked its owner to remove the distaff (apparently the distaff was an insurmountable barrier to a spirit). After it had been taken away, in token of her gratitude, she told the woman to go to a nearby lake, where she would find a small round blue stone, with a hole in it. "Give it to your son, Coinneach," she said. "By its aid he will be able to read the future."

In some of the stories, the stone was white; it came to Coinneach via a farmer's wife for whom he was working and who tried to poison him. And as in one form or another, the stone appears in every version, it seems likely that he did own something of the sort, which he always carried. He may have used it as modern seers use a crystal or cards or some object—as a focus for concentration of the activities of the sixth sense. Or it may have been a gimmick, a theatrical prop, or perhaps it was a form of insurance against the unpleasantness which often was the lot of a seer in those days. The power of divination, he claimed, was in the stone, not in himself; a pebble could not be prosecuted for sorcery.

To begin with, he worked as a farmhand, but before long his reputation as a prophet had spread so widely that he was called in to predict the future for wealthy families on the Scottish mainland, at substantial fees. Coinneach Odhar, yeoman, had become the Brahan Seer.

Many of his prophecies, under the circumstances, were concerned with domestic affairs, of interest only to the men and women to whom they referred. But his inner eye was focused not just on the near at hand in time and space; it ranged over two or three hundred years, with pinpoint accuracy of detail in many cases. Sometimes the wording is bizarre or the phrasing oblique, when he is attempting to describe inventions or developments for which no terms had as yet been coined. He said, for instance, "Fire and water shall stream through every street and lane of Inverness," which translates without too much difficulty into a reference to the installation of gas and water pipes to every part of the town. "Long strings of carriages without horses will run between Dingwall and

Inverness, and even more wonderful, between Dingwall and Skye," he said, foretelling the railway which 200 years afterward carried "horseless carriages" to the places mentioned. Predicting the building of the railway through Muir-of-Ord, he said that "a chariot without horse or bridle" would run there "when there are two churches in the parish of Farrintosh, and there is a man with two thumbs in the Black Isle, and a man with two navels in the neighborhood of Duneen." These three specified signs occurred in the appointed places when the Muir-of-Ord railway was constructed.

One hundred and fifty years before the Caledonian Canal was cut, Coinneach foretold that "ships would sail round the back of Tomnahurich Hill." He saw Strathpeffer established as a spa; people would flock from many parts to drink the waters of a well there, he said.

In 1849 the Ness Bridge was swept away by a great flood, just as the seer had forewarned two centuries earlier. The bridge would be crowded with people, he said, among whom would be a man on a white horse and a pregnant woman. No lives, so far as was known, were lost in the disaster, although Matthew Campbell, riding a white horse, who was crossing the bridge as it crumbled, had a narrow escape. He only just reached the bank in time, carrying with him a woman he had caught up in his arms to save her being swept into the river. There is no record of her condition . . .

Coinneach foresaw and was saddened by the depopulation of the Highlands, which has taken place within living memory. "Ancient proprietors of the soil shall give way to strange merchant proprietors. The whole Highlands will become one vast deer forest—people will emigrate to islands yet unknown which will be discovered in the boundless ocean," said the seer. The island of Lewis would be cleared of the greater part of its inhabitants, and concerning Scotland generally, he foretold the proliferation of "whiskey and dram shops," policemen and commercialism, "travelling merchants so plentiful that one can scarce walk a mile on the highway without seeing one of them."

Another and more gloomy glimpse into Scotland's future was given in one of Coinneach's most enigmatic prophecies. He said that "a dun hornless cow will appear in Minch [off Carr Point in Gairloch] and will make a bellow which will knock the six chimneys off Gairloch House." After this "the whole country will become so utterly desolated and depopulated that the crow of a cock shall not be heard . . . after which deer and other wild animals shall be exterminated by horrid black rain."

The "hornless dun cow" it is thought could be the seer's attempt to describe a submarine (which of course he had not seen); the "bellow" a powerful detonation, possibly from one of the fleet of atomic submarines based in Holy Loch nearby. The "horrid black rain" could be a form of radiation fallout. According to the prophecy, the detonation or bellow which is to be the signal that this uneasy time is at hand, will "knock the six chimneys off Gairloch House." In the seer's day, Gairloch House was a wattled-turf-and-hurdles construction, thatched with turf. It had no chimneys. The present, rebuilt Gairloch House has six chimneys.

Many of Coinneach's predictions concerned his own neighborhood; of those relating to events further afield was his prophecy concerning the inexplicable removal of the massive Stone of Petty, which weighed eight tons, from its site, marking the boundary of Culloden and Moray, into the sea. In 1663 the seer said the stone would be found "as far in the sea as it now is away from it and no one will see it moved or be able to account for its transportation." On February 20, 1799, the Stone of Petty was mysteriously removed during the night and was discovered the next day 260 yards out to sea.

While in those parts, when walking over the area where the battle of Culloden, disastrous for Scotland, would be fought, the seer broke into lamentation. "Thy bleak moor," he said, "shall, ere many generations have passed away, be stained with the best blood in the Highlands . . . it will be a fearful period, heads will be lopped off by the score, and no mercy will be shown or quarter given on either side."

The pessimistic tenor of so many of his predictions does not seem to have discouraged consultants, although few of them could have been found cheering the prospects which, according to the seer, were ahead for them and their families.

The Mackenzies, he said, would lose their possessions at Lochalsh, which would "come into the hands of an Englishman, generous and open-handed. He will have one son and two daughters. After his death, the property will revert to the Mathesons, the original possessors." In a later century, Lochalsh was sold by the Mackenzie family to an Englishman, a Mr. Lullingstone, who made himself very popular because of his kindness and generosity. He had no family when he bought Lochalsh; then, after seventeen years of marriage, a son and two daughters were born. After Mr. Lullingstone's death Lochalsh was sold to Alexander Matheson, then MP for Ross and Cromarty.

For a chieftain of Skye he predicted a disaster which was to come through an heir who would be born when "there is a fair-haired Lochiel, a red-headed Lovat, a squint-eyed, fair-haired Chisholm, a big, deaf Mackenzie, and a bow, crooked-legged MacGille-chailum, who shall be the great-grandson of John [or little] Beg of Ringa [Ringa is on Skye]. He shall be the worst MacGille-chailum ever to be known." And when all the Highland lairds listed in Coinneach's prediction had the characteristics he had specified, there was a MacGille-chailum who was the worst—and last—of his race. Through him all the ancient inheritance of the family was lost.

Coinneach's most famous prophecy ran true to form; it has become known as the Doom of the Seaforths. It was also the last prophecy he made; after it his own doom overtook him.

Apparently, the seer was at the peak of his fame when the Countess of Seaforth sent for him. The third Earl of Seaforth had gone to arrange some business matter in Paris and had sent her no letters or news of any kind during an unexpectedly long stay abroad. The countess was anxious to know if the seer could tell her if her husband was safe and well and what was keeping him away.

Having put his blue (or white) divination stone to his eyes, Coinneach who was famous for prophecy, not for tact, laughed heartily. The countess, he said, need have no fears for her lord's health or happiness. He was having the time of his life. The seer refused at first, in spite of pressing, to go into his vision in detail. Finally, after being threatened with unpleasant punishments if he did not obey her, Coinneach told her that her husband was in a luxurious Paris chamber, in company which he evidently was enjoying; there were no signs that he had any intention of leaving it. The countess still wanted to know more—with whom was her husband? What was he doing?

The seer had been described as shrewd and clearheaded, a cynic, often sarcastic, one who did not suffer fools gladly, and —perhaps because of egotism—he did not trouble to hide his impatience with them. No doubt dismissing the countess as a possessive woman, trying to keep check on a husband who was enjoying a little freedom from her surveillance, he allowed himself to be irritated into describing the scene in the Paris room—and he was famous, as we know, for his flair for detail.

He saw the earl, he said, in a magnificent room, its chairs and sofas covered with velvet or cloth of gold, its paintwork gilded, its walls hung with fine pictures. In the room a beautiful woman was sitting; on his knees before her was the Earl of Seaforth, his arms around her waist.

There probably was an undercurrent of malice which the countess would sense, in Coinneach's manner, as much as to say "You made me tell you, and if you don't like it, you can't blame me." But of course, that was exactly what she did; Coinneach's shrewdness obviously did not include a knowledge of women's ways. He had committed a major blunder; he had made her lose face before her friends and retainers; he had started a scandal which would echo all around Scotland. Beside herself with rage, she called him a liar and a slanderous charlatan, accused him of having vilified a mighty chief in the presence of his vassals, sullying his good name through false divination. Because of Coinneach's lies and his spurious claims as a prophet, he would be put to death.

Coinneach, who was accustomed to have himself and to have his predictions treated with respect, could not believe that the countess was serious. He thought that she was making a show to impress her friends and clansmen. It must have been a horrifying moment for the seer when he was seized and taken out of the castle to his execution. According to some versions, this was postponed for some days after the scene in the castle. A stone slab on the present road running between Fortrose and Fort George Ferry, near the Chanonry Point, marks the spot to which finally he was taken and forced headfirst into a barrel of boiling tar—a method of dealing with witchcraft. The execution was supervised, it is said, by local clergy.

Before he died, Coinneach produced his divination stone. Putting it to his eye, he said: "I see into the far future and I read the doom of the race of my oppressor, and die mourning. The long-descended line of Seaforth will, ere many generations have passed, end in extinction and in sorrow. I see a Chief, the last of the house, both deaf and dumb. He will be the father of four fair sons, all of whom he will follow to the tomb. He will live careworn and die mourning, knowing no future Chief of his clan shall reign at Brahan or at Kintail. He himself shall sink into the grave, and the remnant of his possessions shall be inherited by a white-hooded lassie from the East, and she shall kill her sister. As a sign by which it may be known that these things are coming to pass, there shall be four great lairds in the days of the last deaf and dumb Seaforth—Gairloch, Chisholm, Grant, and Ramsey, of whom one shall be buck-toothed, another harelipped, another half-witted, and the fourth a stammerer. Chiefs distinguished by these personal marks shall be the allies and neighbors of the last Seaforth, and when he looks around him and sees them, he may know that his sons are doomed to death, that his broad lands shall pass away to the stranger, and that his race shall come to an end."

As he finished his last prophecy, the seer threw his divining stone into a pool or small loch nearby, saying that whoever found it would inherit his gift of divination, indiscreet use of which had brought to him so terrible a penalty.

It seems that he might have escaped it if the execution had been delayed only a few hours. On the day of the seer's death, the Earl of Seaforth came back to Scotland, to be greeted with the story of Coinneach's prophecy and its sequel. Seaforth, horrified by the unjust condemnation of a man, and for a triviality, to a death of such cruelty, rode without rest or food to Chanonry Point, hoping to reach it before the sentence was carried out. His horse died under him; he had to walk the last few miles, arriving in time to see rising from the ness a column of thick black smoke, Coinneach's funeral pyre.

The truth of the vision, telling of which had brought him there, was verified by the Earl of Seaforth, who told his wife that every detail of the seer's description was exact. His companion in the Paris apartment was Lucy Walters, mistress of Charles II and mother of his natural son, the Duke of Monmouth. Perhaps realization of the enormity of what she had done weighed on the countess' conscience; at any rate, a few years later, she threw herself from the tower of Brahan Castle. The Earl of Seaforth seems to have lived uneventfully until his death in 1678. The seer's presage of doom had been not for him but for his descendant, who would be the last of his line.

In 1754 Francis Humberston Mackenzie (created Lord Seaforth in 1797) was born, and Coinneach Odhar's prophecy was fulfilled. Lord Seaforth was neither deaf nor dumb in early childhood; he became deaf when he was about fifteen years old, after an attack of scarlet fever. Later on in his life, he also became dumb. Of four Scottish lairds who were his neighbors, Sir Hector Mackenzie of Gairloch was buck-toothed, Chisholm of Chisholm was harelipped, Grant of Grant was half-witted, and MacLeod of Ramsey stammered. Here were the signs, foretold by the seer in 1663, of the imminent ending of the Seaforth line.

Perhaps Lord Seaforth dismissed them as coincidence. At any rate he did not go out of his way to avoid danger, even if it meant a risk of bringing Coinneach's prophecy to pass. He raised a regiment with which he fought in the French Revolutionary Wars and came through without so much as a scratch. He married; he had ten children, six daughters, and four sons. One son died in childhood; two others died later. The last remaining son, the heir, who had a wasting disease, was sent to the south of England to be treated by a specialist. Daily bulletins of his condition came to Brahan Castle; at one period, the invalid seemed to be making progress. But when the family piper heard the good news, he sighed and said, "Na, na. He'll never recover. It's decreed that Seaforth shall outlive all his sons." And in a few days the Seaforth heir was dead.

On January 11, 1815, the last of the Seaforths sank "into the grave," in the words spoken by the Brahan Seer 200 years earlier. But this was not the end of the story of loss and sorrow foretold by Coinneach; the "doom" was as yet only half accomplished.

Lord Seaforth's eldest daughter, Mary Frederica Elizabeth Mackenzie, had married in 1804 Admiral Sir Samuel Hood, KB, who was later appointed commander in chief of the East Indian station. He died there, about the same time as his father-in-law died in Scotland. Lady Hood returned from the East white-coiffed in the mourning fashion of the day for widows. The "white-hooded lassie from the East" of the seer's prediction had come back to take up her dwindling inheritance.

And now, for one reason or another, the family's "broad lands" began to pass out of their possession into strangers' hands. The "gift land of Kinsale" was sold, as Coinneach said it would be, because of some losses in estates in the West Indies; other sales followed.

Sometime later, Lady Hood married again—a Mr. Stewart, who took the name of Mackenzie, since there were no male heirs in his wife's family. They still lived at Brahan Castle, where the Seaforth tragedy culminated when Mrs. Stewart-Mackenzie was driving her sister Caroline through woods on the estate in a pony carriage. For no reason ever discovered, the ponies took fright and bolted; the carriage overturned; the two women were thrown out. Mrs. Stewart-Mackenzie was badly shaken and bruised; Caroline was so seriously injured that she died.

The lord lieutenant of Ross, Duncan Davidson of Tulloch, in a letter dated May 21, 1878, mentioned the Brahan Seer's predictions: "Many of these prophecies I heard upwards of seventy years ago, and when many of them were not yet fulfilled, such as Lord Seaforth surviving his sons, and Mrs. Stewart-Mackenzie's accident near Brahan, by which Miss Caroline Mackenzie was killed."

Coinneach Odhar had known that these things would happen 200 years before they actually occurred. He described the scenes of his predictions as vividly as if they were part of his own experience. How could he see so clearly so far ahead, things which sometimes had no connection with himself and no identifiable significance?

One of his prophecies was that "a bald black girl shall be born at the back of Gairloch church." It was fulfilled when a well-known young woman was taken in labor at a communion service there and delivered of a dark girlchild before she could be removed. The prediction was accurate, but the interesting point about it is that it should have been made at all. It was not related to any person or family for whom he was looking into the future; the vision seems to have come to him without reason or purpose. Perhaps as he was strolling past the church, the incident which was to happen many years afterward registered in some way on his consciousness, its unexpectedness intrigued him, and he recorded it.

We simply do not know enough as yet about the working of the sixth sense to begin to find the answer to such questions as, for instance, why some apparently unimportant events should be foreseen when others of much greater significance may go apparently unnoticed, or why in some races, such as the Scots, the faculty of prevision is so active.

About 400 years before the time of Coinneach Odhar, Scotland had produced another seer almost as famous as he; Thomas the Rhymer was born about 1220 on the estates of the Earl of March, whose vassal he probably was. All the prophecies with which he is credited may not have been his; the fact remains that they were made, and made long before the events occurred to which they related—which seems to be the most important issue. And Archbishop John Spottiswood (1565-1639) at least, in his *History of the Church of Scotland*, came down in support of Thomas' authorship. He says that the Rhymer's prophecies "may be justly admired, having foretold to many ages before, the union of England and Scotland in the ninth degree of Bruce's blood, with the succession of Bruce himself to the crown, being yet a child, and other divers particulars which the event hath satisfied and made good."

Thomas foretold the death of King Alexander III of Scotland in prophetic hyperbole typical of the period. Lord March had asked Thomas in a joking way "what another day was to bring forth"; Thomas, in very different vein, replied, after sighing deeply, "Alas for tomorrow, a day of calamity and misery. Before the twelfth hour shall be heard a blast so vehement that it shall exceed all those that have yet been heard in Scotland; a blast which shall strike the nations with amazement, shall confound those who hear it, shall humble what is lofty and what is unbending shall level to the ground."

Lord March, who thought he was referring to the weather, expected a storm, but the next day was so fine and clear that the earl ridiculed Thomas as a humbug, prematurely, as it turned out. As he was sitting down to his midday meal, just before twelve o'clock, the earl was disturbed by the sound of a horse galloping into the castle yard. The rider was a messenger bringing news of the death of King Alexander, who had been thrown over a cliff at Kinghorn.

The Brahan Seer and Thomas the Rhymer 141

Doom was the theme of Thomas' most famous prediction, as it was of the Brahan Seer's: the doom of the house of Mar. It took several centuries to work out, as did Coinneach's forecast of disaster for the Seaforths. Sir Bernard Burke in his *Ulster King at Arms: Family Romance* (1853) quotes the prophecy:

> Proud Chief of Mar: Thou shalt be raised still higher until thou sittest in the place of King. Thou shalt rule and destroy, and thy work shall be after thy name; but thy work shall be the emblem of thy house, and shall teach mankind that he who cruelly and haughtily raiseth himself upon the ruins of the holy cannot prosper. Thy work shall be cursed and never finished, but thou shalt have riches and greatness, and shalt be true to thy sovereign and shalt raise his banner in the field of blood. Then, when thou seemest to be highest, when thy power is mightiest, thou shall fall; low shall be thy head among the nobles of thy people. Deep shall be thy moan among the children of dool [dolor or sorrow]. Thy lands shall be given to a stranger, and thy titles shall be among the dead. The branch that springs from thee shall see his dwelling burnt, in which a king is nursed, his wife a sacrifice in that same flame; his children numerous, but of little honour; and three born and grown who shall never see the light. Yet shall thine ancient tower stand, for the brave and true cannot be wholly forsaken. Thou proud head and daggered hand must dree thy weird, until horses shall be stabled in thy hall and a weaver shall throw his shuttle in thy chamber of state. Thine ancient tower, a woman's dower, shall be a ruin and a beacon, until an ash sapling shall spring from the topmost stone. Then shall thy sorrows be ended, and the sunshine of royalty shall beam on thee once more. Thine honours shall be restored; the kiss of peace shall be given to thy Countess though she seek it not, and the days of peace shall return to thee and thine. The line of Mar shall be broken but not until its honours are doubled and its doom ended.

According to Sir Bernard Burke, the first stage of the prophecy was fulfilled in 1571, when the then Earl of Mar was appointed regent of Scotland and guardian of James I. He began to build himself a palace in Stirling, which was never finished. It was called Mar's Work. A descendant of his, who fought for the Stuart cause, lost his lands and his titles when the Pretender was defeated. Alloa Tower, which was owned by this Lord Mar's grandson, James Francis, was burned; his wife, Lady Francis, who died in the fire, left three children, all of whom were born blind. Fifty horses were stabled in the hall of Alloa Tower during the French war scare; a weaver was found working in the ruins. And out of the "topmost stone" an ash tree was growing.

In 1882, during George IV's visit to Scotland, the earldom of Mar was restored to Erskine of Mar by the King. His (Mar's) grandson was given the title of Earl of Mar and Kelly, dual honors. The unsought "kiss of peace" was given to his wife when Queen Victoria, meeting Lady Mar by chance in Stirling Castle, was attracted to her and kissed her.

10. Astrologer Royal and Prophecies About Monarchs

John Dee, Queen Elizabeth's astrologer, that fascinating character, man of mystery and of pathos—in that the great promise of his early days crumbled in the end to nothing—lived in a period when interest in prophecy was at peak in his country. Everyone, from those in the top income group to the lowest-paid worker, wanted to consult an astrologer. Such a man, if he was genuine, had had training in mathematics, astronomy, and philosophy, and a man of such learning was entitled to charge a high fee, which meant that only the better-off of the community could be his clients. The less-affluent relied on "almanacs and prognostications," popular publications known as "the poor man's way of using practical astronomy," as astrology was often called at that time.

An almanac would almost certainly be found in the average sixteenth- and seventeenth-century home—as well, of course, as a Bible—and no other book. In 1600 about 600 almanacs and prognostications were published. Pamphlets of prognostications supposed, for example, to be the predictions of Merlin appeared from time to time. Calendars and almanacs were intended for the use of students of astronomy, law, or medicine; almanacs at one time probably were synonymous with calendars. The word originates from the Arabian term *al-manakh,* meaning calendar. Roger Bacon, probably the first English writer to use the name, applies it in his *Opus Majus* to tables of apparent motions of the stars. And it appears twice in Geoffrey Chaucer's *The Treatise on the Astrolabe*.

About 1539, all three—calendar, almanac, and prognostication—were issued together as one publication, annually. The cost for one year was about 1*d.*; for thirty years, 4*s.* 8*d.*

Dee was growing up while the interest in divination was at its height; this perhaps was a stimulus for the development of his occult gifts, which may have been inherited from his Celtic forebears, the Dees of Nant-y-groes, Radnorshire. Opinions vary on who was his father; he may have been a London vintner, Rowland Dee, but John Strype, the seventeenth-century historian, says Dee senior was a gentleman usher to Henry VIII. Henry apparently treated him badly; in an attempt, it is said, to make amends, Henry's son and daughter showed special favor to John Dee from time to time. Edward VI, to whom he dedicated one of his books, gave him a pension of 100 crowns a year. Dee exchanged this for a living at Upton-upon-Severn, a bad bargain for him. It turned out to be an unhealthy place, with a stipend much smaller than the pension offered by Edward.

In November, 1542, John Dee went to St. John's College, Cambridge, where for three years, he says, he studied for eighteen hours daily, allowing himself two hours for meals and recreation and four for sleep. In May, 1547, he went to the Low Countries to confer with notable scholars. He studied the arts and sciences at Louvain, where he took his LLD, and became a friend of Gerardus Mercator. Since he brought back to England with him an astronomer's brass staff, a great globe constructed by Mercator, and an astronomer's brass ring, he probably made his first significant contact with astonomy-astrology (the terms were then synonymous) at that time.

After his return to England in 1551, he built up a repu-

Astrologer Royal and Prophecies About Monarchs 145

tation as an astrologer. For a time things went smoothly; then he fell foul of Queen Mary, who disapproved of his "occult practices." She had him arrested and imprisoned on suspicion of plotting against her. Perhaps she had heard his predictions about her marriage; perhaps she was angry with him because it may have seemed to her more like a curse than a prophecy. Dee had said when he was told of the mooted alliance: "Woe to the two nations: Sorrow and dolour: Disaster by water and persecution by fire. And our Queen shall die childless."

When his predictions about Mary Tudor had been fulfilled and her sister came to the throne, Dee's fortunes took a turn for the better. He had been in correspondence with Elizabeth for some time before her accession and had cast her horoscope, foretelling that one day she would be queen. Before she was crowned, she sent Robert Dudley to ask Dee to name the most propitious day for the ceremony. Having made his calculations, Dee chose January 14, 1559, a date, he said, which offered prospects of success and of a great reign.

Dee was given an official position at Elizabeth's court; he was known as "hyr astrologer," whom she consulted about anything and everything. A comet appeared; she sent for and questioned him on whether it foretold that the scourge of Germany, Gustavus Adolphus, whose career of destruction the astronomer Johannes Kepler had predicted, would attack England. Dee told her that although the comet was supposed to be an omen of the northern prince's depredations, Britain would not be affected.

Then a wax image of the queen was found in Lincoln's Inn Fields, with a great pin stuck in its breast. She seems to have panicked; Dee was commanded to go at once to Lincoln's Inn and make a report on it. Prudently taking Mr. Secretary Wilson with him as witness, Dee looked the image over. It was not, he thought, dangerous; it had not been made in malice by a skilled magician.

Dee and Secretary Wilson took a barge to Richmond to report to the queen, whom they found sitting in her garden near the steps of the royal landing stage. Lord Leicester and the lords of the Privy Council were in attendance when Dee told her that in his opinion the affair of the wax image was nothing more than a practical joke. No harm would come of it, he said, and she seems to have taken his word for it. During the years she had known Dee, she had come to believe in and to rely on his prescience.

None of the voyages of the merchant adventurers—Martin Frobisher, John Hawkins, and the rest—was undertaken until Dr. Dee had been consulted about the most favorable sailing date. It was Dee's advice which set the scene for the great battle with the Armada. When news reached England of the vast fleet which Philip of Spain was assembling for the invasion of England, as everyone knew, Francis Drake's plan was to attack the Spaniards while they were still in their home port. Elizabeth refused her consent to the expedition until Dee gave his opinion of it. His findings were that its success was doubtful; Elizabeth told Drake the venture must be called off. Much against Drake's will, apparently, he had to wait until, when the Spanish fleet was entering the Channel, the auspices were favorable enough for Dee to give the all clear for action. He had already foretold the coming of the Armada, its probable date, the areas in which defenses should be set up.

His psychic powers had begun to manifest themselves about 1581. An entry in his diary for May 25 of that year reads: "I had sight in Chrystallo offered me and I saw." As a rule he had to rely on Edward Kelly, the medium with whom he worked for a number of years, for such visions; Dee, as he often said, "could neither 'see' nor skry [crystal-gaze]." At least four years before the execution of Mary Queen of Scots, in 1587, Uriel (one of the spirit guides with whom Dee communicated through Kelly), described her kneeling on a scaffold; a "tall, black-clad man" was standing beside her. There was also a "sea full of ships." Foreign powers were providing ships "against the welfare of England, and these shall shortly be put to practice," he said. In 1581 the Spanish Armada,

Astrologer Royal and Prophecies About Monarchs 147

which attacked England in 1588, would not have been heard of in this country.

About this time, he is said to have "laid a storm" for Sir Everard Digby. He also foretold to Goodwife Faldo, a neighbor of his at Mortlake, where he had been living since 1569, that she would recover a basket of clothes which she had lost through carelessness—and the place and the way in which it would be found. To the butler of a friend, who thought he had been robbed of a bundle of his master's plate which he was bringing by boat to the owner's house, Dee predicted that the plate would be found. On a day specified, the butler must go back, said Dee, to the boat in which he brought the plate. There he would meet a man who had taken the basket by mistake. The butler obeyed instructions; the plate was found.

Innumerable horoscopes were cast by Dee; among them is a chart he made for his son Arthur, who would, he said, "have good fortune from a prince." Some years after John's death, Arthur Dee was recommended by James I to the Emperor of Russia as a physician. Arthur went to Moscow, where he lived for some time; "supporting twelve children [and his wife, of course] in luxury."

Alchemy fascinated John Dee. He studied and practiced it for a time, but stronger than the urge to produce gold was the urge to find a source of cosmic wisdom, through which the purpose of human life could be uncovered. This was the reason for his efforts to make contact, through the medium Edward Kelly, with the angels Michael and Uriel and with spirits of discarnate human beings. Kelly was necessary to Dee, who had no mediumistic gifts himself; Kelly seems to have been genuine in this respect. In others, he was untrustworthy—a liar, as Dee knew, a forger, and a grave robber. His ears had been cropped as punishment for one of his misdemeanors; he had a cap with long sidepieces which concealed the mutilation. Dee apparently never discovered why he always wore it.

Together Dee and Kelly produced a great deal of psychic

phenomena, much of which seems to have been genuine. His two main hopes, to find the secret of transmuting base metal into gold and the revelations of higher wisdom, were, like so much that happened in Dee's life, will-o'-the-wisps, leading him on with promises which never fully materialized. The pension offered by Edward VI, the pledges given to him by Elizabeth of money and preferment, which all seemed so splendid in prospect, in the end came to little or nothing.

Apart from financial ups and downs, he had to contend with troubles arising from the superstitious fears which were roused by his occult work. Ever since his student days at Cambridge, a reputation for dabbling in dubious magical practices had clung to him, never quite dispelled by the prestige of the positions he held or by royal patronage—a reputation which began when Dee, who was playing a small part in a presentation of Aristophanes' *The Peace*, apparently flew to the rafters on the back of a huge beetle. It was probably all done with mirrors, Dee being a master of the science of optics and the owner and maker of distorting glasses and lenses, but there was gossip that he had used the black arts for his levitation. Later, the stories of his séances with Kelly brought this old tittle-tattle back to people's minds; the faction which was jealous of his influence with the queen built up public feeling against him as a magician to a point where a mob raided his house in Mortlake while he was away in Germany and destroyed his magical instruments and many of his books. When he came back, it was to face an accusation, arranged by his enemies, of blinding one child and killing another by magic. At the hearing, the court threw out the charge.

The thread of frustration running through Dee's life reached its climax under James I, who dismissed him from a post given him by Queen Elizabeth as being an "ally of Satan." Although he was then eighty, Dee, furiously denying the charge, insisted on being tried for witchcraft. James, who knew very well that a public hearing would only have established the harmlessness of Dee's researches and his long story

Astrologer Royal and Prophecies About Monarchs   149

of loyal service to Crown and country, had the petition dismissed.

At the time of his death, December, 1608, public feeling toward Dee was summed up in the epitaph given him by his neighbor, Goody Faldo: "A mighty good man he was." He must have been a handsome one; John Aubrey described him as tall and slender, with a "very faire cleare rosie complexion" and, later, a long white beard. At Mortlake he is buried between two of Queen Elizabeth's servants, a Mr. Holt and a Mr. Miles.

Dee was probably the greatest astrologer retained by a monarch of that century; he was not the last or the first. Queen Anne had an astrologer on her payroll, but after her reign there is no record that the office was ever filled again, although "unofficial" prophecies continued to be made, as they had been all through history, concerning the kings and queens of Britain.

The possibilities of Edward the Confessor's accession were negligible when Bishop Brihtwold prophesied to this son of Ethelred the Unready by his second wife, Emma of Normandy, that he would be king, reigning for many years and leading a pure life. Brihtwold saw Edward hallowed to the kingdom by St. Peter in a vision; he heard Edward ask who would come after him, and St. Peter's reply: "The kingdom of England belongs to God. He shall provide a king according to his pleasure."

Brihtwold—or St. Peter—was right about Edward's accession and his reign. He was succeeded by Harold, the son of Earl Godwin, whose short period of kingship ended at Senlac in the fighting against the Normans. As for which, if either, of these was the divine provision, there is no indication; William at least does not seem to have been the people's choice. Not long after his seizure of England's crown, he seized also a great tract of the villeins' land in Hampshire, which he turned into a game reserve. His New Forest gave him increased scope for hunting and increased unpopularity; a prediction which was not far from a curse became current at this time:

> William's forest shall be his bane.
> There shall sons of his house be slain.

Some years after this prophecy was made, William's second son, Richard, was killed in the forest. Then a grandson of William's, the natural son of his heir, Robert Curthose, died there. Finally came the shooting of his successor, William Rufus, by accident, some said; others said that since he was a witch, his death was a ritual sacrifice. If it were so, that might account for the king's being left where he fell when the arrow struck him. Apparently none of his entourage even made sure that he was dead before riding away, perhaps chary of interfering with coven affairs. Rufus' abandoned body was found some hours afterward by a charcoal burner named Purkiss, who, apparently concerned that the king should be buried decently, wheeled the corpse on his hand cart to the nearest church. Afterward he complained bitterly that his vehicle was never returned to him.

Eleanor of Aquitaine, wife of Henry II, had a prophetic dream, which was recorded by the Archdeacon of Wells, Thomas Agnell, about her son Henry, the "Young King." At the time Eleanor was a prisoner in Salisbury Tower (the cathedral was not yet built), which can still be seen in the turfed crater lying within the ruins of the castle. In June, 1183, she dreamed she saw the Young King lying on a couch, his hands together in the pose of an effigy on a tomb. He wore a splendid sapphire ring; on his head was the crown he had worn when crowned King of England in June, 1170, by order of his father, Henry II, who at that time divided his domains among his sons—except John. A second crown, a crown of light, cast a glow on his smiling colorless face.

Agnell, who had been sent by the king to tell Eleanor of her son's death, says that she knew the purpose of his errand before he could tell her of it. She described the dream which

Astrologer Royal and Prophecies About Monarchs 151

she had had some weeks earlier to Agnell, who was able to confirm all its details.

The Young King had died in France within a few days from an illness with which his doctors had been unable to deal; his last moments had been of a remarkable peacefulness. Knowing he was going to die, Henry had sent a message by the Bishop of Agen to his father, asking his forgiveness for rebelling against him, which the king at first was unwilling to give. At last, persuaded to change his mind by the bishop, Henry gave him a magnificent sapphire ring to take to his son in token of their reconciliation. The Young King put on the ring; although he gave orders that it was to be removed after his death, it could not be taken from his finger and was buried with him.

Henry's rapprochement with his dying son was one of the few such episodes in his family life, which was as stormy as any in the history of British kings. His sons, Richard and Geoffrey, were always at odds with their father, helped by King Philip Augustus of France, to whom Richard did homage for his lands in that country, in front of his father, as a gesture of defiance. Henry's wife, Eleanor, worked against him, and for this he imprisoned her; his youngest son, John, whom Henry believed to be loyal beyond question to him, stayed with him when all his vassals deserted, but when after a truce in the war between them, Philip of France sent to Henry, as agreed, a list of traitors in the English camp, John's name headed it.

Henry had foreseen these events long before they happened. Giraldus Cambrensis says that in a room in the palace of Westminster was a painting of an eagle and four eaglets, three of which were tearing at the eagle's back and wings with talon and beak. The fourth (and smallest), perched on the parent bird's neck, was trying to peck out its eyes. The king, looking at the picture, said that the four eaglets were his sons. "They will persecute me until I am dead. The cruelest of all, the one who will hurt me worse than the other three, is the youngest—my favorite."

A prophecy which was made to Henry IV personally or about which he was told forecast that he "would die in Jerusalem." The king, an ardent crusader, who had dreamed all his life of being able to enter the Holy City and recapture the Holy Sepulcher, while preparing for the campaign which he hoped would fulfill his dream, remembered the warning. He gave orders for all possible precautions to be taken for his safety when the goal was finally reached.

In 1412 a great council was convened at the Whitefriars Hall in London, to make decisions concerning armaments and ships for this expedition to the Holy Land. All through the winter discussions went on, in spite of the fact that the king was a very sick man. Early in 1413, while praying at the shrine of St. Edward the Confessor, he had a violent fit and had to be carried to the abbot's house at Westminster and put to bed before a fire. For some hours he lay in a coma; when he became conscious, he asked where he was, and was told the house of the Abbot of Westminster.

"I shall not die here," he said. "It is foretold that I am to die in Jerusalem."

His condition grew worse, but before he lapsed into unconsciousness, he asked if the room in which he was had any special name. "The Jerusalem Chamber," they told him.

He died in the Jerusalem Chamber on March 20, 1413.

Henry V turned prophet temporarily at the birth of his son. Looking down at the newborn child, he said, "Good Lord; I, Henry of Monmouth, shall small time reign, and much get; Henry, born at Windsor, shall long time reign and lose all, but God's will be done."

In the year of the death of King James I of Scotland a prophecy was made which might have changed the course of the history of his country if he had taken it seriously. The prediction pronounced that a king would be slain that year in Scotland.

On the night before his assassination, James was playing chess with one of his knights, who was nicknamed the "King of Love." The king, in high spirits, quoted the prophecy to him, saying jokingly: "There be no kings but you and I. Look well to your safety; mine is provided for."

During the festivities one of James' squires told him that he had had a dream in which he saw one of the king's knights, Sir Robert Graham, kill him. The king said he had had a similar dream but did not take it seriously.

Late that night a loud knocking awakened the guards. A woman was at the door, demanding to be taken to the king; she had something to say to him of great importance. When she was told to go away and come back in the morning, she said, "You shall all repent that I was not allowed to speak to the King."

Before morning, James had been stabbed to death by Sir Robert Graham and his fellow conspirators.

The disaster of the Battle of Flodden Field was foretold to King James IV while he was preparing for the campaign of which it was the ending. James was praying in Linlithgow church, when a man in a blue habit, girdled and wearing sandals, forced his way through the press of nobles, calling loudly for the king. When he reached James, he did not salute or greet him in any way. Speaking in an authoritative voice, he told the king that the campaign he was about to begin would end disastrously. "Cancel your plans," he said, "and give up your illicit amour. Otherwise you and most of your supporters will perish on the field of battle." Before the king or any of his lords could ask the blue-habited man who he was or whence he came, he disappeared, and no one saw him go.

Prophetic omens foretold ill fortune for Charles I from his first hour on earth. He was born on the day on which Lord Gowrie and his son, the Master of Gowrie, were executed—some said murdered—by order of James I. Their dismembered corpses were carried past the palace where the royal baby was; their heads were impaled on spikes in the Tolbooth. The wise women of Edinburgh pronounced that the synchronization of these bloody happenings with Charles' birth was the worst possible augury for his future. They predicted that he would be sickly, and would suffer dismemberment or beheading.

When preparations were being made for his coronation, it was found that not nearly the amount of purple velvet required was available. The material could be obtained only from Genoa; because delivery of an order from that city to London would take at least 150 days, it would arrive too late for the ceremony. So white velvet was used, instead, in spite of the protests of a member of the council, who said it was a bad omen. "White is the color in which victims are dressed."

According to Welwood in his *Memoirs* (1718) some forecast of ill fortune was made to both Charles and Lord Falkland when they tried to foretell their future by the *sortes Virgilianae* method of divination in the Bodleian Library, Oxford, though he does not say what the warning was.

The *sortes Virgilianae* are a do-it-yourself form of oracle; to consult them, all that is necessary is a book of Virgil, a thumb or a pin to mark the place where the book is opened at random, and a knowledge of Latin so that the lines on which pin or thumb rests can be read.

It is apparently a very old method of divination. In *Erotomania* (1640) Ferrand mentions the "kinde of divination by opening of a booke at all adventures [*i.e.*, at random], and this was called the Valentinian Chance, and by some, Sortes Virgilianae, of which the Emperor Adrian was wont to make very much use." Home in *Demonologie* (1650) says of it: "For sorcery, properly so-called, viz. divination by lots, it is too much apparent how it abounds. . . ."

According to Aubrey's life of the poet Abraham Cowley, the *sortes Virgilianae* foretold his father's fate to Prince Charles (later Charles II). Aubrey says:

> In December 1648, King Charles the first being in great trouble, and prisoner at Caerlsbrooke, or to be brought to London to his Trial; Charles Prince of Wales being then at Paris, and in profound sorrow for his father, Mr. Abraham

Cowley went to wayte on him; his Highness asked him whether he would play at Cards, to diverte his sad thoughts. Mr. Cowley replied, he did not care to play at cards; but if his Highness pleased, they would use *Sortes Virgilianae* (Mr. Cowley always had a Virgil in his pocket). The Prince accepted the proposal, and prick't his pinne in the fourth booke of the *Aeneids*. The Prince understood not Latin well, and desired Mr. Cowley to translate the verses, which he did admirably well.

> At bello audacis populi vexatus et armis,
> Finibus extorris, complexu avulsus Iuli,
> Auxilium imploret, videatque indigna suorum
> Funera; nec, quum se sub leges pacis iniqae
> Tradiderit, regno aut optata luce fruatur,
> Sed cadat ante diem mediaque inhumatus arena.

> But, vex'd with rebels and a stubborn race,
> His country banish'd and his son's embrace,
> Some foreign Prince for fruitless succours try
> And see his friend ingloriously die;
> Nor, when he shall to faithless terms submit,
> His throne enjoy, not comfortable light,
> But, immature, a shameful death receive,
> And in the ground the unbury'd body leave.

George Villiers, Duke of Buckingham, so closely influenced and was influenced by the fortunes of Charles I that fulfillment of a prophecy made to him affected Charles so deeply that it can be treated as if it concerned the king personally.

The Keeper of the Wardrobe at Windsor had a vision of an old friend who had been at college with him in Paris, the late Duke of Buckingham. "Tell my son," the father said, "that he must make himself popular, or at least soothe the embittered minds of the people, otherwise he will not live long." On three different occasions, the vision came to the royal wardrobe keeper, who finally went to London and asked Sir Ralph Freeman to help him arrange an interview with the duke. The duke met his father's friend in a private room where there was no possibility of the warning, which was passed on in a conversation lasting an hour, being overheard.

He apparently was not seriously disturbed by his father's prediction; his mother, with whom he discussed it, wept bitterly, imploring him to do as he had been advised. Neither his attitude nor his way of life in the months following his father's appearance showed any signs of the improvement he had been urged to make. Less than a year after it was made, the prophecy was fulfilled; George Villiers was assassinated.

Bad omens gathered around James II as they had around his father. To begin with, the crown was too small for his head and often had to be prevented from falling off. Then the window of a London church on which his coat of arms had been painted suddenly fell down without discoverable cause. When Sir Edward Sherborne, at the Tower, received the signal from the abbey that James had been crowned, he took out the great flag which bore the king's arms. No sooner was it hoisted than the wind blew flag and flagstaff into the Thames.

The monarch concerned, of course, was often the last to hear of prophecies or omens of ill fortune. It could be unhealthy for a seer to make gloomy predictions; Robert Allen, the astrologer, was lucky only to be severely censured for foretelling in 1551 that Edward VI would die two years later. John Woodhouse, another astrologer, took care not to make too definite his pronouncement concerning "troubled times" that, "beginning on 20th January 1601, would continue till 18th November 1603. Sundry great persons, lawyers, rulers, etc., the middle-aged and lusty, are especially threatened." He came very near to pinpointing the time of Queen Elizabeth's death.

Johannes Kepler, the German astronomer and astrologer, was more or less contemporary with these men (he was born in 1571 and died in 1630). He made a prediction known as the "prophecy of the six M's," which ran: "Magnus Monarchis Matthias Menso Martis Morietur [The great monarch,

Astrologer Royal and Prophecies About Monarchs 157

Matthias, will die in the month of March]." The Emperor Matthias died in March, 1619.

For most of his life, Kepler was poor. Yet when, in 1620, James I sent an ambassador, Sir Henry Wotton, to him, asking him to come live in England under his patronage—a proposal amounting to the offer of a post as court astrologer and astronomer, Kepler refused to leave his country. He probably felt that poverty was preferable to the pitfalls in the path of a royal astrologer.

About two years before his death, he did accept an equivalent position, offered him by Albrecht W. E. von Wallenstein as a result of the accuracy with which Kepler had cast the horoscope and described the (then unknown to him) appearance and character of Wallenstein's wife, the Duchess of Friedland. Wallenstein gave him a comfortable pension and a pleasant house; at least he was free at the end of his life from the driving penury which earlier had forced him, as he said, "to defray the expense of the Ephemeris for two years by composing a vile prophesying Almanac, which is scarcely more respectable than begging, unless it is saving the Emperor's credit, who abandons me entirely, and would leave me to perish from hunger."

Kepler's tutor in astronomy and astrology, Tycho Brahe (1546-1601), was official astrologer to Rudolph II, Emperor of Austria, who not only provided him with a handsome pension and a country estate, but equipped an observatory for him. Brahe, in return, named the Rudolphine tables, which he had constructed and which were in demand among astronomers, after his patron.

In 1563, when he was only seventeen, he made a prophecy which was to become famous. He said that in 1665 a plague "must come, because it took place in the beginning of Leo and not far from the nebulous stars of Cancer, two of the zodiacal signs which are reckoned by Ptolemy 'suffocating and pestilent.' " The Great Plague swept Europe from 1665 to 1666.

Another of Brahe's prophecies concerned the appearance of the Lion of the North (Gustavus Adolphus), King of Sweden, who devastated most of Central Europe in a supposedly religious war. In 1572, Tycho registered the appearance of a new star in the constellation Cassiopeia; this he said was the sign of the birth of a "valorous prince, whose arms would dazzle Germany, but who himself would disappear in 1632." Gustavus Adolphus was born in Finland in 1594; in 1632, he was killed at the Battle of Lützen, having defeated the armies of General Wallenstein.

Nearly 200 years before Gustavus was born, John of Capistrano made a prophecy about the year 1622, which was recorded in his book *Astronomy*. In that year, he said, "The great Lion of Midnight goes forth and returns no more to his house, but he will have accomplished that which was ordained. Many of those who deem themselves wise will declare 'he cannot'; others will say 'have I not told you so in advance?' Those who will suffer most severely, however, will be blind and will take the Lion for a rooster, whom no eagle may fear. Nevertheless in the year 1622 the Lion will roar so loudly that all earth will shudder and all mankind be terrified." Capistrano's timing was not quite accurate, but his prevision was remarkable. At the time he made his prediction, neither Sweden nor any other Scandinavian country had made impact of any kind on Europe's affairs.

Gustavus Adolphus, virtual dictator of northern Europe during his short career, was only thirty-eight when he died in the year predicted. Another dictator, Oliver Cromwell, king in everything but name, died on the day foretold by a Colonel Lindsay of the parliamentary army. Colonel Lindsay said that Cromwell would die on September 3, which the dictator had always considered his "fortunate day," the date on which he had won his famous victories at Dunbar and at Worcester. And on Friday, September 3, 1658, Oliver did die—a day on which there was a very high wind, so it is recorded.

About the middle of the seventeenth century, in the library

of a house belonging to one Salizarus of Heidelberg, a prophecy was found which foretold the career—and appearance—of William of Orange:

"There shall a great King arise, having a long forehead, high brows, large eyes, and an eagle's nose. He shall gather a great army and destroy all the tyrants of his kingdom . . . he shall wage war even unto the fortieth year, bringing unto subjection the Islanders . . . he shall obtain a double crown . . . going overseas with a great army."

The united crowns of England and Scotland formed the double crown; when William was born, the midwife, Mrs. Tanner, saw three crowns over his head. The third probably was the crown of Ireland, which William was determined to add to the double crown.

William's nephew, Queen Anne's son, the pathetic, hydrocephalic Prince William, who died while still a child, seems to have been gifted with the "sight." Several times he made predictions which were fulfilled. He foretold the death of his nurse, who, having left the palace, was then living in another part of London.

The horoscope of William Frederick, George III of England, is a blueprint of the events of his life. Also, it gives supporting evidence to the astrologers' claim that the occurrences and circumstances of an individual's life are governed by the planetary influences dominant at the moment of birth. If this is true, the ups and downs experienced by two people born at the same time and in the same place would follow roughly the same course, although naturally the details would be modified by the environment of each life.

In the year 1738, on June 4, in the parish of St. Martin's-in-the-Fields, two boys were born almost at the same minute. One was William Frederick, grandson of the King of England; the other James Hemming, whose father was a tradesman. From that June day these two lives followed a similar basic pattern, only the details varying, according to the social environment of each individual.

In October, 1760, William Frederick became George III,

which was the main event of his life. In October, 1760, James Hemming opened his own business, the equivalent to him in his circumstances of kingship to William in his. Both men were married on September 8, 1761. Both men died on Saturday, January 29, 1820, within, it seems, less than an hour of each other. In the February of that year newspapers were full of the death of the king; the same newspapers carried a small obituary of James Hemming, ironmonger.

No astrologer could ask more.

11. Witches' Warnings

Aradia, daughter of the moon (or witch) goddess, Diana, traditionally gave to her colleagues in the craft twelve powers; among them was the gift of prophecy, or divination. History shows that Aradia kept her promise. The witch of Endor's accomplishments in seership were proverbial. Macbeth's witches must have produced equally accurate forecasts; otherwise their stock would not have stood as high with him as it undoubtedly did. He constantly asked their advice, not only on the occasion of the meeting described by Shakespeare, on the "blasted heath." The Hardmoor, as this heath is called, was known even in those days of sparse populations, as solitary; its wildest, least frequented part is thought to be the spot where Macbeth consulted the "weird sisters." They were in fact not sisters; they were the two most famous witches in Scotland; they lived on either side of the Thane of Glamis, one at Collace, the other at The Cape. The heath is in the two parishes, Dyke and Moy; the boundary of the counties of Elgin and Forres crosses it. A stone in the parish of St. Martin's marks the exact meeting place. Dunsinane—or Dunsinnan—Castle was built on their advice. Practically impregnable, they foretold it would keep Macbeth and his family safe forever, or until "Birnam wood do come to Dunsinane," which Macbeth took to mean forever.

The witches' prophecy came true, Macbeth's security did last until Birnam Wood was brought to Dunsinane, by his enemies who carried hundreds of its lopped-off branches as camouflage for their attack, so that the whole forest seemed to be advancing upon Macbeth.

Cornwall has always been a stronghold of witchcraft, white and black. The "white" witch acted as antidote to her "black" sister, curing disease in human beings or cattle, generally remedying misfortunes called down by "ill-wishing" or "overlooking." To Cornwall belongs the relatively rare distinction of a witch trial at which a verdict of not guilty was recorded for the defendant in Exeter, in September, 1696. The witch, Elizabeth Homer, alias Turner, was accused on a number of counts, including prophecy; evidence of the kind accepted in those days was forthcoming on all this. The Lord Chief Justice who tried the case, however, according to Archdeacon Blackburne, who attended the trial, seemed not at all impressed by the depositions of the witnesses, and so, says Blackburne, "the jury brought her in not guilty."

A shepherd who practiced witchcraft near Torquay was not so lucky. The then sheriff of Cornwall, Sir John Arundells of Trevice Manor House in the Torquay district, accused this man of witchcraft. Sir John, apparently uninterested in the fact that the shepherd was a "white" witch, sentenced him to a long term of rigorous imprisonment—and the shepherd warned him that no good would come of the injustice. The shepherd, after he was set free, used to arrange to pass Sir John as often as possible on the highway, keeping his eyes fixed on the sheriff as long as he was in sight, muttering under his breath, "When upon the yellow sand, Thou shalt die by human hand."

After some months, these almost daily encounters disturbed Sir John so much that he moved into a house some way from the district where the shepherd worked. Sir John lived peacefully for a time; then there were local uprisings. As sheriff of the county, he had to lead an attack on St. Michael's Mount, during which he was badly wounded. As he lay dying on the sands of Marazion, at the foot of the mount, the shepherd appeared. The last words Sir John heard were: "When upon the yellow sand, Thou shalt die by human hand," which the shepherd whispered over him.

Britain's most famous witch, Mother Shipton, was famous because of her prophecies. There were several claimants to her name and fame; one of whom lived near Wychwood Forest in Oxfordshire, not far from the prehistoric circle of the Rollwright Stones. Probably all the other Mother Shiptons were also outstanding seers, but since no records of their predictions are discoverable, the Yorkshire Mother Shipton's title is not in serious question.

She was born near the Dropping Well, Knaresborough, Yorkshire, in July, 1488. Her mother's name was Agatha Southill; her father's name was unknown; according to legend, he was more than mortal. He rewarded Agatha for becoming his mistress by giving her the power to kill or heal, to raise storms and tempests, to command men and animals, to foresee and to foretell the future.

Agatha's circumstances soon changed for the better; no one quite knew how. She would often be away from home for several days at a time; her absences intrigued her neighbors so much that they bombarded her with questions about where she went and why. At last they so much annoyed Agatha that she called up a wind which blew them out of her house and into their own homes. This incident and other displays of her powers were relayed to the local magistrates, who had her brought before them on the charge of being a witch. The accusation was not proceeded with, nor was it made again in her case.

Soon after the birth of her daughter, Ursula, Agatha retired into a convent, where she died. Ursula, who had been left in the care of the parish nurse, was sent to a school where her ability to learn quickly made her a star pupil. The other children teased her unmercifully because her appearance was freakish—she had a long, crooked nose, goggling eyes, big bones, misshapen legs—but as Ursula apparently had inherited her mother's powers, her persecutors' hair was pulled; they were pinched and punched and knocked down by invisible hands. The end result was a decision that Ursula and the school would do better apart; she does not seem to have been sent elsewhere to finish her education.

Perhaps her looks improved as she grew older; at any rate, when she was twenty-four, a man named Tobias Shipton, of Shipton, near York, fell in love with her and married her; nothing else is known about him, but from that time onward more and more is known about Ursula, his wife. As her reputation for accurate prediction spread, people came to consult her at first from all over the county, then from all parts of the country. Her charges were moderate; unfortunately she had a maidservant who prevented clients from seeing Mother Shipton until they had handed over a bribe, often larger than the clairvoyant's fee.

This went on until Mother Shipton discovered her maid's chicanery in a curious way. The heir to a great estate had asked Mother Shipton whether his father, who was seriously ill, would recover. Since she refused to tell him anything at all, he offered the maid a substantial sum if she would persuade her mistress to answer his question. The girl tried in every way she could think of to worm some sort of reply out of Mother Shipton but without any success. Determined not to lose the money she had been promised by the young man, when he came next day to hear Mother Shipton's prediction, the maid handed him one contrived by herself, which ran:

> The grave provided hath a room.
> Prepare for death; thy hour is come.

The young man took this as an indication that his father would die, and then he would inherit the family wealth and estates. He was delighted, but when with his father's recovery, his hopes vanished, he became so depressed and melancholic that he developed a serious illness. The father, in a state of great anxiety about the health of his son, who was his only child, as well as his heir, consulted Mother Shipton about his condition. She told him:

> They who for others' death do gape out
> Their own unlook'd for comes about.
> Earth he did seek, ere long shall have
> Of earth his fill within his grave.

The prophecy meant nothing to the father, who did not know of his son's visit to Mother Shipton or its purpose. A fortnight later, the young man died; afterward one of the servants in whom he had confided told the whole story to the father, through whom it reached Mother Shipton.

Mother Shipton's earlier prophecies concerned the personal affairs of the men and women who consulted her. Later she predicted historical events; the first of these forecasts related to and was fulfilled in the reign of Henry VIII. Mother Shipton said, "When the English Lion shall set his feet on the Gallic shores, then shall the Lillies begin to droop for fear . . . the princely Eagle shall join the Lion to tread down all that shall oppose them, and though many Saggataries shall appear in defense of the Lillies, yet shall they not prevail, because the dull animal of the north shall put them all to confusion; and though it be against his will, yet shall he cause great shame unto them."

In plain English, Mother Shipton was saying that when Henry VIII invaded France, he, together with Maximilian, the German emperor, would defeat the French, in spite of the gallant resistance of their cavalry ("the Saggataries"), which happened, as foretold. The English cavalry ("the dull animal of the north") would bring confusion on the enemy, and great shame on them, which the "dull animal" would do "against his will." This part of the prophecy was fulfilled in the sense that the English cavalry attack which won the battle was not ordered, nor was it planned. Before the fighting began, King Henry's horse, having been struck accidentally, bolted toward the French lines. The cavalry, thinking he was leading a charge, spurred after him; the French forces broke and were defeated.

Mother Shipton nearly found herself in serious trouble over her next prophecy, which concerned Thomas Cardinal Wolsey, whom she called "the Mitred Peacock." She said, "The Mitred Peacock shall now begin to plume himself, and his train shall make a great show in the world. . . . He shall want to live at York, and shall see it, but shall never come thither. . . ."

Cardinal Wolsey, who was Dean of Lincoln and Almoner to the King, Bishop of Tournai, and lessee of the revenues of Bath, Worcester, Hereford, St. Albans, among others, who held in succession the sees of Durham, Winchester, and York, had a train of 800 gentlemen, knights, and servants, which certainly did "make a great show." He surrounded himself with a splendor and pomp rivaling Henry's own, until he lost the royal favor and much of his wealth. He decided to withdraw to York; when he heard of Mother Shipton's prediction that he "shall never come thither," it angered and disturbed him so much that he sent three gentlemen of his retinue in disguise to find out if she had made such a prophecy and to threaten her with terrifying penalties if she reiterated it.

There is a difference of opinion about who the three messengers of the cardinal were, but the basic facts of what took place that day in Mother Shipton's house near York are more or less the same in each version of the interview. William Lilly, the astrologer who made a study of Mother Shipton and her prophecies, said that the witch's visitors were the Duke of Suffolk, Lord Darcy, Lord Percy, and a local man named Beasley, who acted as guide.

Mother Shipton welcomed the deputation, gave them cakes and ale, and, when they asked if she had predicted that the cardinal should never see York, replied, "No, I said he might see it, but never enter it."

They told her, "When he comes, he'll surely burn thee."

Whereupon she threw a linen kerchief into the fire, saying, "If this burn, so shall I." After fifteen minutes she lifted it out of the flames, unsinged, evidence of her powers which so impressed the three men that they all asked her to prophesy for them.

To the duke she said, "My love, the time will come when you will be as low as I am, and that's a low one indeed." She told Lord Percy: "Shoe your horse in the quicke, and you shall doe well, but your body will be buried in Yorke pavement and your head shall be stolen from the barre and carried into France." Lord Darcy was warned: "You have made a great gun, shoot it off, for it will doe you no good, you are going to warre, you will paine many a man, but you will kill none."

As Mother Shipton had foretold, the Duke of Suffolk was beheaded, as was Lord Percy, whose head "was stolen . . . and carried into France." And Cardinal Wolsey, on his journey to take up residence in York, reached Cawood, from which he could see the spires and towers of the city, eight miles away. While he was at Cawood, Lord Northampton, bringing a warrant for his arrest on a charge of high treason, overtook him and forced him to turn back. So he never entered York. Northampton's orders were to conduct Wolsey to the Tower; the cardinal, already a sick man, died on the way to London, so being saved from trial and the inevitable sequel —execution.

After his visit with the cardinal's party, Master Beasley apparently consulted Mother Shipton frequently. One of the predictions she made to him was: "Before the Ouse Bridge and Trinity Church meet, they shall build in the day and it shall fall in the night—until they get the highest stone of Trinity Church to be the lowest stone of Ouse Bridge."

In course of time, a gale blew down the steeple of Trinity Church, York; a flood wrecked Ouse Bridge. Stone from the steeple was used to repair the bridge, but every night the work done in the day fell to pieces until one of the masons, remembering Mother Shipton's prophecy, used the highest stone of the steeple in the foundations of the bridge. After that, it stood firm.

One of her longest prophecies in verse was made to the Abbot of Beverley, to whom she had given so many accurate forecasts that he begged her to make a series of long-range predictions. After a good deal of cajolery by the abbot, Mother Shipton described events which would happen through the centuries ahead. She ended with a warning note: "The world then to an end shall come, in nineteen hundred and ninety-one," eight years before the date set for a global cataclysm by most of her rival prophets.

She made innumerable prophecies for the period between her own time and this final debacle. Of the reign of Edward VI, she said, "This Prince that never shall be born, Shall make the shaven heads forlorn." Edward was not born in the accepted physical sense; he was taken from his mother by an operation which was a primitive version of the modern Cesarean section—and which resulted in her death. The "shaven heads" were the monks and friars who were homeless when abbeys and monasteries were seized during the Reformation, which was stringently prosecuted during Edward's reign.

Mary would succeed her brother, said Mother Shipton; when she was queen, "mitres shall rise and heads fall down, And streams of blood run Smithfield down. England shall join in league with Spain. . . ." Then: "A maiden queen full many a year, Shall England's warlike sceptre bear. . . . The western monarch's wooden horses, Shall be destroyed by Drake's forces." In June, 1561, the steeple of St. Paul's was destroyed by fire. More than twenty years before, Ursula Shipton had predicted: "Great London's triumphant spire, Shall be consumed with flames of fire," following this with a prophecy of the end of Mary Queen of Scots. "More wondrous yet, a widowed queen, In England shall be headless seen."

Events in the reigns of James I, Charles I, and Charles II

were foreseen by Mother Shipton: "the first coming of the King of Scots [James I] shall be at Holgate Town, but he shall not come through the Bar." So many people were gathered at Holgate Bar when James arrived that he had to take another way into the town. She mentioned the crowning of Charles I—whom she called the White King (Charles was robed white for his coronation), his marriage to "the lillies" (Henrietta Maria of France), his overthrow and execution. Then the Wolf (Oliver Cromwell) "with blood usurp the Lion's den." Another king would succeed; in his reign there would be a great plague. And after the plague would come a fire. "After that," said Mother Shipton, "a ship shall come sailing up the Thames till it comes against London, and the master of the ship shall weep, and the mariners shall ask him why he weepeth, seeing he has made so good a voyage, and he will say, 'Oh, what a goodly city this was, none in the world comparable to it. And now there is scarce left any house that can let us have a drink for our money.'" Not one house was left standing between the Tower and the Temple when the fire's work was done.

Onward through time ranged the vision of Mother Shipton's "third eye," seeing that "around the world thoughts shall fly, In the twinkling of an eye, Through hills men shall ride, And no horse or ass at their side, Under water men shall walk, . . . in the air shall men be seen, Carriages without horse shall go, And accidents fill the world with woe . . . fire and water [steam] shall more wonders do . . . a house of glass shall come to pass, in England [the Crystal Palace] . . . when below Thames bed, Shall be seen the furnace red, When its bottom shall drop out, making hundreds swim about." *Blackwood's Magazine* of 1846, commenting on this prophecy, says: "The Thames tunnel had been pushed in the middle of the river bed, when, coming to a loose portion of the clay, the roof fell in. The Thames burst through its own bottom, the tunnel was instantly filled, and the workmen were forced to swim for their lives."

Having given a date for the world's ending, some four centuries ahead, she looked onward about four decades to her own end, which she said would come in 1561. In that year, having said farewell to her many friends, she died in her bed at the age of seventy-three.

At Clifton, just outside York, the stone erected in her memory and its inscription are evidence of the high esteem in which Mother Shipton was held. These are the words carved on her memorial:

> Here lies she who never ly'd
> Whose skill so often has been try'd
> Her prophecies shall still survive,
> And ever keep her name alive.

Unremarkable as is the stone, with its doggerel inscription, it is probably unique—the only memorial in Britain which praises the memory of a witch. More usually its perpetuation would be a cairn of stones to mark the place of execution. All witches in those days, even if they had never been known to do anything but good, were classed as evil, simply because they belonged to the craft; a Scottish witch, who had never attempted to harm anyone, was put to death in 1616 because of one example of "foreseeing." Jonka Dyneis was the wife of a fisherman; one day when he was out in his boat, six miles offshore, Jonka went into a trance and cried out that he was in danger. She was found leaning against the wall of her house, apparently beside herself with grief. When questioned, all she could say was: "If our boat be not lost, she is in great hazard." For this crime she was brought before the bailie, who ruled that it was an example of "phairie control," for submitting to which he sentenced Jonka to death.

12. Curses Fulfilled

Fifteen centuries before the birth of Christ, one of the greatest of the Hindu philosophers said, "As long as a man has faith in a blessing, so long will he believe in a curse." In other words, if a force exists, it can be used constructively or destructively, according to the purpose of the operator; if blessings work, then curses must also work. The basic active power is necessarily the same in both cases.

Curses—and blessings, of course—were believed in unquestioningly for many centuries. Then modern science said that only ignorant, superstitious people could credit these ideas, which were obviously survivals from man's remote past. Lately, because of the discoveries of parapsychology and the power of the human mind, some scientists admit the possibility that concentrated thought force, impregnated with strong hate or love, could transfer to an object a good or bad influence, much as a piece of iron reacts to magnetism. The human will, being the greatest of all magnets, when used according to the law which governs it could attract constructive or destructive conditions which would manifest on the physical level. This is a theory based on the knowledge that all forms of matter, from rocks and earth up to the human body, are made up of atoms, vibrating at a set rate and having a kind of intelligence—an intelligence which the adept of the past and the trained mind of today can direct to a fixed purpose.

Perhaps this sounds like fairy-tale stuff, as unaccustomed ideas often do. As the great chemist the late Sir William Crookes said in a lecture on the then new and incredible theories of the composition of matter: "Gentlemen, I know what I am going to tell you is an impossibility according to the established laws of nature. Nevertheless it is true."

And so with the curse. A tremendous body of evidence exists to show that "this impossibility according to the established laws of nature" is a reality. We can deny it; we can say that what works is coincidence, not a curse. In the first place, not all the evidence can be false; in the second, it would be more than coincidence if all the happenings in all the cases were coincidental. And as for denial, in the light of parapsychology's recent discoveries concerning the mysterious activities of thought force, Schopenhauer's words seem to sum up the situation: "Your denial does not argue that you have superior intelligence; it simply proves you ignorant of the latest acquisition of knowledge."

The ancient Egyptians were masters of the art of the curse. By means of the ritual known as tying, which is represented in the ideographic Egyptian language as a knotted rope, and by the word, a reiterated mantra or affirmation, a condition was linked with an object or individual. The word was—and still is—considered one of the most important factors in magic. The two major sources of its power were the association of the meaning of the word with its sound or vibration of its utterance. The word had to be spoken in a certain tone, called Ma-Khru, or the just voice, the word of truth, which released the power of the creative or destructive force of vibration. The words of power, which were part of the inner mysteries of all theurgical teachings, were formed in Egypt from combinations of ideographic letters, retained even when the grammatical and phonetic systems of writing were developed.

The curse invoked for the protection of a mummy must have been in great demand among ancient Egyptians, who believed literally in the resurrection of the physical body.

Curses Fulfilled 173

The next incarnation, they were convinced, would make use of its atoms and electrons, though those, of course, were not the words they used. Sir Ernest Wallis Budge mentions this attitude to the body in his translation of the Nilotic country's *Book of the Dead* and of a ritual (curse) used for its protection:

> There is little doubt that when the body was laid to rest in the tomb the priest pronounced certain words or formulas, or prayers over it, and it is probable that the recital of these words were accompanied by the performance of certain ceremonies . . . we are within our rights to assume that they were addressed to the God of Gods of the community on behalf of the dead, and that they contained petitions for the welfare of the departed in the world beyond the grave. . . . Certain portions of texts which have been incorporated into religious works of a later period show that the life which the Egyptian hoped to live after death was one similar to that which he led on earth, and it is clear that he thought the preservation of his natural and material body to be in some way absolutely necessary for the attainment of this life.

Not every corpse seems to have been given the safeguard of this ritual. There are mummies all over the world, but no mention of high mortality among archeologists, although perhaps the sudden death of some of these men may not have reached the press. Then, too, in some cases the officiating priest may not have been good at his work. Besides having knowledge, in order to make an effective spell, it is essential to be able to raise the consciousness to a high peak, and to inflame it as advised by that great expert Abramelin the Mage: "Inflame thyself with prayer."

In some cases, the tying ritual seems to have been effective. Lord Carnarvon's death after the opening of Tutankhamen's tomb was dramatically swift and sudden, which is logical. The power of the curse would be directed chiefly against him as the organizer and prime mover of the project; one or two of his colleagues also died.

The thick plate-glass case of a mummy in the British Museum has twice broken into fragments, without discoverable cause, according to a reputable scientist and writer. Apparently this happened in the 1920's; the mummy does not seem to have been active again since then. Naturally the authorities of the museum officially know nothing about the affair.

A mummy curse worked unerringly on an Egyptologist acquaintance of my family's, who uncovered the tomb of some not very important Pharaoh—I forget of what dynasty. He was given permission to take the mummy to England; for some reason he decided that he wanted only the head—in spite of warnings on papyruses found in the tomb that anyone who mutilated the mummy of this Pharaoh would die by injury to the part of the body desecrated.

The professor, who thought curses as credible as fairy stories, brought the Pharaoh's head to England—where there was an outbreak of poltergeist phenomena in the house he stayed in. The head went with him to the sugar plantation he owned in the West Indies. He was a good employer, and his workers had no grievances; nevertheless, when he was riding around the estate, a band of these men set on him, dragged him from his horse, and beat out his brains with chains. One of his sons had an accident while out on his motorcycle. His head was seriously injured. A younger son, who fell out of a window onto his head, was badly but not fatally hurt. Ill luck followed the family so persistently that the professor's widow sent the Pharaoh's head home to Egypt. After that things began to go right again.

Today, although few of us know as much about it as did the ancient Egyptians, cursing is not a lost art. And machines seem to make as good media for malediction as were more seemingly likely objects—wax figures, symbols, and so on—used many centuries ago for the same purpose.

The bright red touring car in which the Archduke Franz Ferdinand and his wife were driving when they were assassinated in Sarajevo in June, 1914, carried a curse, though no one seems to know how or why it came into being.

Curses Fulfilled

The murder triggered the First World War. About a week after it had broken out, the commander of the Fifth Austrian Corps, General Oskar Potiorek, seized the house of the governor of Sarajevo, where the red car had been garaged. Twenty-one days after the general took over the car, he was defeated catastrophically at Valjevo, losing his command as a result. Sent back to Vienna in disgrace, he lived there in poverty, finally went mad, and died in a workhouse.

A captain who had served with Potiorek was the next owner of the opulent red car. Nine days later, driving along a country road, he ran into and killed two Croat farmworkers, swerved into a tree, broke up the car, and was dead when he was taken out of the wreckage.

The car was repaired; at the end of the war the new governor of Yugoslavia became its owner. In four months while driving in it he had four accidents, through one of which he lost his right arm. He ordered the destruction of the car, but was persuaded to sell it to a Dr. Srkis, who was intrigued by the idea of owning the historical vehicle. No rational person could believe in the curse it carried, he said; its evil reputation was founded on a series of tragic coincidences.

For six months it seemed that he was right. Then the car and its driver were found at the side of a road. The car was upside down, only slightly damaged. Beside it was the doctor's body. He had been crushed to death when the car rolled over on him.

It was then sold to a wealthy jeweler, who drove it without incident for a year, then committed suicide. Another doctor bought it, but before it could do him any harm, he sold the car. He found that patients, nervous of the curse it carried, were leaving him.

Its next owner was a Swiss racing driver. In it he competed in a Dolomite road race, during which the car ran off the road. It hit a stone wall, over which the driver catapulted and was killed.

A wealthy Sarajevo farmer bought it, had it repaired, and drove it for several months. One morning it broke down; since no efforts could get it started again, the farmer persuaded the owner of a passing car to tow him to the city. Just as they set off, the engine roared into life; the car, leaping forward, broke the towrope. It hurtled down the road, overturning on a sharp bend, where the owner was thrown out and killed.

Battered as the car was, a garage proprietor, Tibor Hirshfeld, bought it, repaired it, painted it blue, and drove it around. One day, when driving six friends to a wedding party, he crashed into another car. Tibor Hirshfeld and four of his friends died in the accident.

Then the Austrian government, probably because of its association with Archduke Franz Ferdinand, had it repaired and housed in a Vienna museum, where it was unlikely to do any more damage. It had been the cause of the death of fourteen people; it had been a factor in the beginning of a war— and in a war it was destroyed. An Allied bomb dropped on the museum which housed it, exorcising finally the curse of the red car.

The career of the *Scharnhorst* follows much the same pattern as that of the red car. She, too, was a piece of machinery —*lèse-majesté,* perhaps, to describe a battle cruiser as such —which like the car, carried a hoodoo. She was a 40,000-ton weapon of supreme efficiency, but her popularity rating with the German Navy was in inverse ratio to her potentialities. She was jinxed, the men said; no one wanted to serve in her, in spite of her speed, her extra-long-range guns, her electronic equipment, which enabled her to find her targets before they found her.

She was in the ship builders' yard, just over half-completed, when she first showed her mettle. Wrenching away from her supports, she rolled over on her side. Sixty-three workmen were crushed to death, 110 injured, by her antics. Raising her was a slow business; fresh gangs of workmen continually had to be drafted. No one wanted to stay on the job; word had gone around that the *Scharnhorst* carried a jinx. It took three months, but at last she was dredged up.

Then, the work of building completed, the steel leviathan was ready for launching.

The *Scharnhorst* was the last word in naval weapons. Her send-off was an opportunity not to be missed by the Nazis of impressing allied, neutral, and enemy nations with the strength and superiority of German arms. To make the launching a star occasion, Hitler, Göring, Himmler, all the high-ups of the party, rallied to the dock where *Scharnhorst* lay—or should have lain. The *Scharnhorst,* Hitler's pride, had not waited for him. During the previous night she had launched herself, smashing up a couple of barges in her progress.

The first foray in which she took a publicized part was the seizure of Danzig. A news film, showing the *Scharnhorst's* mighty guns reducing the port to pulp, was circulated to the world by the Germans. Not included in the film were the explosion of one of these guns which killed nine of her crew, and the scene in another gun turret, where the air conditioning failed and twelve men died.

At the siege of Oslo, the *Scharnhorst* came off worse than any of the other German battleships. Afire in at least a dozen places, she had to be towed away by the *Gneisenau*. Limping home during the dark hours, hiding from British bombers by day, one night she reached the mouth of the Elbe. Across her path, indistinguishable in the pervading blackness, lay one of the world's greatest liners, the *Bremen*. She was not picked up by the *Scharnhorst's* supposedly superlative radar equipment; no one knew why. Too late the ship's watch saw her and gave the alarm; a few seconds afterward he died in the collision, which sent the *Bremen* into the Elbe mud. The *Scharnhorst* was put out of commission for so long that by the time she was afloat again, Hitler's sands were running low.

She was sent, as soon as she was seaworthy, to attack an Allied convoy in the Arctic Sea. For the *Scharnhorst,* with her weapon range and speed, it should have been an easy assignment; even so, because of her established reputation as a jinx, the authorities might have chosen another ship for the action, if one of the same caliber had been available. But the *Bismarck* had been sunk; the *Tirpitz* was a gutted hulk in a Norwegian fjord; it had to be the *Scharnhorst*, hoodoo and all, or nothing. The night on which she slipped out of the Elbe, this time avoiding the *Bremen*, was as dark as the night of their collision. Pitch blackness made invisible the coast of Norway as she made her way to her rendezvous; it hid her from Allied patrol planes, but it also hid from her a small British ship, hove to for engine repairs. As the *Scharnhorst* thundered past, so close to the small craft that she rocked in the battle cruiser's wash, the British captain gave the alarm. Almost within minutes, the fleet was on the *Scharnhorst*'s track.

The *Scharnhorst* far outclassed in speed the British force; she bolted away into the night before there was time to do more than fire a few shots in her direction. The captain of one of the ships in pursuit, literally making a shot in the dark, since he had no clue to the *Scharnhorst*'s course, sent a broadside at 1,600 yards after her. At that moment apparently, she swerved. She swung into the exact trajectory of the shell. While she was still reeling under the impact of several tons of high explosive, the British ships, having found her range, hit her again and again, until she sank.

Two of the few survivors of her crew made landfall in a rubber dinghy. But they did not escape the jinx of the *Scharnhorst* so easily; some months afterward they were found dead, killed by the explosion of an emergency oil stove.

An impersonal malevolence seems to be the motivating force of both the *Scharnhorst* and the red car jinx—not directed at any individual, but against everyone coming in contact with its vehicle. Some curses are much more direct in purpose; they are invoked by a person, for a definite reason, as was a curse which operated in Sicily about fourteen or fifteen years ago.

At the end of the 1940's there was a campaign on that island for the capture of Salvator Giuliaro. He was the most famous bandit of modern times, head of an organization to make Sicily independent, virtually its king. Seizure of Giuliaro, dead or alive, was made a priority by the authorities—but somehow neither the government officials, secret service men, *carabinieri,* or Army officers who tried to locate him came to grips with him. All they got was some form of ill luck.

Then the twenty-seven-year-old Giuliaro was found dead, riddled with bullets. No one knew how it had happened or who had shot him; no one claimed the reward for discovering him. His mother, kissing the wounds on her son's body, said, with his blood on her lips, "My blood . . . they have betrayed you." And she cursed the betrayers.

Eventually Gaspare Piscotta, once a close friend of Giuliaro's, was arrested on a charge of murdering him and other crimes. On February 9, 1954, while in prison awaiting trial, Piscotta suddenly screamed as if in agony; within an hour he was dead. No physical cause was discovered. Three weeks afterward, eight people who were suspected of having had a hand in Giuliaro's betrayal were taken ill suddenly and violently.

According to the primitive code of Sicily, this was proof of their guilt; a curse, if it is to work properly, must have a just basis. If it destroys or injures an individual, that individual must have done the wrong which caused the curse to be made.

The Hapsburg dynasty was cursed twice—and it would be said with some just reason—once by a Hungarian priest, when Hungary was made part of the Austrian Empire, once by the Countess Karolyi of Hungary, whose son was executed during her country's revolt against its invaders. The Emperor Franz Josef was the object of both curses; it was he who had ordered the ravishing of Hungary and the young Karolyi's death.

In an agony of grief at her son's death (emotion is always an essential to successful spell making) the countess cried out: "May heaven and hell blast his [Franz Josef's] happiness. May his family be exterminated. May he be smitten in the persons of those he loves. May his life be wrecked, and may his children be brought to ruin."

One by one the misfortunes she called down on him materialized. Franz Josef's brother Maximilian, well-meaning but weak, who was drawn into the ill-fated Mexican venture by the power-seeking mediocrity Napoleon III of France, was shot by a revolutionary firing squad in Mexico. His wife, Carlotta, hearing of his death in Rome, where she was trying to persuade the Pope to help her husband, went mad.

Franz Josef married a beautiful, gifted woman with whom at first he lived happily; but their temperaments were opposed, and soon they began to drift apart. Elizabeth is said to have taken lovers; there were rumors that she was psychotic. The emperor had a stern, forbidding streak in his character, which may have alienated his wife and later his son Crown Prince Rudolf. He thought Rudolf irresponsible; they quarreled often and bitterly. At last the emperor more or less cut himself off from his son, which had the effect of turning Rudolf into a full-time playboy. Scandals of all dimensions were current about him; the last and greatest broke when he was found shot dead with his current mistress, Baroness Maria Vetsera, in his hunting lodge at Mayerling.

For some time after the loss of her son, Elizabeth was physically ill; when she recovered, she lived as a recluse. Then wanderlust set in; she spent most of her time traveling outside Austria. When she was visiting Geneva in 1898, as she walked from her hotel to board a lake steamer, she was stabbed by an anarchist. She died a few hours afterward.

Tragedy after tragedy undermined Franz Josef's family. Sophie, Duchesse d'Alençon, was burned to death in Paris; the Archduchess Matilda died in the same way when her ball dress caught fire. Archduke John of Tuscany disappeared on the high seas; Archduke Wilhelm Franz Karl was killed by a fall from his horse; the mad King Ludwig of Bavaria drowned himself. Count Ludwig of Trani committed suicide.

Other relatives became eccentric or meddled with malcontents' plots and got into difficulties. The women contracted marriages which Franz Josef considered unsuitable to members of the Hapsburg dynasty.

The year 1914 saw the emperor's heir and his wife shot dead in Sarajevo by a Serbian student, Gavrilo Princip. This was the beginning of the curse's culmination, reached after Franz Josef died, having dragged out his embittered, lonely life to its eighty-ninth year, when a revolution swept away the remnants of the imperial family and made Austria a republic.

Hungary figures in a curse which destroyed another king. The king was Alfonso XII of Spain, who received a beautiful, valuable, but not altogether desirable gift—a ring, carrying a curse which operated if it were taken out of Hungary. On their wedding day Alfonso gave it to his bride—who died soon afterward. He presented it to his sister-in-law, who died within a short time. Then Alfonso was reckless enough to wear the ring himself—he was dead within twelve months; the ring was sent for exorcism to a Madrid church.

Alfonso courted disaster by ignoring the curse; so did the owners of the Hope Diamond, which probably carried a more active hoodoo than any other precious stone on the market. It was—or is—one of the most perfect blue diamonds ever to be discovered, weighing forty-four and a half carats; in size one inch by seven-eighths of an inch. Its original setting was the forehead of a Buddha statue; the curse laid on it warned that: "This stone has been consecrated to God. The profane who touch it shall suffer dire misfortune or violent death."

The trail of murder, madness, and violence which marked the progress of the diamond from owner to owner began when Jean Baptiste Tavernier, the great French traveler and jeweler, brought the stone back with him from the East and sold it to Louis XIV in 1668. Louis, delighted to own such a magnificent diamond, rewarded Tavernier with letters of nobility for having procured it. Tavernier purchased the barony of Aubonne, near Geneva. After a year of misfortunes, he died in Moscow in 1689, in poverty.

Willem Fals of Amsterdam, who was employed by Louis to cut the stone, had no sooner begun work on it than everything went wrong: His business, which was a prosperous one, declined; his son committed suicide. He himself died, utterly ruined.

Louis XIV did not die until 1715, by which time he had almost destroyed France. The war he carried on for years bled her white, ending after a series of defeats with the ignominious Peace of Utrecht. Both Louis' son and eldest grandson died prematurely.

The reign of Louis XV, *Le Bien Aimé,* who inherited the blue diamond, was one of disaster, financial troubles, and widespread misery. Excesses and too-frequent debauches weakened his constitution so that when an epidemic of smallpox broke out in 1774, he, having no powers of resisttance, caught the disease and died in that year.

Louis XVI then became the diamond's owner. It was one of Marie Antoinette's favorite pieces of jewelry; occasionally she lent it to her close friend, the Princesse de Lambelle. All three died during the Reign of Terror.

The name of its next possessor is recorded as Francis Beaulieu. After his death by starvation in prison, there is no trace of the diamond's career for some years, until it appeared suddenly on the market and was bought by the banker Thomas Hope for $90,000. His descendant, Lord Francis Hope, after a series of losses and misfortunes, sold the stone in 1901.

The diamond seems to have been relatively inactive during the Hope ownership. Its next owner, the New York jeweler, Samuel Frankel, was not so lucky. Almost as soon as the stone came into his hands, his firm got into financial difficulties, verging on bankruptcy. Before he completely lost his business, he got rid of the diamond to a Colin Broku. Although Mr. Broku sold it to Prince Kanitovsky almost at once, he did not escape its attentions; he went mad and committed suicide soon after the sale was completed.

Prince Kanitovsky gave the Hope Diamond to his mistress, a

lovely girl who was an actress at the Folies Bergères. On the first night of a new play she appeared on the stage, the fabulous stone, the estimated value of which was more than that of the theater and its contents, blazing in her corsage over her heart, in which no doubt there was an answering blaze of pride.

Lorena Laduc's moment of triumph was soon over. As the spotlight focused on her, her lover, who was sitting in a box, shot her, the diamond marking his target. It was an unreasoning, motiveless murder, committed while the prince was gripped by a sudden attack of madness. He was never arrested for the crime. Two days after Lorena's death and before suspicion was directed to him, a party of Russian terrorists who broke into his house stabbed him to death.

The diamond was then taken over by a Greek named Montharides. A short time after he made the purchase, he, his wife, and two children were captured by brigands, who threw them over a precipice.

For a time the whereabouts of the jewel were not known. When next seen it was decorating the décolletage of Salma Zubata, the French favorite of ex-Sultan Abdul-Hamid, for whom he had bought it.

The curse of the stone had been putting in a little overtime work before it came into Salma's hands. The sultan had sent it to a jeweler, Abu Sabir, to be polished; when Abu swore the stone had not reached him, he was imprisoned until such time as he came to his senses. In the meantime, it was found in the possession of the dungeon keeper. He died mysteriously by strangulation. Arrangements for its safekeeping seem to have been so haphazard that a palace eunuch was able to steal it, but the theft was discovered, the thief arrested, and summarily hanged from a Constantinople lamppost.

After this sanguinary interlude, the diamond having been returned to the sultan, he presented it to Salma. Soon afterward she was shot dead by the sultan when a party of Young Turks broke into the palace, presumably to save her from a more unpleasant form of death. The Young Turks took the stone with them when they left the royal quarters; they sold it to a Mr. Habib, who was drowned soon afterward off Singapore. The sultan escaped from his term of ownership of the diamond with his life; he lost only his kingdom, from which he was deposed soon after the palace coup.

In 1911, Edward McLean, owner of the Washington *Post*, bought the Hope Diamond from Cartier, the famous French jewelers, for $260,000. His wife, who knew its history, objected so strongly to the purchase that he decided to cancel it. Cartier sued him; eventually he agreed to take delivery of the diamond for $180,000 in January, 1912, greatly against Mrs. McLean's will. Soon afterward McLean's mother died of pneumonia; this was only the beginning of the curse's work in this family.

The McLeans had a son, Vinson, a baby two or three years old when the Hope Diamond came into their possession. There was no other child on either side to inherit the McLean or Walsh fortunes, which were considerable; the McLeans were newspaper proprietors and owners of the Washington public transportation system; the assets of the Walshes (his mother's family) included the Camp Bird gold mine, one of the richest in Colorado. Without realizing any of these expectations, the boy was already enormously wealthy, in his own right, having been left the bulk of the estate of a Walsh uncle killed in a car crash. Vinson's possessions were estimated at more than $150,000,000; he was known as the "richest baby in the world."

So many precautions were taken to keep him safe that at times the little boy must have been bored with restrictions. He was not allowed to move around without an armed guard; every house in which he lived had a steel fence outside which he must not go. But one day, somehow, he did go outside the fence. He was playing near the gates of his father's house when a car, driven by a woman, hit the "hundred million dollar baby." He was injured so badly that he died a few hours later.

There is, or was, in existence another blue stone in quality and color identical with the Hope Diamond. The great gem expert Edward Streeter, who examined it, believed that it was carved from the parent stone when it was originally cut by Tavernier. It possesses another salient characteristic belonging to the Hope Diamond—a curse which operates on similar lines.

The smaller gem is known as the Brunswick Blue Drop Diamond; from the time it came into the possession of this family the House of Brunswick experienced tragedy and misfortune.

The first blow fell when Duke William Charles Ferdinand was wounded mortally at the Battle of Jena, 1806. Soon afterward, his heir died; his second son abdicated. Frederick William, the next in line, was killed at Quatre-Bras. The Duke of Cumberland, who became Duke of Brunswick when his kinsman, Duke William, died in 1884, lost his heir in a motor accident. The second son, in whose favor he abrogated his right to the title in October, 1912, married the only daughter of the German Kaiser. After the 1914-18 war, the duchy was absorbed by the German Republic; the House of Brunswick came to an end.

Another instance of the power of the word to impregnate an object with a force which apparently can produce effects on the material level was given to me by Gerald Yorke, the Oriental scholar and research worker in occultism.

After the death, around fifteen years ago, of Aleister Crowley, whom Mr. Yorke knew well and who had at one time a great reputation as magician and master of occult arts, a man who had been a colleague of Crowley's bought a collection of the Magus' formulas. Mr. Yorke, who knew that Crowley had willed his formulas to a certain museum, strongly advised against their purchase; the other man, in his anxiety to possess them, took no notice of Mr. Yorke's warning.

He got them—but with them came a bonus. He developed an obscure disease, which could not be diagnosed and which no treatment seemed to affect. He became steadily worse; at last he was so ill that in the hope of saving himself he decided to send the formulas to the museum specified in Aleister Crowley's will. He handed them over to Mr. Yorke, who arranged for their delivery. Mr. Yorke says that while they were in his house, pending collection, his wife, who until then had never had an abscess, nor has had one since, developed a painful swelling on the neck, which disappeared as soon as the manuscripts were taken away. So did the illness of the man who had bought them.

At Christie's, the famous London auctioneers of antiques and *objets d'art,* an unlikely place for acknowledgment of the power of the word, conditions laid down by a spell were respectfully followed before the selling of a Charles II silver field trumpet in October, 1967.

The trumpet, known as the Luck of Woodsome Hall, according to tradition must be blown on important occasions; otherwise misfortune follows. Two previous owners who ignored the charge did not live to regret their omission. One was killed in a hunting accident; the other committed suicide.

Christie's auctioneer, taking no chances, asked the musicologist Eric Halfpenny to provide the essential blow, after which the trumpet could be safely sold. It was bought by Michael Dalgleish for his thirteen-year-old son, who is not likely to commit a breach of the terms of the tradition.

Instances of another type of curse, the curse laid on a whole family, from generation to generation, were common in the past. Today fewer examples are found; perhaps the blanket curse belongs to the days of great estates and houses. And perhaps, too, in some cases the curses have worked too well. The families have disappeared.

The direct line of the Sheridans, for instance, no longer exists. A curse laid on the family that the heir would never inherit, that he would die on or about his twenty-first birthday, was fulfilled in each succeeding generation. When Clare Frewen, the sculptor and Winston Churchill's cousin, married a Sheridan, who (as a second son) became head of the family, she had a child, a boy. He was the heir; there would not be a second son because her husband had been killed in the 1914 war. If the curse were fulfilled, the line must die out. The crucial date, his twenty-first birthday, came and went; he was still alive. Perhaps, at last the curse was lifted. . . . A few weeks after attaining his majority, Clare Sheridan's son, who was touring in Europe, caught pneumonia and died.

Derwentwater, another family on which a curse of extinction was laid, has died out so completely that it might never have existed. A warning sign would be given, said an old prophecy, when the fulfillment of the curse was at hand:

> When a green oak leaf is turned to red
> The last earl shall die in his gory bed.
> The fox and the owl shall inhabit his halls,
> The bat and the spider shall cling to his walls,
> His lands from his house the strong arm shall sever
> And the name of his race be extinguished forever.

The Derwentwaters were a Catholic family. James, the last earl, was pressed by his co-religionists to take part in the Jacobite rebellion against George I, with which he was not at all anxious to be involved. Finally, against his better judgment, he joined the insurgents. It is said that he came to the decision while riding around his estate; having made it, he halted his horse on a reach of the stream known as Devil's Water. Looking up, he saw among the green foliage of an oak one prematurely red leaf.

Both James and his younger brother, Charles, fought with the Jacobites at Preston; both were captured by General Henry Lumley, commanding the king's forces. James was sent to the Devereux Tower in the Tower of London. Nine days afterward, at his trial, he pleaded guilty to insurrection, but pleaded in extenuation inexperience and that he had advised colleagues captured with him to plead guilty and throw themselves on the king's mercy. For him there was none; he was sentenced to death.

Numbers of petitions were made for his reprieve. Three of his co-prisoners were released, but George I, influenced by

Robert Walpole, who said he had been offered a bribe of £60,000 for James' life, refused to spare him. James Radcliffe, Lord Derwentwater, died by the ax on the scaffold on Tower Hill on February 24, 1716. He was twenty-seven years old.

His younger brother, Charles, born on September 5, 1693, was also found guilty and sentenced to death. He was imprisoned in Newgate; it seems likely that he would have been pardoned, but having a chance to escape with thirteen fellow prisoners, he took it. He safely reached the Continent, where he joined the Stuart family, for a time acting as secretary to Prince Charles Edward.

In 1724 he married Charlotte, the rich widow of Thomas Clifford. Both before and after his marriage, Charles made numbers of secret trips into and out of England, without discovery, until November, 1745, when he was captured off Dogger Bank in a French ship carrying arms to the Young Chevalier.

Taken to the Tower, he was condemned to death under the previous sentence. His brother having been attainted ("his lands from his house the strong arm shall sever"), he was not legally a peer. His judges, although not prepared to forgive Charles' one indiscretion committed as a boy twenty-odd years earlier, made the grand gesture of waiving the technicality. Charles Radcliffe, the last of his direct line, was beheaded as a peer, instead of being hanged as a commoner, on December 8, 1746. That day saw the curse—"The name of his race be extinguished forever"—and the prophecy of a gypsy fulfilled. Reading his hand at a fair when he was a boy of fifteen or sixteen, she told him all she could see for him was a bloodied ax, with the blade turned toward him.

13. Dreams: Doorway to the Unconscious

We spend a good half of our life in the almost unknown world of dreams which lies behind us, stretches ahead of us, and which science is only now beginning to explore systematically. The conscious mind which we use in dealing with everyday activities—career, household, or social affairs, all the multitudinous problems connected with work or play—is a relatively small part of our mental equipment. It has been likened to the top of an iceberg; what is visible above the sea's surface is as nothing to the mass beneath the water.

The subconscious mind is analogous to this submerged area; its extent is unknown, its potentialities only guessed at. Its resources of power, wisdom, knowledge, and ideas are beyond the range of conscious thought. The subconscious is the center through which precognition and every form of extrasensory perception operate. We would live more fully, more happily, more safely, it seems, if we could only tap its power.

The conscious mind, ceaselessly active, prevents most of us from glimpsing our hidden depths. Few of us have the time to practice techniques which control the flow of material level thought so that we can make contact with the deeper self deliberately.

Yet there is another way of making this contact with which

the conscious mind cannot interfere—through dreams. The source of many of these may be pent-up emotion—anxiety, frustration, resentment, sex—or the body registering its protest against a disorder of organ or function (which can be useful in the detection and prevention of disease). But there are also dreams which may solve a problem, indicate a course of action, warn against disaster, or reflect the future. Most of us do not seek this dream contact; it just happens. And when it happens, often we are none the wiser, because we cannot interpret the hints and nudges given to us in symbolic form by the subconscious.

But as research into the stuff of dreams progresses, no doubt we shall learn their language. Then it will be possible to draw knowingly and at will upon the limitless reserves of the collective unconscious which a body of scientific thought today believes can reach us through the pipeline of the subconscious and the message of dreams. The mystery of dreams —what they are, and why they come, their proverbial elusiveness, "fleeting as a dream"—has intrigued us, the dreamers, through the centuries. Among the scientists who now are making one of the first mass attempts to solve the enigma is a panel of psychiatrists, doctors, and psychologists, whose findings are correlated by Peter Fairley, the London *Evening Standard* science editor, in the Premonitions Bureau established by that paper.

Ninety percent of the premonitions come in dreams. The Aberfan disaster was predicted accurately by a number of people. A London woman, a piano and ballet teacher, has a record of correct forecasts which rivals the Delphic oracle's achievement: "so exact they are cast-iron" is Mr. Fairley's description of them. She predicted the Alaskan flood and disaster; the events she foresees usually take place within a month of her prevision.

Then there is a forty-two-year-old post office night worker. He foretold a Cyprus air crash one month beforehand, described how it happened (which was afterward checked and found correct), forecast the number of dead. The locality of

Dreams: Doorway to the Unconscious 191

the accident was not mentioned, but six major points in his prophecy identified the place with the crash. A premonition which came in a dream to his sister-in-law, Arabella Barrett, was recorded by Robert Browning in 1863. On July 21 of that year, Miss Barrett dreamed that she was with her sister, Mrs. Browning, who had died in 1861. "When shall I be with you?" she asked Mrs. Browning, who told her: "Dearest, in five years." Arabella died in June, 1868.

At the beginning of this century, the eruption of Mont Pelée in the West Indies was foreseen in a dream by Fernand Clerc, a sugar planter. St.-Pierre, the town at the foot of the Naked Mountain, had had a population of about 40,000 for many years, during which time the volcano had shown no signs of activity. M. Clerc decided to forget his dream.

He remembered it on May 5, 1902, when a stream of lava from the mountain poured over a sugar factory, burying twenty-five workers. At once, M. Clerc packed his family and portable possessions into his carriage and, taking no notice of friends who laughed at him for an alarmist, drove as far away from the city as he could. Three days afterward, on May 8, the volcano erupted in earnest. In less than five minutes the town was covered entirely with lava, the streets were six feet deep in ashes, and 39,999 of its population were wiped out. The one survivor was August Ciparis, a Negro who was a prisoner in an underground cell, where he was found still alive some days later by American journalists.

The life of a British passenger on the SS *Waratah* was saved through a dream presaging a disaster for the ship in which all aboard her would lose their lives. He told his dream to a number of the passengers and to the captain as the ship neared her next port of call, Durban. The passengers laughed at him; the captain said the vessel was in good seaworthy condition; nothing was likely to happen to her. Nevertheless, the man who had had the dream disembarked at Durban. Within a week, the *Waratah* was listed overdue at Lloyd's. Nothing was ever heard of her; no one knows what happened; whatever it was, no one survived the disaster. All that was ever found were pieces of wreckage carrying the ship's name.

In Sweden, Herr Berndt-Hollsten, managing director of the illustrated newspaper *Saningsmannen*, was known as the Man Who Dreamed True. From a child he had seen future events in his dreams. When, in June, 1950, he saw in a vision during sleep a big Army bomber crash 100 yards away from himself and his son at an air display to which he had taken the boy, he wrote down the dream the next day, showing the précis to his family and to friends. Three weeks later, there was an air display at Bromma which Ian-Ake, his son, wanted to see. As they watched, an Army bomber somersaulted, then crashed 100 yards away from them, exactly as he had seen it in his dream. Herr Berndt-Hollsten often dreamed of railway accidents, which always happened, but rarely "got" the place where the accident would occur. One night, he saw himself walking through a thick forest, at the edge of which ran a railway line. He saw a train crash, about which he told his wife and office colleagues the next morning. The evening papers carried banner headlines: RAILWAY DISASTER IN FOREST. MANY KILLED.

Even when names of places and other details come clearly through to a dreamer, prophecies of disaster are often not taken seriously. The Tay Bridge catastrophe was foreseen by numbers of people, but the authorities took no action, probably feeling that a dream was too slender a thread on which to hang an investigation.

Before a Leicestershire Charity Cup football match between the Syston Imperial Club and the Wigston Field Juniors in which he was to play, David Hubbard dreamed that it would end with the death of a player. When he begged the Syston Club to put off the game, he was laughed at; the match took place as arranged. One of the team, Roger Yates, Hubbard's close friend, was carried off the field with a broken leg. Less than thirty-six hours afterward he died from complications.

A Derbyshire woman, Mrs. Mary Raynes of Belper, dreamed

in 1959 that her husband lost both legs in a car accident. He was not a car driver; he laughed at his wife's "nonsensical" dream. The next day an Indian, Shashikant Gundavala, took him for a drive. The car crashed, killing the Indian; Mr. Raynes' legs were so badly injured that although he did not actually lose them, he lost the use of them.

A dream of a murder, though it came too late to save the victim's life, led to the arrest of his killers. About the middle of the last century when the West of America was still wild, a miner, Lloyd Magruder, was camping at night on the buttes of the Clearwater River. Three of his companions, D. C. Lowry, James Romaine, and David Howard, set on Magruder. Lowry killed Magruder with his ax, using so much force that in order to lever out the blade, he had to put one foot on his victim's chest. Before collecting the loot for which they had murdered Magruder (about 35,000 dollars in gold and a laden freight wagon), they killed the four other men in the party, throwing all the bodies, still wrapped in their sleeping blankets, down a conveniently near and deep canyon. There was not even a shanty within 100 miles of the spot and nothing, they thought, to connect them with the murders.

That night, Hill Beachy, owner of the Luna Hotel in Lewiston, Idaho, where Magruder often stayed, dreamed that the man of whom he had become a close friend was killed and robbed. In vivid detail he saw the slayer's face, the ax blow, the struggle to free it. Next day, the Walla Walla stagecoach was due to call at Lewiston. Among the travelers buying tickets in the Luna Hotel for the journey, Beachy recognized the man in his dream.

Dreams not being legal evidence, he could do nothing to stop the man and his two companions from leaving Lewiston. A few days later he heard that some packhorses had been left by these men on a ranch by the Clearwater, which then had been running too high for them to cross at the ford. Beachy persuaded the sheriff to come with him to the ranch; the pack animals were there. And there, too, left by one of those incredible blunders murderers are supposed always to make, they found Magruder's saddle, revolver, and personal gear. Later, when the bodies of the murdered men were discovered in the canyon, the postmortem showed that Magruder had been killed by a single ax blow. On Magruder's chest was Lowry's bloody footprint, made when he was struggling to disengage the ax.

The men were arrested in San Francisco. Brought back to Idaho territory, they were tried by the first district court ever to be held there, on January 5, 1865, found guilty, and hanged on March 4, 1865—because of a dream.

More often than not, dreams seem to be on the side of justice. Another instance of a murder solved in the sleeping state happened in London in the reign of William III. A man named Stockden, a Grub Street grocer, was murdered on December 23, 1695. No clue to his killer was discovered; then a Mrs. Greenwood made a statement to a magistrate that Stockden had appeared to her in a dream, telling her that one of his murderers lived in a house in Thames Street, which she described. Stockden visited her again, this time showing her a portrait of a man whose name he gave as Maynard, saying that he was the killer. Maynard, when questioned, apparently lost his head, admitting to murdering Stockden with the help of three accomplices; the face of one of these was shown to Mrs. Greenwood by Stockden, when he appeared to her in a third dream. The man who was arrested through her identification was eventually hanged, along with Maynard and a third confederate.

More dreams seem to be concerned with death and disaster than with any other theme. Dr. Louisa Rhine, wife of the great parapsychologist Dr. J. B. Rhine, suggests in *Hidden Channels of the Mind* that the reason may be that the subconscious considers them "newsworthy." They satisfy the inner urge for excitement, which shows itself in the way a crowd materializes whenever there is a street accident and in the popularity of horror films and crime reports in the newspapers.

A precognitive dream of this type came to Baron Charles

de Richter, when he and his wife were traveling to Nice by train on an afternoon so hot that the baron became drowsy and fell asleep. He dreamed that Isadora Duncan, the dancer, whom he knew well, kept repeating to him, over and over, the words "I have a rendezvous with death." When he arrived at Nice station, he was met by a friend, who gave him the news that Isadora had died in an extraordinary accident. She had been strangled by a Spanish shawl she was wearing, which somehow had become entangled in the steering wheel of the car in which she was driving.

A presage-of-death dream came to a girl of seventeen whose sister was happily married to a musician. In the dream, which was very vivid, her brother-in-law was out shooting with a boy whose face she could not see. As the boy climbed through a fence, his gun went off, the discharge hitting Eddy (the brother-in-law) in the hip. He bled to death before a doctor arrived. In her dream the girl thought she was asleep and was awakened by the sound of her mother screaming. As she ran down the hall, a woman, whose face again she did not see, was there; her mother, who stood in the dining-room doorway, had a telegram in her hand, telling her of her son-in-law's death. The dream disturbed the girl so much that she described it in a letter to her sister, which arrived on a Saturday morning. She and her husband treated it as a joke; on Monday morning Eddy died just as prefigured in the dream, which proved to be an exact blueprint of the actual event. The telegram with the news of his death arrived at the mother's house; a friend who had called in was with her when she and her daughter met in the doorway in the hall.

Sometimes depth of feeling for the subject of the death-and-disaster dream seems to be the spark that sets off in the dreamer the premonitory process. Sometimes the precognitive knowledge or warning of danger may concern casual friends or even strangers.

In the first category is the dream of a woman during the night before a Good Friday, on which her husband was to join a shooting party. She had tried in vain to persuade him to change the date of the shoot; she was a religious-minded woman, and to go out with the guns on Good Friday seemed to her a shocking thing to do. Before he set off, she begged him again to cancel the shoot. The night before, she said, she had dreamed that as she stood at the front door, she watched a cart drawn by a white horse go by on its way to the hospital; in the cart was her husband. She was still trying to make him change his mind when his friends called to collect him for the trip, and he went off with them.

Apparently about midday, they ate a picnic lunch on the bank of a small river. When Mr. X (the dreamer's husband) had finished his sandwiches, he felt thirsty. Bending over the stream to get water, he pushed against his gun, which, as the trigger knocked against a stone, went off. Mr. X fell back, calling out that he was shot. One of his friends ran off to try to get help; near at hand he found a man with a cart drawn by a white horse. When the injured man had been lifted into the cart, its driver was given instructions by Mr. X's friends on the best way to get to the hospital without passing through the street where Mr. X lived. But the carter, missing his way, drove past the X's house; the wife, standing in her doorway, saw the cart pass, as she had seen it in her dream. That night her husband died in the hospital.

In neither of the following two instances was there any deep emotional tie which could make likely a precognitive experience. The first case is the dream of a New York woman, in which she saw a thirty-four-year-old neighbor and friend, the father of four children, lying in his coffin in the living room of his house. When the children came running in, she asked the widow if she could help her by taking them home with her for the time being. The next morning the dreamer told her husband about her vision. He advised her not to think about it and not to talk about it. Three weeks later, the man next door died suddenly from a heart attack. His widow brought his four chidren to stay with the dreamer until the widow was able to have them home again.

Dreams: Doorway to the Unconscious 197

In the second case, a Kentucky woman who had got up early one April morning to give her second baby its bottle went back to bed and dozed off. She said it seemed as if she heard the street door open; having got up to find out who was there, she saw climbing the stairs a girl named Betty, to whom she had not written for some months. The baby's arrival and its care had kept her so busy that she had been out of touch for some months with most of her friends—Betty, who had been ill with tuberculosis, among them.

She said that she did not feel there was anything unusual in Betty's unannounced appearance, nor was she surprised when the girl put an arm around her and told her she couldn't pass by without calling in to see the two babies she had heard so much about. In the nursery she went from one cot to the other, saying she couldn't make up her mind which baby was the more appealing, the blond or the brunet. Finally, she said she must go, telling her friend, "Don't bother to come down; I can let myself out." Soon after this incident, the babies' mother made amends for her neglect with a letter to Betty describing how she had "seen" her, to which she was surprised not to receive, as usual, a prompt answer. About a month later she heard from Betty's father, who managed a branch of an American company in England, saying that his daughter had died on the date and at the time mentioned in the account of the dream sent to Betty.

Probably one of the strangest factors of such dreams is that they give warnings about disaster ahead for people with whom the dreamer is not intimately connected. There seems to be no logical explanation for them in most cases—but the reason for dreaming even a "straightforward" dream, which may give important information, often not available through ordinary channels, is just as inexplicable. Why does the dream come? Sometimes as an answer to a problem turned over to the subconscious deliberately, much more often unsought and unexpected by the dreamer. General George B. McClellan, for instance, had no thought of being aided supraphysically in a task which must have seemed almost hopeless, yet he had a dream which affected the course of American history.

President Lincoln (who dreamed of his own death a week before it happened) had called in General McClellan to rally the demoralized Union forces. Late one night the general fell asleep at his desk, awakening at once, so he thought, to find the room filled with light. Framed in the light, he saw the face of George Washington; he heard him say, "General McClellan, do you sleep at your post? Rouse you, or ere it can be prevented, the foe will be in Washington. . . . You have been betrayed, and had God willed it otherwise, ere the sun of tomorrow had set, the Confederate flag would have waved above the Capitol and your own grave. But note what you see. Your time is short." Then as if a living map were unrolled, all the troop positions of the Confederate troops as they marched on Washington were shown him, as well as the maneuvers planned for the future. In his dream, he took up a pencil and noted down everything he had seen.

Washington went on to speak of the part America should play in establishing a "Universal Republic." Then McClellan awoke, to find on the map beside him the notes he had made in his dream of the Confederate Army's movements. Knowing his enemy's plans, McClellan was able to forestall them. When they were finally defeated, the Portland (Maine) *Evening Courier,* reporting the success of the Union troops, reported also the dream which had made it possible.

A Norfolk man, named John Chapman, owed his considerable wealth to a dream, which occurred three times, telling him to go to London Bridge, where he would meet a man who would make him rich. Chapman, who was a Swaffham tinker, set out on what everyone he knew told him was a crazy venture. His belief in the reality of his vision was not shaken, nor was he tempted to turn back, even when his tiny capital ran out, leaving him without means to buy food or drink or shelter for the final stage of his journey. Reaching London Bridge at last, he began looking about for the man who would give him wealth. All that day he walked up and down, without catching a glimpse of gold. He thought despairingly that the people who had told him his pilgrimage was a fool's errand were right. There being no point in waiting any longer, he was taking a last look around, before he began his homeward journey, when a man came up to him. "Would you mind telling me," said this man, who looked like a well-to-do citizen, "why you have been walking up and down, sometimes standing still, looking at passersby? I have been watching you for some time, and it has completely puzzled me."

Chapman's answer was that he was there because of a dream. The man seemed to find ridiculous the idea that anyone would stand about on London Bridge for no reason except the directions of a dream. "I had one myself the other night," he said, "a very vivid one, but what a fool I would be if I followed its instructions." He went on to say that he had been told to hurry off to a town called Swaffham, in which lived John Chapman, a tinker. The tinker had a garden; if the dreamer dug under the only tree growing there, he would find a crock of gold. For a moment, staggered by the way in which this dream linked up with his own, Chapman was on the point of blurting out his own story. Instead, prompted by caution, he agreed that it did sound improbable.

As soon as the man had gone, John set off for Swaffham. Exhausted and footsore as he was when he arrived, he went into his garden before he ate or rested. He had dug about a foot into the earth under his one tree when the spade struck against something hard—an earthenware jar, which he found, when he opened it, was full of gold pieces. On its lid was inscribed: "Dig deeper; under me doth lie one richer than I." No very strenuous effort was needed to uncover a second pot, about double the size of the other, also crammed with gold coins.

John Chapman's rags-to-riches story is commemorated in the marketplace of his hometown, by a sign which reads: "The tinker of Swaffham who did by a dream find a treasure." In Swaffham church are his memorials—a prayer desk, carved with figures depicting him, his wife, and his dog, and the north aisle itself, which he had built in 1485 as a thank offering for his good fortune.

The late Sir Ernest Wallis Budge found fortune, if not a crock of gold, through a dream. From a child his great ambition was to become an authority on Oriental languages, which he studied so intensively that he attracted the notice of Prime Minister William Gladstone, who was himself an expert in the classics. Gladstone, finding that the Budges could not afford to send their son to a university, arranged for the boy to enter Christ's College, Cambridge, as a noncollegiate—or charity—student.

His work on his chosen subject was thought so promising by his tutors that he was asked to enter an Oriental languages competition, run by Professor Archibald Henry Sayce, then the acknowledged greatest authority on ancient tongues. Four questions had to be answered at some length by the competitors; the prize for the winner was a fellowship (known as an Exhibition), which would mean to Budge that he could stay on at Cambridge and so take a long step toward his goal.

Budge slaved so hard to ensure that he would know something about any question that could be asked in the examination that on the night before it was to be held his brain went on strike. He could think just coherently enough to realize that unless by a miracle he could pull himself together, he would not be able to sit for the crucial examination, let alone win the prize. He went to bed so mentally and physically exhausted that he fell asleep at once. And he dreamed he was sitting for the examination, but not in the usual type of room; it looked to him like a shed of some kind. A tutor came in with the test questions; they were written on long slips of green paper, which he took from an envelope in his pocket. There were also texts to be translated.

In his dream Budge knew that he could answer the questions easily, but when he saw that the texts were written in multilingual cuneiform Assyrian characters and in the obscure Akkadian language, he panicked, thinking that he could not translate them. And if he failed the test, the golden opportunity offered by the prize would be lost. He woke up, then fell asleep again almost at once—to dream the same dream. Again he awoke, sweating with fright; again he slept. The dream was repeated a third time; when he awakened from it, he saw by the bedside clock that the whole sequence of dreaming and wakening had taken only about a couple of hours. The time was just after 2 A.M.

Mulling over various features of his dream, he remembered that he had seen those texts which had to be translated in Henry Creswicke Rawlinson's *The Cuneiform Inscriptions of Western Asia.* The book was in his study; in it, as he had thought, he found the texts. Until he had to leave for the test, Budge studied them so carefully that he almost knew them by heart.

Although he arrived at the examination hall well before time, it was already full. Budge was shown into a room which opened out of the hall near the service quarters. It had a roof which made it look like a shed, a battered table, one chair. Budge had seen it before—in his dream. He recognized the face of the tutor who came in, bringing an envelope, from which he took four long green slips of paper. When Budge looked at them, questions and texts for translation were exactly as he had foreseen them.

That day was the turning point of his life and the beginning of his great career. After winning the competition, he was able to go on with his work and research until he became a world authority on ancient languages and Oriental subjects. Perhaps his most famous achievements are his translation of the Egyptian *Book of the Dead,* the *Teachings of Amenhotep,* and of the hieratic papyruses in the British Museum, where he later was appointed keeper of the Department of Egyptian Antiquities.

Robert Louis Stevenson was one of the relatively rare people who, as I mentioned earlier in this chapter, can make the subconscious work for them through dreams. Some of his best stories and novels were written for him, as it were, while his conscious mind was sleeping. As with Sir Ernest Wallis Budge, a dream which came to him at the crucial point in his career put him on the path to fame and success. Stevenson had written a short story around the dual personality theme, which he called "The Travelling Companion." At that time he was a known but not well-known writer; the editor to whom he sent the story returned it with a note saying that although it was ingenious, its plot was weak. Stevenson thought the editor was probably right, but after weeks of revision he still could not make the plot salable. He seems to have forgotten for the moment, as happens to all of us at times, the obvious answer—his ability to turn a problem over to his subconscious. Suddenly one night he remembered how often in the past his deeper mind had provided him with just the necessary material. Before he went to sleep, he read and re-read "The Travelling Companion." Beside his bed was paper and pencil; as soon as he awoke the next day, he noted down the plot he had dreamed, the dual personality story which became a world best seller and made him famous—*The Strange Case of Dr. Jekyll and Mr. Hyde*.

Dreams have opened the way to discoveries valuable in many branches of science, such as that of the remains at Glastonbury Abbey which were found because of a series of vivid dreams.

An important piece was added to the pattern of paleontology (study of prehistoric forms of life) by the dream of a brilliant ichthyologist Louis Agassiz, which he describes in his book *Recherches sur les Poissons Fossiles*. He was working to free from the stone bed where it had lain for millions of years a fossil fish, particularly interesting and valuable because it belonged to a species then unknown. Having no clue to the exact shape of its body, he found that to separate the fossil's outline without damage from the stone was unusually difficult. After trying to solve the problem in every possible way without success, he decided to let the fish stay as it was.

A few nights afterward he had a dream in which he saw the fish swimming about alive. The dream was so clear that

Dreams: Doorway to the Unconscious 203

he thought it might give him some clue to the fossil's body structure, but when he examined it, it seemed to have no relation to his dream. A second time the dream came; again he studied the fossil with the same result. After its third repetition, Agassiz, waking in the night, made a sketch of the prehistoric fish as he had just seen it.

In the light of day, the drawing seemed to him a fantasy, useless as a key to the restoring of the fossil. There were anatomical details which he had not come across before, and for this reason, he thought they had never existed. Still, with his sketch as blueprint, on the chance that he might get some result, Agassiz chipped away at the fish's stony surroundings, until presently a screenlike layer fell off, disclosing the fossil. It stood out boldly, as if carved, a unique specimen of a species until then unknown, an exact replica of his dream drawing.

Dr. Hermann Hilprecht, celebrated Oriental scholar and authority on Assyria, was given through a dream information which he needed for the completion of his book *Old Babylonian Inscriptions*. At the same time, details about the ancient kingdom were supplied which then were not known to any living person.

To complete his manuscript, Dr. Hilprecht had to transcribe the inscription on two agate fragments, which came from the temple of Baal at Nippur. He believed they were finger rings; they were broken and so small that the engraving on them was indecipherable. The next day was the deadline for delivery of the manuscript; with the strongest magnifying glass he could find, Dr. Hilprecht worked late into the night trying to wrest their secret from them.

At last, still sitting at his desk, he fell asleep. He woke, he thought, to see standing beside him a tall man, whom the doctor recognized by his robes as a priest of Baal. He told Dr. Hilprecht to come with him. "I will help you." At this point Dr. Hilprecht noticed that he was sitting, not on the chair in his study, but on a massive stone step; he could feel a hot wind blowing around him. He followed the priest along an empty street of deserted buildings and then into the largest and most splendid of these, set a little apart from the rest.

"You are in the temple of Baal at Nippur, between the Tigris and the Euphrates," Dr. Hilprecht was told. He could see enough of the vast, dimly lit hall around them to recognize it by its main features, reconstructed by archeologists. "Can you tell me," he asked his guide, "the whereabouts of the secret treasure room of the temple—which no one since your day has been able to discover?" The priest led him across the main body of the temple, down a dark passage, at the end of which was a small room, where stood a strong wooden chest. It was empty except for a few fragments of agate.

They had been part of a votive cylinder, the priest told Dr. Hilprecht, to which the fragments on which he had been working also belonged. "When we were ordered to make a pair of earrings for the god Ninib [Ninurta], the only agate we could find was this cylinder. Here in this room it was cut into three pieces one of which was lost; each carried part of the original inscription."

"What was this inscription?" Dr. Hilprecht asked.

In the thick dust which covered the walls of the room, the priest wrote in Sumerian script: "To the god Ninib, son of Baal, his lord, has Kurigalzu [the king who sent the votive cylinder to the temple], pontifex of Baal, presented this."

Even as Dr. Hilprecht read the words, they faded. The temple of Baal was gone; he was back in his Philadelphia study, the priest still beside him. On the desk, a sheet of paper on which was written the word "Nebuchadnezzar" caught the doctor's eye; two eminent Egyptologists had translated it as "Nebo, protect my work as a mason." The priest said: "The correct translation is 'Nebo, protect my boundary.'" Then Dr. Hilprecht awoke.

Having been given the missing part of the inscription, he was able to deliver his book on time. Later the agate fragments were identified as part of a cylinder, as the priest had said they were; his version of the meaning of the name Nebuchadnezzar was accepted by modern scholars; the site of the treasure room was found to be exactly as shown to Dr. Hilprecht in the temple of Baal by his hierophant.

Many scientists think that entities and colorful settings which are features of some dreams (as of Dr. Hilprecht's) may be dramatization of the subconscious mind or have perhaps a symbolic meaning.

The last Lord Seaforth had a dream the prophetic burden of which was given by the (possibly) symbolic figure of an old woman. The late Colonel John Constantine Stanley, who married Susan Mary, eldest daughter of the late Keith William Stewart-Mackenzie of Seaforth, gave an authenticated account of the dream:

"The last Lord Seaforth was in full possession of all his faculties. When about twelve years of age scarlet fever broke out at the school at which he was boarding . . . some fifteen or twenty boys who had taken the infection were moved into a large room where they were treated. . . . One evening after dark, the attendant nurse, having left the dormitory for a few minutes, was alarmed by a cry. She instantly returned and found Lord Seaforth in a state of great excitement. After he became calmer, he told the nurse that he had seen, soon after she had left the room, a hideous old woman come in. She had a wallet full of something hanging from her neck in front of her. She paused on entering, then turned to the bed next the door, and stared steadily at the boy lying in it. She then paused at the foot of the next boy's bed, and after a moment moved up to the head, and taking a mallet and a peg from her wallet, drove the peg into his forehead. Young Seaforth said he heard the crash of the bone, though the boy never stirred. She then proceeded round the room, looking at some boys longer than at others. When she came to him, his suspense was awful . . . in years after he could never forget the moment's agony when he saw her hand reaching down for a nail and feeling for his ears. . . . The nurse laughed at the lad's story and told him to go to sleep. When the doctor came an hour later, he observed that the boy was feverish and excited and asked the nurse if she knew the cause, whereupon she reported what had occurred. The doctor . . . returned to the boy's bedside and made him repeat his dream. He took it down in writing at the moment. The following day nothing eventful happened, but in course of time, some got worse and a few died, others suffered only slightly, while some, though they recovered, bore some evil trace and consequence of the fever for the rest of their lives. The doctor found to his horror that those whom Lord Seaforth had described as having a peg driven into their heads were those who died from the fever; those whom the old hag passed by recovered, and were none the worse, whereas those she appeared to look at intently or handled, all suffered afterward. Lord Seaforth left his bed of sickness almost stone deaf, and in later years, grieving over the loss of his four sons, absolutely and entirely ceased to speak."

This was the Lord Seaforth of whom the Brahan Seer foretold some two centuries before his birth: "I see a Chief, the last of the house, both deaf and dumb."

Another factor in the enigma of the dream pattern is timing. Now and then the manifestation of the prophetic vision exactly coincides with the beginning of the event it presages. An instance of this is the dream of Arlette, mother of William the Conqueror. Arlette, daughter of Fulbert, the tanner of Falaise, worked as a washerwoman by the river. There she was noticed by Duke Robert the Devil (the Magnificent) of Normandy. Arlette was brought to his bed; that night, toward dawn, she awoke, crying out that she had dreamed a great tree was growing out of her body. It was so tall that it reached the sky; its branches spread over all Normandy and over England. That night William the Conqueror was conceived.

He was born in 1027. Duke Robert, who was away, knew nothing of the birth until his son was a year old. Then he heard tales of the wonderful child in the house of Fulbert the tanner, of how, when the boy was delivered, the midwife had prophesied over him. He had been put on the floor because his mother bled; he clutched the rushes there so tightly that they could not be taken from his fist. The midwife said,

"There's a little lord that will take his seizin; what he has he'll never let go." William was taken to the castle, where he was brought up by his father; to Arlette, Duke Robert gave a house, to which he came often.

Arlette dreamed of her son's great future in the hour of his conception; the dream of John Williams of Scorrier in Cornwall, mining engineer, came to him some hours after the event which it seemed to foretell had happened. On the evening of May 11, 1812, Spencer Perceval, Prime Minister and Chancellor of the Exchequer, was shot dead, as he went into the House of Commons, by a man named John Bellingham, who hid behind a door. That night John Williams dreamed the whole episode three times, as clearly as if he had been an eyewitness. He made a statement concerning it, witnessed by the Reverend Thomas Fisher and Charles Prideaux Brune, which was (and still may be) kept at Prideaux Place, Padstow. Dr. Abercrombie, to whom Mr. Williams told the experience, made a record of the dream exactly as he had heard it from Williams:

"Mr. Williams dreamed he was in the House of Commons, where he saw a small man in a blue coat and white waistcoat. Then, as he watched, a man in a brown coat with yellow buttons drew a pistol from his coat. He fired at the small man, who fell, blood pouring from a wound a little below the left breast. Mr. Williams heard clearly the report of the pistol, saw blood fly out and stain the waistcoat, saw the colour of the man's face change." He watched the murderer seized by men who were present, "observed his countenance," asked who had been shot, and was told "the Chancellor."

Mr. Williams, waking in the night, told his wife of the dream. She advised him to go to sleep again; he did, only to dream the same dream. He woke his wife again; the same thing happened again. In Falmouth, the next day, Mr. Williams told everyone he met about his strange experience; he told his daughter and son-in-law, who said that the Lord Chancellor would not be in the House of Commons. When Mr. Williams described the man who had been shot, the son-in-law said he had described the Prime Minister and Chancellor of the Exchequer—whom Williams did not know and had never seen; nor had he ever been in the House of Commons.

While the dream was being discussed, Mr. Williams' son Michael came in from Truro, seven miles away, full of news brought by a man who had just arrived on the mail coach from London. This man, who had been in the House of Commons on May 11, said that Mr. Perceval, Prime Minister and Chancellor of the Exchequer, had been shot by a man named Bellingham. Six weeks later, Mr. Williams made his first (bodily) visit to the House of Commons, where he pointed out the exact spot on which he had seen Bellingham standing and the place of Perceval's collapse. These details were checked and found correct, as were Williams' descriptions of the dress of Perceval and of his murderer.

So far as one can see, Mr. Williams' dream, interesting though it was as an example of psychic "sight," had no practical purpose. It could be of no use in preventing the crime it pictured; the dream came after the crime had been committed. The murderer was arrested on the spot, there was no need to turn to the dream for clues to his identity, but there is no logic in dreams.

At this stage of our knowledge and development, dreams seem to be uncontrolled and uncontrollable manifestations of the sixth sense. Omens are even more inexplicable. Why should the actions of birds or animals or the reactions of inanimate objects foretell death or disaster—omens are almost always of unpleasantness—for human beings? The easy answer is that they don't, but the enormous body of well-authenticated evidence that they do makes the easy answer difficult to accept.

One of the few omens of good, instead of bad, fortune was the beating of Drake's drum on a November day in 1918. On that misty day the British fleet, led by the *Royal Oak*, which was flying a silk banner made by Devon women, carrying a crew chiefly of Devon men, was on patrol in the North Sea.

On her bridge was Admiral Grant, Captain McLachlan, and other officers. About 9 A.M., the German fleet was sighted through the haze, and at that moment a drum began to beat in the *Royal Oak*; the sound was of a small drum beaten in rolls. At first the officers, who were expecting the German ships to open fire, paid no attention to it. Later Admiral Grant mentioned it to Captain McLachlan; the captain listened and was puzzled, as was the commander. The ship's complement was at action stations; the decks were cleared for action. Messengers were sent to every part of the ship to track down the drummer; he could not be found, and every man was accounted for. The drum continued to beat. Then the commander went around the ship, checking the whereabouts of the crew—each man was where he was supposed to be.

All this time the British fleet was closing in around the Germans; all the time the drum went on beating. By 2 P.M. the enemy fleet was encircled and helpless; the British ships dropped anchor 15 miles off the Firth of Forth. Then the drum stopped; no sound of it was heard again. The Germans had sent a signal of surrender.

Birds or animals which appear in certain places at certain times are, it seems, heralds of disaster. The perching of a cormorant on the steeple of Dornoch church in 1816 was a death omen, the people of the parish said, of the minister—who died a few days later.

The sculptor Raymond Briton Riviere, son of the artist and grandson of the famous Victorian painter William Riviere, told me that the death of a member of the family was always foretold by the appearance of a bat in full daylight. On a clear summer's morning, as he and his father were walking on Dartmoor, a bat flew into his father's face. At the inn where they were staying they found a telegram telling them of the death of Raymond's grandfather.

According to the late Nell St. John Montagu, a clairvoyant famous in the 1930's, the behavior of the rooks which congregated around Leamlara, her husband's historic house in southern Ireland, was an omen of the fortunes of his family. For nine centuries, the Standish-Barrys had lived at Leamlara, built on the site of a castle, and the rooks (or crows, as the southern Irish call them) had lived in the rookeries on the estate. The size and number of them were a legend in County Cork, and of great importance to the Standish-Barrys. According to an ancient tradition, so long as the "crows" came back each night, circling three times around Leamlara before settling down in their treetops, so long would the family always have an heir.

Mrs. St. John Montagu used to find the legend comforting when her son, Charles, almost before he could walk, began to court every kind of danger. He climbed abnormally high trees; as he grew up, he rode recklessly to hounds, swam in risky places, did acrobatics while riding his motorcycle. An old dairymaid used to tell her not to worry. "Shure, don't the crows come home ivery night? So long as they do, the young master won't be afther coming to any harm."

Every night, while her son grew into a young man, the sky would be black with the "crows" returning to the Leamlara rookeries; every night they circled the woods three times. Then, one morning, the "crows" flew off as usual, but that night the rookeries were empty, deserted for the first time for centuries. Not one of the birds ever returned to Leamlara—and how had they known even before it happened of the heir's death?

The Cotters of County Cork were warned of death or danger ahead by the sound of a galloping horse, so Mrs. St. John Montagu was told by a member of the family. As they sat talking by the fire on a stormy November night, Mrs. St. John Montagu heard, above the drumbeat of the rain and roar of the wind, the sound of horse hooves, in the house, it seemed, but galloping away from it. Her companion, Tommy Cotter, was listening tensely; then, as gradually the echo of the hoofbeats seemed to die away, he relaxed. He said that when that happened, they were a warning only of danger. The story began, he said, some centuries before when an ancestor of his had been convicted of some offense and sentenced

Dreams: Doorway to the Unconscious

to death. "A great friend of his, who owned the house where we now are, through influence at court, got a reprieve for him—which only arrived in County Cork on the day before the date of the execution. My ancestor's friend set off for Dublin, riding so hard that his mount—his favorite horse—died under him. Eventually he reached the prison a few minutes before the time set for the execution, to find that through some chicanery, it had been put forward a quarter of an hour. His friend was already dead.

"His would-be rescuer had the body of his horse brought back here and buried somewhere in the house; no one has discovered exactly where. Ever since then, the sound of galloping hooves has been a danger signal to the Cotters."

The next day Tommy Cotter was in a friend's car, which he insisted, in spite of Cotter's protests, in driving much too fast on a dangerous cliff road. Tommy Cotter managed to jump out of the car just before it overturned, injuring its driver badly. If he had not heard the warning of the galloping hooves the night before, Tommy Cotter was certain he would never have avoided the accident.

Some months afterward, workmen who were reflooring the room in which Mr. Cotter and Mrs. St. John Montagu had been sitting that night, told Mrs. St. John Montagu that they had found the skeleton of a horse under the boards. Since she was certain it could only be the remains of the horse which had died in the attempt to save the life of the Cotters' ancestor and which his master had buried there, she asked that the bones should not be disturbed—and they were left where they were found.

Her final experience of the Cotter family omen came a few years later, when Sir James Cotter, the elder brother of Tommy, asked her to give him a reading with the crystal. At first she could see only a galloping riderless horse. Sir James looked so healthy that Mrs. Montagu felt that the warning, if it were a warning, could not apply to him. She looked into the crystal again; this time details concerning Sir James' business affairs were pictured there. A few weeks afterward Sir James, who was on his honeymoon, dropped dead.

14. Modern Seers (I)

Between the end of the nineteenth century and the present time, prophets have proliferated. They made predictions as remarkable in accuracy and detail as the pronouncements of great seers of the past or even more remarkable, an upward trend which could be linked to the approach of the Aquarian age.

A few years before the beginning of the twentieth century a Scotsman, Robert Laing, an Oriental scholar and fellow of Corpus Christi College, Oxford, made a prophecy as exact and detailed as the predictions of Nostradamus or the Brahan Seer. In April, 1885, in Jerusalem, he met four artists—Bruno Piglheim, Joseph Krieger, Karl Frosch, and René Reinke—who, with Frau Piglheim and Frau Frosch, were staying at the German hospice where he was lodging.

According to Herr Frosch, after dinner one evening, Robert Laing told them that because he was interested in the fact that they all were to work together to produce a panoramic painting of Jerusalem, he had "enquired into their future fate." To Frosch and Piglheim, he said, "You two will quarrel and become mortal enemies over your work." Piglheim, he added, would "come to grief over it."

The artists wanted to know how—was he to fall off a scaffolding, or would there be an accident of some other kind? Laing said, "The picture will be completed. But something will occur, something related to the matter, this picture, and as a result you, Piglheim, will come to grief." This would happen in a few years, he added.

To Frau Piglheim, who had protested that after a period of years, twenty perhaps or thirty, it was quite possible that her husband would die, Laing answered, "No. When I speak of a few years, I mean five or ten. It may take ten years, but no more. Whenever I see anything clearly it comes to pass within about a ten-year period."

Frosch asked about his own future. He was told: "You will paint the panorama three times, but you will do well."

As for the reason he and Piglheim were to become enemies, Laing explained that it would happen because of the picture. Frosch, he said, would travel to many countries on business connected with it: "I saw sea and a ship, and that means a distant voyage. On the deck of the ship you stood with two other artists. . . . I noticed those men particularly, for they wore curious cloaks and felt capes such as I have never seen either here in Jerusalem, or in England. It seemed to me you had been seasick; you looked quite ill. One of these panoramas you will bring to England, perhaps as a result of a commission—I discerned that quite clearly. . . . Thenceforth you are going to be sued because of the picture —the prosecution will originate in London. It will come to a lawsuit and will follow you, even to Germany."

Frosch asked two more questions—what would happen as a result of the prosecution, and what else would come to him? The answer to the first query was: "Nothing; the prosecution is all there is to it," and to the second: "You will do well."

Laing told one of the other artists, Herr Reinke, that in spite of his having come to Jerusalem for the purpose of painting the panorama, he would not work on it at all. Krieger asked if he would get married. "Yes, but the marriage will not turn out well. You will soon be divorced."

To Herr Frosch, the Scotsman repeated that he would do well after about five years, in which many unpleasant things would first happen to him; he would find Munich—

of which he was very fond—uncongenial because of these episodes; he would leave the town and make his home elsewhere.

Before they left one another, Robert Laing asked the artists to write down all he had said. This was in 1885; in 1891 Herr Frosch made a statement giving details of Laing's prophecy and its sequel to Dr. Baron Karl du Prel, well-known authority on psychical research. So much that Laing foretold had already happened, said Frosch, that he wished to make a deposition, which could be used to check whether the remainder of the predictions were fulfilled.

He told Du Prel that he had already made the long journey in connection with the panorama—he had gone to America. With him in the ship were two colleagues, German painters, who wore shepherds' cloaks, fastened with metal clasps as big as saucers, which attracted a good deal of attention. Frosch was seasick for about five days.

Reinke did not work on the panorama. Frosch painted it four times; one of the four paintings was sent, without his consent and without his knowledge, from America to London; as a result, he was sued in Munich for plagiarism. The day before the hearing, his lawyer, Dr. Wimmer, told him the trial would not take place. At the last moment the complaint against Frosch was withdrawn, although by so doing, the plaintiff became liable for costs.

Frosch and Piglheim did quarrel over the panorama. Krieger did get married; his divorce was proceeding when Frosch made his deposition. So far the program outlined by Laing had unfolded according to plan. Frosch's deposition, made before a notary, signed by witnesses, of whom Dr. du Prel was one, sealed with five individual seals, was left in the notary's custody for eight years. In 1899, power of attorney to open the document was given to Dr. Walter Borman, also celebrated for research in psychic matters, Dr. du Prel having died in the meantime.

Dr. Borman, making investigations on how many more of the predictions listed in the deposition had been fulfilled,

Modern Seers (I) 215

found that the panorama, painted eventually by Frosch, Krieger, and Piglheim, had been one of the chief exhibits at an exhibition in Vienna. On the night of April 27-28 it had been completely destroyed by fire. Piglheim, who, since he had worked on the panorama, had taken to expressing life's hardships and sufferings in his pictures, made a tremendous effort to re-create it in increased beauty—which failed. And on July 15, 1894, he died of a heart attack in Munich, nine years after Robert Laing had foretold that within ten years great misfortune would come to him in connection with the panorama.

Herr Frosch, his wife, and Herr Krieger all were puzzled that there was no mention in the deposition of the destruction of the panorama. They all felt certain that Robert Laing had predicted some calamity for it; Herr Frosch was sure he had mentioned it in his statement to Dr. du Prel. They could only suppose that he had omitted this part of Laing's prophecy by mistake when he compiled the deposition.

Equally detailed was the prophecy made to Marshal (then General) Carl Gustav Emil von Mannerheim in 1917, when he was convalescing at the Hotel London in Odessa from the effects of an injury. Among fellow guests was Lady Muriel Paget, who had been with a Red Cross unit in Rumania. Having been assigned to a motorized hospital section in Odessa, she was waiting there for orders from London. One day she gave a tea party, to which Baron Mannerheim was invited. A surprise item for her guests was a clairvoyant who foretold their futures.

In the *Memoirs of Marshal Mannerheim*, the baron says that having had no experience of psychic matters, he was not much interested in the clairvoyant's predictions. Each guest was told to write out four questions, which were handed to the psychic, who, sitting in a cubicle leading off the main room, apparently went into a trance.

The marshal's first question was about his daughters, Anastasie and Sophie, about whom he was anxious, having had no news of them for some time; the second was also about members of his family. The third was personal; the fourth was to do with the war, but exactly what he had wanted to know concerning it, he could not remember when writing his *Memoirs*.

His daughters, the clairvoyant said, were well; the elder was doing humanitarian work. The younger would cross "perilous seas, but would come to no harm." The rest of his family was well. For Mannerheim himself, nine detailed predictions were made, about which he told Lady Muriel after the session.

First, a long journey was foretold; afterward he would be given command of an army, which he would lead victoriously. Then would come honors and a high position (No. 3), which he would resign voluntarily (No. 4). The fifth prediction promised that soon after this, he would visit two important Western countries on a vital mission, which would be successful (No. 6). A position higher than he had held earlier would be his (No. 7), but (No. 8) he would not keep it long. Finally, many years afterward, he would once more achieve greatness (No. 9).

At the time, just before the Bolshevik Revolution, Mannerheim was a lieutenant general in the Imperial Russian Army—what was left of it. The travel and the Army command were events likely to happen to a man in his position; they could have been foretold without the aid of second sight. Predictions 3-9 seemed as improbable of fulfillment as the first two were probable in Mannerheim's situation at the time.

However, step by step, the predictions were fulfilled.

(1) From Odessa, Mannerheim went to Petrograd (as it was then), leaving it as soon as he could for Helsinki. Finland was by now a free country. Mannerheim decided his place was there, rather than with the Russian Army.

(2) Communist elements in Finland were preparing for a coup to enable them to take over control of the country, which then would be absorbed into the Soviet system. Mannerheim organized resistance to this movement so successfully

that in January, 1918, he was made commander in chief of the defense forces (No. 3). In May, 1918, he won a victory which ended the war of liberation.

(4) Mannerheim had stipulated before accepting the post of commander in chief that no other country should be asked or allowed to intervene in Finland's affairs. Behind his back, telling him nothing of what was toward, the Senate appealed for assistance to Germany. It came, with excellent short-term results; its long-range effects were not so acceptable. A legend, which still flourishes, was created that the German forces had had to be called in to liberate Finland because her own army was inadequate for the task. And, too, Finnish prestige suffered, giving Soviet Russia a weapon, of which she later made full use.

Mannerheim had foreseen this. Outraged by what he considered double-dealing by the Senate, he decided to retire; his sense of duty to Finland overcoming his personal feelings, he made up his mind not to leave his post for the time being. Later, although great pressure was brought to bear on him to stay in his post, he resigned.

(5) Soon afterward, Finland's domestic affairs having been stabilized, Mannerheim was sent on missions to England and to France with the purpose of establishing diplomatic relations between these countries and his own; he also went to Sweden to settle a dispute there.

While he was in London, he met Lady Muriel Paget, who reminded him of the predictions made to him in Odessa. Everything he had been told had come true up till then, he told her—both the prophecies about his personal affairs and about his family. His elder daughter had become a Carmelite nun ("humanitarian work"); the younger, crossing France to Sweden and to Finland through mined waters, had arrived safely.

(6) Mannerheim was so successful in presenting Finland's case to the Allies that she was recognized as a sovereign independent country, instead of being incorporated with Sweden, as had been mooted.

(7) and (8) On December 12, 1918, Baron Mannerheim was made regent of Finland, a position, as the prophecy had specified, higher than that of commander in chief of the Army. He resigned from it less than a year after his appointment, on August 16, 1919, when Kaarlo Juåho Stahlberg became President.

(9) Mannerheim was unanimously elected President of the Finnish Republic in 1944.

The clairvoyant's accuracy score in the Mannerheim prophecy was 100 percent. In spite of this astronomically high figure, the baron apparently was no more impressed by it than he would have been by a train running on schedule. Psychic phenomena to him were curious experiences, and that was all. He did not even give the name of the clairvoyant, which appears a little grudging. If her performance on this occasion was a fair sample of her gift, it put her in the same class as great seers such as Cheiro, the palmist-prophet.

Cheiro—the pseudonym of Count Louis Hamon—was a fabulous character. There have been others whose powers perhaps equaled his, but none in our time has reached and remained on quite so high a peak of fame as he achieved. He was born on November 1, 1866, on the outskirts of Dublin. When he was about twenty-three, he went to India, coming back to Britain after studying with Brahmin priests for two or three years. Cheiro had everything: He was tall, good-looking, distinguished, brilliant, charming. Soon people from all over the country, of all sorts and conditions, including royalty, were scrambling for a consultation with him. He seemed able to see ahead as easily as most of us can see across the road, and what he saw came to pass.

In 1894 and again in June, 1911, Cheiro warned the famous journalist and psychical researcher W. T. Stead (who edited the *Review of Reviews*) that he would be drowned in April, 1912. Stead lost his life when the *Titanic* sank in that month and year.

Cheiro called to see Lord Kitchener at the War Office on July 21, 1894, to take an impression of his hands. He told Kitchener that he would have to cope with the heaviest responsibilities of his career in 1914, when he would be sixty-four years old. Lord Kitchener asked when he would die. "When you are sixty-six," was the answer, "but not as you might expect, being a soldier, in battle. Your death will be the result of storms or disaster at sea; there is a chance of capture by the enemy and exile from which you will never recover."

In 1915, when Kitchener was at Dunkirk, he was told by Commander Balincourt that a friend of his had been killed nearby. Kitchener, as the Exchange Telegraph reported on June 10, 1915, said he was not afraid of sharing his friend's fate: "I know I shall die at sea." A year afterward on June 5, 1916, Kitchener, then in his sixty-sixth year, was aboard HMS *Hampshire* when she sank in the North Sea. He was not among the survivors.

A year or two before the events occurred, Cheiro foretold the Boer War, the death of Queen Victoria, an attempt on the life of the Shah of Persia, the assassination of King Umberto of Italy. To King Edward VII he predicted the day, the date, and the year of his death.

In June, 1902, the king was so ill that his coronation had to be postponed. Although Cheiro had told him that he would not die until he was sixty-nine, he was so depressed about his health that Queen Alexandra sent for Cheiro to reassure him. The king recovered; he was crowned on August 9. He was taken ill again in the spring of 1910. This time there was no recuperation; the king, then in his sixty-ninth year, died on Friday, May 6, as Cheiro had prophesied.

In 1925, Cheiro said, "In 1926 a treaty of the most far-reaching importance will be revealed between Russia and a combination of interests antagonistic to Great Britain." In March, 1926, a treaty was signed between Soviet Russia and Germany. For May of that year (1926) he foretold a strike in America, the Channel Island earthquake in July, a substantial tremor in England, fire which destroyed many large houses in Britain.

The First World War, he said, would break out in 1914, in midsummer. By this reckoning, since it did not begin until August, it was a little overdue, but it finished according to Cheiro's schedule, in November, 1918. He had said that it would "last about four years" and that afterward the Central European powers would collapse. The Russian Empire would break up, as would its monarchy; he warned of "the downfall of the Csar, and the massacre of himself and all his immediate family." He had already told the czar, who had visited him incognito in about 1913 and whose identity Cheiro did not know, that his death would be violent, "caused by war."

Cheiro made a number of predictions about members of the House of Hanover, the title of which was changed by royal proclamation to the House of Windsor on July 17, 1917—a very unfavorable date, according to him. He was interested in the dynasty because it had, he said "a remarkable occult history," beginning with the horoscope of George I. Cast by the famous astrologer Pard Zepi, who was infatuated by George's imprisoned duchess, it foretold that the king would die a year and a day after his wife. The birth chart, kept for many years in the muniment vaults of the royal family at Hanover, set the date of his death as June 11, 1727. On that day the king died in his carriage while driving into his German principality. His duchess, whom he had imprisoned for thirty-two years in Ahlen Castle because of her amour with Count Philipp Christoph von Königsmark, had left him a widower on June 10, 1726.

The period of April to July, as Cheiro pointed out, is a period of significance for the Hanoverians, or Windsors. George I died on June 11; George III was born on June 4; Queen Charlotte on June 7. George IV died on June 28. May 24 was Queen Victoria's birthday; her eldest son, Edward VII, was born on June 23 and died on May 5. George V was born on June 3; Queen Mary on May 28. They were married on June 6. The Duke of Windsor's birthday is June 23; Queen Elizabeth II's is April 21. Six coronations or accessions between the reigns of William IV and Queen Elizabeth II took place in May or June.

George V's horoscope showed clearly that he would be king, according to Cheiro. His would be a troubled reign, war clouds, unrest in England, bad trade conditions—and from 1928 to 1930, unfavorable personal indications. "A critical time and a period of deep anxiety for the whole Royal family, and for the British Empire. This will be a period when his Majesty will be particularly exposed to danger of illness and accidents of all kinds, especially those caused by or from the air." In November, 1928, George V was seriously ill; the illness lasted until the summer of 1930. There was pneumonia, dangerous inflammation of the lungs and bronchi.

The years 1927, 1928, 1929-32 were favorable neither for England nor for the royal family, except for the then Duke of York. Cheiro remarked: "In his case, it is remarkable that the regal sign of Jupiter increases its power as the years advance, which as I have explained, was also the case of his royal father, before there was any likelihood of his coming to the throne."

Of the then Prince of Wales, Cheiro said: "His astrological chart shows perplexing and baffling influences that most unquestionably point to changes likely to take place greatly affecting the throne of England. . . . The Prince of Wales in his signs parallels in a strange fashion his ancestral namesake, George, Prince of Wales, afterwards Regent. . . . His disregard of Court ceremonial caused estrangement from his father, George III; his restless mind found an outlet in travel . . . he had a wonderful knack of catching and holding popular love. . . . His relations with the fair sex to this day remain somewhat of a mystery. . . . The present Prince of Wales has piqued curiosity many times by rumours of marriages that have faded away into the air . . . it is well within the bounds of possibility, owing to the peculiar planetary influences to which he is subjected, that he will in the end fall a victim to a devastating love-affair. If he does, I predict that the Prince will give up everything, even the chance of being crowned, rather than lose the object of his affection."

For the years 1926-30 Cheiro predicted that adverse conditions would affect almost every country in the world. England, Germany, and Japan would suffer from frequent, devastating outbreaks of fire, explosions from apparently inexplicable causes, earthquakes, earth subsidences, tidal waves, storms, bombardments by thunderbolts and meteorites of unusual kinds. Disasters by sea, earthquakes, storms would cause loss of life and property in China and India; especially malefic influences would bring to China pestilence, floods, famine, and financial stringency. For India—serious failure of crops, riots, religious disturbances, general upheavals. For France—a series of financial crises, unrest, especially in the Army and Navy, plots, continual changes of government. England's trade would come almost to a standstill; exports would sink to the lowest, unemployment would rise to the highest-known level. Foreign affairs were as unpromising. There would be serious trouble in all Britain's colonies and possessions. India would soon be given her freedom, but "religious warfare will rend that country from end to end, until it becomes equally divided between Mohammedans and the followers of Buddha."

A dictator for Spain, the return to Palestine of the Jews, who would again be known as Israelis, in Britain votes for women and another queen to rule her are fulfilled predictions on the formidable list.

He was as well known in America as in Britain. While in Washington, he was asked by one of his clients to read the hand of her daughter. "I believe you are an impostor," she said, "but do your best—or worst." Cheiro predicted a brilliant—but short—life for the girl, who would marry in a few years a man of another nationality through which she would be in a position in an Eastern country equal to that of a

Modern Seers (I) 223

queen. The prophecy sounded preposterous enough to justify Mrs. Leiter's stricture of Cheiro. She was the wife of a Chicago millionaire; their daughter, Mary Leiter, later married Lord Curzon, became vicereine of India—and died while she was still a young woman.

When Mark Twain was in a hopeless financial position—his debts totaled $94,000 through the failure of the Charles L. Webster Company—Cheiro predicted that he would be rich when he was sixty-eight. The author saw no hope that Cheiro could be right, but on October 22, 1903, Twain signed a contract with Harper Brothers, which assured him an income of at least $100,000 annually.

In 1930, Cheiro made his home in Hollywood, where he retired from professional life, but not before the leading film stars of the day, among them Mary Pickford, Lillian Gish, Erich von Stroheim, and Irene Rich, had consulted him. One of his last predictions was the date and the way in which the famous film director Irving Thalberg (husband of Norma Shearer) would die.

Cheiro organized a school of metaphysics in Hollywood, where he taught his occult philosophy and methods of divination until he died, on October 8, 1936. According to a number of witnesses, all that day the stairs and corridors of his wonderful white house creaked and cracked under the tread of invisible feet, entering and leaving the room in which he lay. A grandfather clock at the foot of the stairs three times struck one o'clock. Cheiro died at 1 A.M. For many hours afterward, the scent of lilies of the valley and roses—his favorite flowers—filled the house, although not a bud or blossom of either plant was in the place at the time.

Since Cheiro's day, probably the most widely discussed and best-known prophecy is Mrs. Jeane Dixon's prediction of President Kennedy's assassination. Mrs. Dixon, who, with her husband, runs a real estate agency in Washington, D. C., has been able to "see ahead" since her childhood. She was told by a gypsy, when she was eight years old, that the lines in her hand indicated that she could become a great seer and mystic. "You have the gift of prophecy; you will see world wide changes," said the gypsy at parting, giving her a crystal ball.

By the time she was nine, people had begun consulting her. Marie Dressler asked if she should open a boardinghouse because she was getting nowhere as an actress. The child told her she would become a star. To Carole Lombard, Jeane said, "Don't travel by plane for the next six weeks." Carole Lombard replied that she was booked to fly in a few days on a war-bond promoting tour. Jeane so strongly urged her to change her booking and go by train or car that Carole Lombard tossed a coin to decide if she should follow Jeane's advice—"heads I cancel the flight, tails I let it stand." The coin's answer was "tails"; the plane crashed; Carole Lombard was killed.

The first warning of President Kennedy's assassination came to Jeane Dixon in 1952, when she was in St. Matthew's Cathedral, Washington. In a vision, she "saw" the date—1960—when a Democrat would be elected, to be assassinated while he was in office. His face was clearly visible to her; she particularly noticed his vivid blue eyes. In 1956 she mentioned this vision to Jack Anderson of *Parade,* who in his account of the interview with her published on May 13 said, "As for the 1960 election, Mrs. Dixon thinks it will be won by a Democrat. But he will be assassinated in office."

After his election, she saw black clouds looming over the White House, into which Kennedy's coffin was being carried. "If only he would wait eight years—for his own good," she said.

Three weeks before November 22, 1963, Mrs. Dixon was lunching with a friend, a well-known Washington society woman, Mrs. Harley Cope. Mrs. Dixon suddenly seemed in great distress; apropos of nothing, she said, "He's going to be shot," and answered Mrs. Cope's question on whom she was talking about, with: "Why, the President, of course."

Between that time and the day of the assassination Mrs. Dixon repeatedly told a number of well-known people of the tragedy which she felt was so close. She asked Kay Hall, daughter of Cleveland philanthropist Samuel Hall, who was a friend of the Kennedys, to warn the President of the danger. Miss Hall apparently relayed the message to Mrs. Alice Longworth (daughter of former President Theodore Roosevelt), but not to Kennedy.

On Tuesday of the fatal week Mrs. Dixon had a vision of the President being shot in the head; she called out, "The President has been shot." On Friday, the day of his death, the White House seemed to her to be shrouded in black. Mrs. Dixon said at breakfast time, "This is the day—this is the day; it has to happen." The name of the assassin, she thought, had two syllables and six letters, the first of which was *O*; then came an *s*. It ended with a "letter that went straight up." The name was Lee Oswald. There came, too, an impression of hands removing Lyndon Baines Johnson's name from the Vice Presidential office.

In 1944, Mrs. Dixon had foretold the time of the death of another U.S. President. Franklin Delano Roosevelt called her to the White House in November, 1944. "How long have I left?" he asked her. She told him: "Six months or less." Five months later, on April 12, 1945, he died in Warm Springs, Georgia.

On another occasion she had predicted to him that China would turn Communist, that after a period of unfriendliness the United States and Russia would become allies against China. The first part of the prophecy was fulfilled when China went Red on September 21, 1949. During her last visit to Roosevelt she told him that racial rioting would break out, increasing in violence. It would not end until 1980.

Years before, Jeane Dixon had foreseen Roosevelt's four victories. Her first prophecy concerning the White House was of the election of Herbert Hoover as President while she was at school. During the war she told Harry S. Truman, then Vice President, that he would become the country's leader and that he would have two periods of office. In January, 1948, contrary to general opinion, she said he would be reelected in

November. Later, in 1952, the Republicans would return to power under Dwight Eisenhower.

America was not the only country the fate of whose leaders Jeane Dixon foresaw. In 1945 she told Sir Winston Churchill, then on a visit to America, that he would be turned out of office by the voters; if he called an early election, he would be defeated—as he was in June of that year. Within six years he was back in power, as Mrs. Dixon foretold, which he held until his retirement in 1955. In 1962 she predicted to Russell Riley the time of Sir Winston's death—the end of 1964. He died in 1965, twenty-six days after the date Mrs. Dixon had given.

In 1956 she was asked to make a forecast of what lay ahead for Jawaharlal Nehru, who had been Prime Minister of India since 1947. Mrs. Dixon predicted that within eight years, he would be succeeded by a man whose name began with *S*. On May 27, 1964, he died; the name of his successor was Lal Bahadur Shastri. Mir Laik Ali would be the first Prime Minister of Hyderabad, she told him. Later he would be put in prison—from which he would be rescued. The events she forecast all happened in the following year. In June, 1947, she had foreseen that one of India's great figures, Mahatma Gandhi, would be murdered on January 3, 1948.

The subcontinent's politics figured in a prediction Mrs. Dixon made in 1946 at a reception given in Washington by Sir Girja Shankar Bajpai, agent-general for India. To a member of the Indian embassy, newly arrived in America, she foretold the partition of India, which would be announced, she said, as it was—on February 20, 1947. The official who consulted her would go over to Pakistan and prosper. That, too, came to pass. This forecast of the partition and its fulfillment caused a sensation when the newspapers reported that Lord Jellicoe, who was in Washington at the time, asked Mrs. Dixon to tell him how she had managed to do it.

Again, international affairs were the subject of a prophecy by Mrs. Dixon, this time in Russia. Joseph E. Davies, the former U.S. Ambassador to Moscow, asked her if she could see what lay ahead for Georgi Malenkov. She predicted that he would be replaced in under two years "by a man with an oval-shaped head, greenish eyes, wavy gray hair and a goatee beard." Davies commented that from her description the man wasn't a Russian type, that USSR premiers were not peacefully replaced: Either they died from natural causes, or they were shot. The man with the goatee beard, Jeane Dixon went on, would not be long in office; his successor would be short and bald-headed. This man would gain power in some way from the launching of what she described as "a silken ball into outer space, which would circle the globe and return to the U.S.S.R." Two years, less one month, later, Malenkov was "peacefully" replaced by Marshal Nikolai Bulganin, who was gray-haired and had greenish eyes and a goatee beard. In 1957, the first sputnik satellite was launched; through it Nikita Khrushchev gained kudos and power. In the following year Marshal Bulganin was deposed by this short, stout, bald-headed man. For 1962, Mrs. Dixon forecast a Russian spaceship flight to the moon. There would be a shake-up in the Kremlin in October, 1964.

Now and again the scope of her psychic powers has been challenged. On one occasion a doubter defied her to choose the winning ticket in a raffle for a car. She picked the right number—a 14,000 to 1 chance. Another time Bob Hope, with whom she was appearing on a television program, told her she could not possibly tell him his score at golf that afternoon or the number of strokes his partner (unnamed) had taken for the game. "You took ninety-two strokes, and President Eisenhower ninety-six," said Jeane Dixon. It was a bad moment for Bob; the figures of the round were a closely kept secret; if Eisenhower knew that Mrs. Dixon had given the exact scoring, he could hardly help concluding that she had been briefed by him (Hope). He had that part of the program cut off the tape.

In the summer of 1961 Mrs. Dixon foretold that Dag

Hammarskjöld would be killed in a "plane crash in mid-September." The date of the air accident in which he lost his life was September 18, 1961.

That autumn Mrs. Dixon predicted another tragedy. Marilyn Monroe, said Mrs. Dixon, would commit suicide "within the next year." Nine months later the film star took an overdose of sleeping pills.

On February 28, 1964, Jeane Dixon foresaw a great earthquake, which would bring devastation to the country "around Canada and Alaska," in the early part of 1965. The date of the earthquake in those parts was March 27, 1965.

War in the 1980's is among her long-term prophecies, a war which Asian and African nations, including Vietnam and Korea, will trigger off against Red China. The end of the papal reign will come "within this century," which ties in with St. Malachy's much earlier prediction of the fall of the Vatican. She sees the beginning of an era of peace in 1999.

15. Modern Seers (II)

If prophecy is the art, as some scientists think, of making contact through the deeper self with the collective unconscious, or the supreme mind, or whatever name you care to give to the field of force in which we live and move and have our being, then Edgar Cayce was a past master in that art. Born on March 18, 1877, on a farm near Hopkinsville, Kentucky, where he spent the first part of his life, he went to the local school, where it seems he learned little or nothing. He never got higher than the ninth grade, and that was the end of his formal education. Yet the psychic readings which he gave displayed not only prevision but also profound knowledge of medicine, geology, psychology, ancient and modern languages, and many other subjects which experts could not fault. These statements were made while Cayce was in a state of deep unconsciousness, as were most of his predictions which amazed and sometimes shocked Americans, who christened him "the sleeping prophet."

The sixth sense functioned to some extent in his waking life, in divinatory flashes and insight. But not until the reasoning mind was dormant did he seem to be in full contact with a source of inexhaustible power and knowledge, not bound by the laws of physical existence, beyond time and space.

He was about seven or eight years old when he had his first psychic experience—a vision of a bright light which filled the clearing in the wood where he was sitting. Out of the light a voice spoke: "Your prayers have been heard. What would you ask of me that I may give it to you?" Apparently neither startled nor surprised by what even then seemed to him a perfectly natural occurrence, the boy answered: "I'd like to be able to help other people, especially sick children—and to love my fellow-men."

The next day Cayce's mind was so full of his experience that he was less able than usual to concentrate on schoolwork. When the rest of his class left, he had to stay behind and write out 500 times the word "cabin," which he had misspelled.

So he began his homework late that evening, and he was tired, and it seemed to him that he could never do it, however hard he tried. His father had said that he would have to stay up until he had finished the scheduled tasks, so he went on plodding away. About eleven o'clock, long past his bedtime, as he was nodding over his books, he heard a voice, the voice which had spoken to him in his vision, saying over and over: "Sleep; we will help you." He slept; when he awoke, he found that he knew every word of the lesson he had tried to learn so long, so hard, and so unsuccessfully.

This was the moment and the manner in which Cayce's deeper mind first made that contact with the universal mind —or consciousness—which lasted, unbroken, for forty years, a unique example of the possibilities and potentialities offered to man through such a linkage.

Soon after the homework incident, Cayce was accidentally hit by a baseball. The semiconscious boy told his mother to poultice the base of his brain with a mixture of certain medicaments. The next morning all traces and effects of the injury had disappeared.

This was the first of the health readings for which he later became famous. Before he left school, he was suggesting remedies, while in semitrance condition, for friends' ailments which always produced results. He was about twenty-four years old when he lost his voice. Able to talk only in whispers, he had to give up his work as a salesman. Since none of the treatments recommended by a succession of doctors had any effect on the condition, he took a job in a photographer's darkroom, where it did not matter if his voice was normal or not. This was the situation when a healer, Al Layne, who was also a hypnotist, put Cayce to sleep, giving him the suggestion that his subconscious mind was able to look at his throat, see what was wrong, and suggest a remedy.

Cayce (or his subconscious) diagnosed the trouble as partial paralysis of the vocal cords, caused by nerve strain. It could be cured simply by suggesting that the body should increase the flow of blood to the affected part for a short time. Layne told Cayce to make this suggestion; as he did so, the throat reddened till it became a deep crimson. When, at Layne's instruction, Cayce gave the autohypnotic suggestion of normal blood flow, the flush faded. When Cayce woke up, he asked what had happened—in a normal voice.

Layne persuaded Cayce to try an experiment to discover if he could use this method to help other people back to health. Layne himself was the guinea pig; no doctor had been able to diagnose or to relieve an illness he had had for years. After putting Cayce to sleep, Al Layne gave him the suggestion that he would examine the body of Al Layne, discover what was wrong with it, and suggest remedies.

The sleeping Cayce described Layne's ailments and prescribed diet and medicaments, using medical terms of which in his waking state he had never even heard. There was not one harmful ingredient among the remedies suggested, and they worked.

A great deal of persuasion was necessary before Cayce would agree to use his powers regularly or professionally. Eventually he was convinced that through them he could be of service to many people in a unique way: In his own family, his wife's life and his son's sight had been saved by his health readings.

Doctors had said that his wife, Gertrude, who had been suffering from lung hemorrhages, could not survive another spasm. One of the medical men working on her case suggested that Cayce should give her a reading. The specialist, who listened to Cayce's trance suggestions for treatment, said it was the "most wonderful discourse on tuberculosis" he had ever heard but didn't see how the remedies prescribed would help her. But they did—and after they were taken, there was immediate improvement in his wife's condition—no more hemorrhages, eventually a complete cure.

His son, Hugh Lynn, when a child, was playing with a flashlight kit when the powder flared up in his eyes. Specialists, after examination of the boy, said that the sight of one eye was gone, the other so badly damaged that if it were not removed at once, his life would be endangered. Cayce said nothing must be done until he had taken a reading. Supervised by his wife, he went into a trance, during which he gave instructions that for fifteen days his son was to be kept in a darkened room, with frequently changed dressings of strong tannic acid solution on his eyes. The doctors, though they had said that the sight of one eye was gone and the other must be removed, protested that the solution would damage the delicate eye tissues—and had no answer when Cayce asked them if they were talking of the sightless eye or the eye which they said must be taken out. After twelve days of the treatment Cayce had prescribed, the dressings were finally taken off. All traces of the injury had disappeared; Hugh Lynn's eyes were in perfect condition. "Daddy, I can see," the boy said.

Records of the case histories of men and women treated by Cayce while in trance present an extraordinary picture of the cure of almost every disease known to medical science, including the so-called incurable diseases. He himself believed no disorder was incurable, if the primary cause could be found.

Again and again his health readings, which were one aspect of the manifestation of the power channeled through him, showed that this power was not limited by time or space. He saw ahead, predicting the course and outcome of

Modern Seers (II)

the illness, or he foresaw events in the lives of men and women or the future of a country or a nation.

In April, 1929, he predicted the Wall Street crash, a prophecy based on a dream about which a broker had consulted him. Cayce foresaw a panic in the money markets, not only in Wall Street, but a closing of boards in other centers. There would be a readjustment of actual specie; while these modifications were being made, higher and lower quotations would be made for a period of months; then would come the final debacle.

Six months later, on October 29, 1929, which is still known as Black Friday, the stock market virtually disintegrated. Wall Street in all its history had never known such a crash. Exchanges in many parts of the country were closed; the U.S. and many other countries went off the gold standard.

In June, 1931, Edgar Cayce was hoeing his garden. Suddenly he dropped his hoe and rushed into the house, where he locked himself into his study. When, some hours later, he reappeared, he explained that out in the garden he had had a vision of the approach of the Second World War, in which millions of men and women would die.

Many of his predictions were concerned with results of earth changes—appearance or disappearance of landmasses, earthquakes, volcanic eruptions. He saw the years between 1958 and 1998 as a period of intensive movement of and beneath the earth's crust. In the first part of this specified time, he said "there would be a change in the physical aspect of the west coast of America." The year 1964 was the year of the worst earthquake ever experienced in that area. According to a weekly science report, it moved mountains—by an average of 5 feet; it lifted some parts of the sea floor 50 feet. The entire North American continent was raised half an inch. Its repercussions were felt on coasts 3,000 miles away, where tidal waves 8 feet higher than normal were recorded. In Iran the land rose and fell like the sea as earthquake waves passed through it.

Cayce saw this great Alaskan upheaval as a curtain raiser

to more drastic destruction caused by earth changes later in this century. The sinking and rising of the sea floor of the Mediterranean would presage catastrophes in other parts of the world. Already the maritime disturbances have begun; there has been a subsidence of the eastern basin of Mare Nostrum, while the sea floor off Morocco has been raised by 3,300 feet.

As a result of the polar shift which, he said, is taking place, ice caps at the Poles would melt, climates all over the world would change, some countries would disappear under consequent inundations, and new continents would rise from the oceans. He forecast, among his schedule of world changes, that the "earth would be broken up in the western portion of America," as it was as a result of the great Alaskan earthquake, 1964; that "the greater portion of Japan would go into the sea," a prediction which seems to be working out. According to one geologist, "one volcanic area in Honshu has experienced 87,000 recordable quakes in a six-month period in 1965-66, with 8,000 of these strong enough to be felt." Nobichiko Obara, the eminent Japanese geologist, says that the Japanese archipelago is sinking steadily into the ocean.

During the forty-year period of global upheavals "the upper portions of Europe will be changed in the twinkling of an eye," and "land will appear off the east coast of America." In August, 1941, he said that most of Los Angeles, San Francisco, and New York would be destroyed during the forty-year period of earth changes.

These changes, which according to him, would result from the tilting of the earth's rotational axis, the beginning of which he timed for 1936, have been confirmed as eminently possible by leading geologists who have checked Cayce's reading on the subject. Apparently, under part of New York there is a fault, which could break under any increased strain; Los Angeles and San Francisco are in an earthquake-prone area.

The signal for the onset of the major devastations he foresaw will be violent eruptions of Vesuvius, on a much larger scale than the mild activity recorded recently.

Cayce, who constantly overstrained his energies, was warned by doctors and in trance by his own subliminal consciousness that he was killing himself by the number of health readings he insisted on giving. He refused or perhaps an inner compulsion made it impossible for him to take things more easily. Even so, however hard he worked—or overworked—he could not do more than dent the pile of requests for help which arrived by each post.

Too late, he went to a nursing home in Roanoke, Virginia, for a rest cure; by then he could neither sleep nor rest. At home again, he said, on New Year's Day, 1945: "I am to be healed on Friday, January 5." That he did not refer to a physical healing was realized by his family and friends. Friday, January 5, was the day of his funeral.

His memorial is the Association for Research and Enlightenment, which was founded by him in his lifetime and continues his uniquely important work at Virginia Beach, classifying, analyzing, and applying his readings, of which there were more than 15,000, dealing with the cure of disease, reincarnation, Atlantis, the future of the world and of its nations.

Only a few of the prophecies of many gifted modern seers are available as evidence of the workings of the sixth sense. Mostly the predictions relate to the personal affairs of the psychic's clients, whose names are never given without their permission, according to the ethical code of the profession.

Out of all the predictions made to the uncountable men and women who have consulted him during his thirty-odd years of practice as a clairvoyant, the doyen of British psychics, William S. King, can mention two—one of them because his client, Lady Dufferin and Ava, herself told the magazine *Nova,* in an interview, what Mr. King had prophesied to her. He had foretold when and where she would meet the man she would marry—and it happened exactly as he had said it would. The other client cannot now be embarrassed by mention of the consultation in which Mr. King described important developments in his career, which at the time he pooh-poohed, but which worked out as foreseen. He was David Lloyd George.

In the early summer of the year previous to the death of Labour Party leader Hugh Gaitskell—before there was any mention of his illness—Mr. King said to me, "Hugh Gaitskell will die early next year." Several months later, when Mr. Gaitskell's health deteriorated, I told Mr. King I hoped he was not going to be right. He answered: "I am, you know." In the following January Mr. Gaitskell died.

In *Woody,* a biography of his mother, also a noted clairvoyant, Maurice Woodruff says that two years before George V died, she told a friend—a Mrs. Perry, widow of a former president of the Royal Society of Arts—that the Prince of Wales would marry a commoner. When later, "Woody" (Mrs. Woodruff) had met Mrs. Simpson, she remarked: "She will marry the King of England."

Among predictions made by himself, Maurice Woodruff mentions his forecast of John Kennedy's election as President before he had even been nominated. On a visit to America, he was asked at a press interview to give the winner of the Kentucky Derby. He knew nothing of the race, had not even seen a list of probable starters; no name came to him, but he smelled a heavy flower scent. There were no floral decorations in the room, no women wearing perfume. "Rose Bowl," said the press when he described his impression, "will be the winner," and so it turned out. And, also in America, on the Bob Crane show just before the Presidential elections, Maurice Woodruff forecast that Lyndon Johnson would become President—adding for good measure that Cassius Clay would beat Sonny Liston.

In India, Professor Raman, editor of the *Astrological Magazine,* foretold the assassinations of Mahatma Gandhi and President Kennedy and the deaths of Jawaharlal Nehru and Lal Bahadur Shastri. Taking another glance ahead, he says that the association of the United Nations will end in 1972.

When the amateur psychic Cyril Macklin as a schoolboy foretold that England and Germany would be at war in 1939, his fellow pupils laughed at him. Only his headmaster believed him. Two years earlier, when the Kaiser abdicated, he had said that "another man would rule Germany later, who would raise hell." In 1927, when he saw a photograph of Hitler in a group, he pointed to him: "That is he." And he foretold the Nazi reign of power. In 1928 he had a vision of London in flames; he wrote down the names of the streets in the city which would be destroyed—a list which twenty-two years afterward proved only too accurate.

Sometime after war had broken out—in 1939, as he had foreseen—Mr. Macklin went to work in a big aircraft factory in southwest London. He had been there about ten months, when, sitting in the canteen with several factory inspectors, suddenly he felt faint. He heard what he describes as "a sound like an X-ray machine starting up." He saw the canteen disintegrate—chairs and tables smashed; blood and broken bodies. Mr. Macklin gave in his notice, leaving the factory just before a direct hit demolished the canteen, the machine shops, and an oil tank.

Next, he went to an Acton factory, which produced automobile components for tanks and trucks. There, becoming a shelter marshal, he was in charge of air-raid practices in the deep shelters. Resting in one of these, with his group, after an air-raid drill, he "saw" an aerial torpedo hit the roof of the machine shop, then drop, via the stairs, into the shelter, slicing off the legs of a woman sitting there. Mr. Macklin gave in his notice. Just after he left, an aerial torpedo hit the factory, then fell into the shelter, where it cut off a woman's legs.

He was getting ready to go on night shift at his next place of employment, a factory in the Wimbledon area, when a voice said to him, "Don't go tonight." Mr. Macklin, who does not argue with his premonitions, stayed at home. In the morning he found that the part of the factory in which he would have been working was not there.

His reputation as a prophet having preceded him to Hoover's factory, which was then given over to the production of aircraft parts, his fellow workers looked at him askance. So did his foreman when, on his first day at work, Cyril Macklin foretold that the factory would be bombed that night. "The first planes will miss the mark," he said. "They'll drop two or three bombs in a lane nearby. Then—by the way, have you got a coke dump?" The foreman nodded. "Two bombs will hit the coke dump. Another will drop just outside the canteen, but it won't explode."

The foreman indicated that if the raid did not take place according to Macklin's prediction, he could expect to find himself very shortly en route for the Isle of Man (where people accused of "spreading alarm and despondency" were sent during the war). Macklin did not make a trip to the island. That night, when the German raiders came, they dropped their bombs in the numbers and in the places he had predicted.

Future events, according to him, unfold in much the same pattern as Edgar Cayce described—world catastrophes, eruptions, submergences, subsidences of the earth's crust, wars, upheavals. After two more major wars will come peace and the establishment of a United States of the world, says Macklin.

16. What Lies Ahead?

Discussing the fulfillment of prophecy with Bishop Newton, Marshal Wade said all predictions were written after the event. The bishop answered that many prophecies beyond all doubt were made and recorded centuries before the event they foreshadowed materialized. "If that point could be proved to satisfaction," said the marshal, "there would be no argument against such plain matter of fact. It would certainly convince me, and would, I believe, be the readiest way to convince every reasonable man of the truth of revelation."

The marshal's conversation with the bishop took place long before the term "ESP" had been coined to describe the functioning of clairvoyance or precognition, long before science had begun to take an interest in these activities. Today the weight of evidence accumulated by parapsychological research could hardly fail to convince even a hardened skeptic such as the marshal probably was, of the existence of an "extra sense" in man which is not limited by time or space. Doubt, when satisfactory evidence is not forthcoming, is said to be "an essential mark of an active mind" but "positive rejection of reasonable proof is the sign either of stupidity or unreasoning prejudice."

According to the laws of the three-dimensional world which for so long have limited the range of our ideas and the outlook of science, prophecy (and all the other results of

ESP) can't happen. But demonstrably they do happen, and I think we shall be guilty of "unreasoning prejudice" if we deny that ESP exists and that prophecies are fulfilled.

The reason that scientists for so long refused to recognize the functioning of ESP in any way is probably due to the fact that because of its nature, it is not easy to produce what they consider "acceptable evidence" of its validity. No manifestation of the sixth sense can be turned on as a tap is turned on. Even the professional psychic cannot be certain of "seeing" what lies ahead for his or her client. And one does not know one is going to prophesy as certainly, for instance, as one knows one is going to sneeze.

ESP is like the wind which "bloweth as it listeth." Sporadic and spontaneous, to produce it under laboratory conditions is next to impossible, although this has been done, and research teams are working now on the possibility of uncovering factors which would bring the faculty under some sort of control. If this could be done, we should be nearer to understanding something of its nature and to discovering the hows and whys of its working.

Or perhaps "rediscovering" is the better word. The prophets of Egypt or Israel and other ancient nations had evolved techniques for directing the vision of the "third eye" into the future. They knew that the human mind must be tuned or set to a certain pitch before it can register impressions from other dimensions, just as radio or television receivers today must be tuned in to certain wavelengths. By meditation and withdrawal for a period from the material world, they cut down the "interference" of the conscious mind; this has always been accepted as essential for successful contact with the level beyond the range of the five senses. This is why messages and visions so often manifest during sleep; the body is relaxed and the surface mind stilled.

Although this condition is recognized as the cardinal prerequisite to the functioning of precognition, we are no nearer to discovering what prophecy is or how it works, or any clue to its source. And why should some people be able to see into the future while others have no idea what the next moment will bring? All through human history, some men and women have had "the sight"; sometimes they were, as in the case of the Sibyls or the shamans, an elite within their nation. Not just anyone who had made a few predictions ranked as a seer; in some countries trial by ordeal established if the claimant was a true prophet or not. The Eskimo candidate was submerged for a long period in icy water; the North American Indians kept their would-be soothsayers in a cubiclelike construction, filled with steam from water poured on hot rocks until the grueling heat made them almost unconscious.

One of the scientists who are trying to find an answer to the questions posed by prophecy and ESP generally, Benson Herbert, MA, has constructed at his Paraphysical Laboratory at Downton, Wiltshire, an apparatus registering data concerned with what he calls the specious present. The concept of specious present supposes that the division between past and future is not, Mr. Herbert says, "an infinitely small point of time, but has a finite extension, which diminishes in proportion to the extent the conscious attention is tied up with external events." It may be possible to establish, he thinks, by controlled experiment that when the specious present interval is longer than the reaction time of the subject (in his experiments this is measured before operations are begun), the subject can react to an event (in this case the sound of a Geiger counter) before this sound is heard and registered by an independent recording device. This would constitute precognition of a limited type—but still, precognition.

During sleep, when the consciousness is not preoccupied with objective happenings, Mr. Benson suggests that the specious present interval is increased, so that we often "see" events of the coming day—as anyone who keeps a record of dreams can prove. In trance, when consciousness of the physical world practically ceases, the interval may expand so that occurrences weeks, months, or years ahead could be foreseen.

So, according to modern theories, the functioning of the precognitive faculty (and all other ESP activities) depends on the degree in which conscious attention is withdrawn from the outer world. It is rather as if one shifted a car's gear into neutral so that the engine could freewheel. Ancient teachings said the same thing, of course, in other words. This is where we came in. . . .

In different terms the findings of ESP research and their implications repeat the doctrines of the illuminati through the ages. These men taught that the world of form was an illusion built up by the false witness of the physical senses; scientists working in ESP research today are echoing the dicta of the mystics. "Scholars," says Dr. Louisa Rhine, in *Hidden Channels of the Mind,* "who are trying to comprehend the universe, have recognized that back of the world as we perceive it must be a reality quite different from the psychological concept of it with which we are familiar. The implications of PSI experiences fit in with the idea of a less limited reality, and they add to the data of observation. The meaning could be that the reality glimpsed through PSI is a truer representation than the one the senses picture."

Science is showing that time and space are meaningless concepts created by the human mind, which for so long has been in bondage to the idea of three dimensions, on the strength of the apparently irrefutable evidence of the physical sense. The invention of the telephone has helped undermine the hitherto solid foundation of the principle that time and space are basic realities, the framework of everything we experience. At this moment, anyone in this country (with access to a telephone and the money to pay for the call) could speak to a subscriber in the farthest part of the globe—say, Tokyo—a conversation which would take no more time than if both parties were talking to each other in the same room. If time and space existed in the way we have been accustomed to consider, then the call would occupy time relative to the distance involved.

And speed plays strange tricks with time, as we know it.

As air travel gets faster and faster, we may find ourselves not only arriving at our destination before we started, but on a global trip meet ourselves, so to speak, coming back. . . .

Investigations of prophecy and other ESP manifestations seem to reveal an *Alice in Wonderland* world, a world in which the events of the physical level have already taken place in another dimension. Where does that leave us? Are we, as Omar Khayyám put it in the *Rubáiyát,* enmeshed in predestination, following a set course, as is a planet in orbit or a train scheduled to run between certain stations? Or have we free will; is it possible—somehow—to avert foreseen disasters?

Opinions differ widely on the subject; instances are brought forward in support of each point of view. Examples often quoted by believers in predestination are the circumstances of the death of Aeschylus, the Greek tragic poet, of Michael Scot, astrologer and confidant of Frederick II, and of a Florentine astrologer, Franciscus Junctinus.

Aeschylus' stars foretold that the cause of his death at a certain time would be the falling of some object on his head. To cheat fate, the poet arranged to spend the danger period in the desert. As he sat on an empty expanse of sand, under an empty blue sky, a bird of prey, apparently mistaking his bald head for a stone, dropped on it a turtle, to break its shell. Not the turtle shell, but Aeschylus' skull, was cracked, and the prophecy was fulfilled.

Michael Scot, who predicted much the same ending for himself from his horoscope (which he had cast), took all possible precautions to keep out of the way of falling rocks, which the stars warned would destroy him. While at prayer in a cathedral, a loose stone fell from the roof onto his head, killing him instantly.

As for Franciscus Junctinus, who had foretold that he would have a violent death, he protected himself from all foreseeable fatalities during the bad aspect shown in his horoscope. At the exact hour of peak danger, while sitting securely—as he thought—in his peaceful library, an avalanche of heavy books inexplicably fell on him. And so he died.

On the other side of the fence are endless instances of disasters avoided, warnings to cancel a trip in airplane, train, ship, bus, which were taken by the would-be traveler, who so escaped involvement in an accident, probably of a fatal nature.

Dr. Louisa Rhine tells the story of a mother who dreamed that a heavy ornamental chandelier which hung in the next room over the baby's cot crashed down and killed the child. In her dream, while she and her husband were standing in the wreckage, she heard rain beating on the windowpane and the wind blowing. The time by a clock in the room was four thirty-five, she noticed.

During the night, both she and her husband awoke. He said, when she told him of her dream, that she had been having a nightmare, advised her to go to sleep and forget it. He was soon asleep again, but she was too frightened by her dream even to drowse. Presently she went into the nursery, picked up the child, and carried her into the bedroom. As she passed the window, she saw that a full moon was presiding over an unclouded sky—which was so different from the weather of her vision that she felt her husband had been right in dismissing it as a nightmare. Nevertheless, she kept the baby with her. About two hours later both she and her husband were awakened by a crash reverberating from the next room. In the cot in the nursery, they found the chandelier; it had fallen just where the baby would have been lying. They looked at the clock; the hands stood at four thirty-five. And as they went back into their own room, they heard rain beating on the window and wind howling around the house.

During the First World War a woman was notified by the company in which her husband was employed as a ship's engineer that because he had been at sea for some time, she could meet him in Philadelphia. The night before his ship was due to dock, she dreamed that it came in, unloaded, reloaded, and sailed for India without her knowing. About thirty hours from India, a submarine attacked and sank the ship. Her husband was the only casualty.

The woman got to the docks just as the ship was tying up. As soon as the gangway was down, she raced to her husband, who was on deck, crying hysterically, "Don't go, don't go, the ship is going down." Her husband, impressed with her certainty of disaster ahead, managed to get the company's permission to leave the ship—which was torpedoed and sunk on the way to India. The crew was eventually picked up after drifting around on a raft for sixteen days.

Sometimes apparently a foreseen disaster can be avoided; sometimes all efforts to escape it are useless. And then there are the cases in which a prophecy was ignored; into which category would it have fallen? Would President Kennedy be alive today if he had canceled his trip to Dallas? On May 23, 1934, a Spanish seer, Tomás Menes, predicted that Chancellor Engelbert Dolfuss of Austria would die violently within three months. On July 25 a band of Nazis set upon Dolfuss at a Cabinet meeting and assassinated him. What would have happened if Dolfuss had been able to take a three months' holiday out of his country? No answer can be given to such questions as yet, but as our knowledge of the workings of precognition grows, through research and expansion of consciousness, no doubt we shall come to understand to some extent at any rate why prophecy seems to have two faces.

Many theories have been put forward as solutions of these problems of prophecy. The kahunas, priests of the ancient religion of Huna in Hawaii, which Max Freedom Long has worked for so many years to rediscover, taught that the future jelled up to a certain point; beyond that point it existed as a blueprint which could be altered. Edgar Cayce thought that by prayer and the pruning of faults in individual or in nation, disasters could be circumvented.

Dr. W. H. C. Tenhaeff, director of the Parapsychological Institute of the State University of Utrecht, points out in his book *De Voorschouw* that there are indications that every man knows his own future in his deepest self. He adds: "The fact that on the whole we know so little of this is explained with the help of Bergson's observations on the curbing functions of the brain"—in other words, the inhibiting action of the conscious mind.

And if—and when—we learn to deal with the blocking action of the conscious mind, so that we can foresee something of what lies ahead for us, will that help us? Dr. Louisa Rhine's answer is that: "If the precognitive ability is developed and directed, as in time it is reasonable to expect it will be, its operation, even on a limited basis, could obviously be of untold value to humanity. . . . From present indications, if imperfect ESP impressions, especially those suggesting danger ahead, could be clarified, intelligent preventive action could follow to the untold advantage of mankind."

But precognition is only of "untold value" if we *are* able to avert the disasters it foresees. Apparently, from ESP experiments emerge hints that this is so. These hints, Dr. Rhine says, "do not suggest a fixed and immutable future; at least not on the practical level. While the universe is firm and not subject to change by human will, the little doings of man glimmer and shift against this stable background and in some manner still inexplicable as it seems contradictory, his tiny will seems upon occasion to be able to defend him and his own against dangers still hidden in the future."

Once again it seems the findings of parapsychology are echoing the teachings of the great initiates, the Magi, concerning predestination. They did not believe in blind fate; man was not a mere cog in the wheels of the universe, nor was predestination a canon of the earlier religions. In each life, the Magi said, certain ordeals, or tests, must be undergone; only through them could human will, intelligence, and character be formed and progress made. But if these tests were foreseen, their purpose recognized, the weakness they were designed to eliminate strengthened, the ordeal would become unnecessary and could be avoided.

Thoth, the great teacher and father of Magism, whom the

Greeks called Hermes Trismegistus, the thrice great, was believed to have taught that: "Fatality is the chain of cause and effect in the order established by Supreme Reason . . . but will is the direction of the forces of the mind in order to reconcile the liberty of the individual with the necessity of things. Action born of the union of mind and will makes fate itself work for the fulfillment of the good or evil desires of the man who knows what he wants, and wants what he knows." And he also said: "Fortunate is the man who knows how to read the signs of the times, for that man shall escape many misfortunes, or at least be prepared to withstand the blow."

Three thousand years later, Origen, the great Christian writer of the third century, paraphrased the Hermetic teaching. "Just as the power of the human will is not rendered useless because of God's foreknowledge of the acts that will be ours in the future, even so the celestial signs by which we may be initiated into the foretelling of that future are not a declaration of loss of freewill. Occult influences demonstrate a tendency, but do not submit us to blind fate. The sky is like an open book in which are written the signs of the past, present and future . . . it is the book of universal life . . . it presents the series of tests which composes the circle of each individual existence. . . ."

In the antiphonal chorus are the voices of Iamblichus, Ptolemy, Francis Bacon, Roger Bacon. Iamblichus defended astrology against the stigma of fatalism; Francis Bacon wrote: "There is no fatal necessity in the stars, and this the more prudent astrologers have constantly allowed." Roger Bacon's opinion, based on Ptolemy's writings, was that an astrologer should not "give any particular and fixed judgment and one sufficing in individual cases; but that his judgment should be a general one, and a mean between what is necessary and what is impossible, and the astrologer is not able in all cases to give a final judgment."

Ptolemy says in his *Centiloquy:* "A skillful person acquainted with the nature of the stars, is enabled to avert many of their effects and to prepare himself for those effects before they arrive."

It seems that illuminati, philosophers, and parapsychologists believe that prophecy can help us avoid the "pitfall and the gin" besetting our life's path. If that is so, it can indeed be of "untold value," but to act as an alarm signal is not its only purpose or, indeed, in some ways its more important purpose. Recognition of its existence reveals possibilities beyond the range of present vision. We may not yet understand why precognition need not imply predestination; the understanding which matters most to all of us is prophecy's implication that the human spirit is not imprisoned in the limited world of the five senses. Prophecy, in assuring us that within us is a power to transcend space and time—which, being independent of the physical vehicle, would logically survive it—makes us free of a universe, as yet uncharted and uncertain, expanding with our expanding consciousness.

The solution to the riddle of precognition lies in the depths of the unconscious. Since we are told that the universe exists in the mind of man, searching there not only may we find an answer to the paradox of prophecy, but we may also uncover a measure of the infinite mysteries of that universe.

"We live in a revolutionary age," said Emerson, "when man is coming back to consciousness."

Index

Abdul-Hamid, Sultan, 183-84
Abercrombie, Dr., 207
Aberfan disaster, 190
Abraham the Patriarch, 78
Abramelin the Mage, 173
Adrian, Emperor, 154
Adrian IV, Pope, 92
Aedd the Great, 54
Aeschylus, 243
Agassiz, Louis, 202-3
Agnell, Thomas, 150-51
Agrippina, 35-36
Ailly, Pierre d', 103
Al Hokim, 79
Alchemy, 147, 148
Alençon, Duc d', 98
Alexander III, King, 140
Alexander IV, Pope, 92
Alexander the Great, 24, 27, 28, 77, 79
Alexandra, Queen, 219
Alexandria, Egypt, 23
Alfonso XII, King, 181
Alfred, King, 65
Ali, Mir Laik, 226
Allen, Richard H., 80
Allen, Robert, 156
Almanacs, 143-44, 157
Altan Khan, 69
Amenemhet, 19
Amenemope, 20
Ameni the Triumphant, 20
Amon, 20, 21
Anderson, Jack, 224
Annals of the Bamboo Books, 83
Annals of China (Allen), 80
Antiquitates (Muratori), 30
Anwari, 79
Apollonius, 32-35, 42-43
Aquinas, St. Thomas, 93
Aradia, 161
Archias, 47

Ariston, 52
Arlette (mother of William the Conqueror), 206-7
Armada, Spanish, 146-47
Arras, Treaty of (1435), 98
Arthur, King, 64
Arundells, Sir John, 162-63
Ascletarion, 32
Ashurbanipal, 16
Aspelta, 21
Association for Research and Enlightenment, 235
Astrology and astrologers, 11, 15, 24, 27-28, 30-32, 37, 38, 52-53, 76-87, 103, 112, 113, 128, 143-60, 247
Astronomical Predictions (Lilly), 114
Astronomy (Capistrano), 158
Atlantis, 12, 235
Aubrey, John, 149
Augury, 56, 82; in ancient Rome, 25-38
Augustine, St., 13
Augustus, Emperor, 27-30, 36, 37
Avicenna (Ibn Sina), 79
Avignon, Marie d', 95
Aztecs, 84-87

Babylon, 79
Bacon, Francis, 247
Bacon, Roger, 144, 247
Bailly, Jean Sylvain, 105, 106
Bajpai, Sir Girja Shankar, 226
Balbus, Cornelius, 26
Balincourt, Commander, 219
Balor, 62
Bancroft, Hubert H., 96
Barbillius, 35-36
Bardic Triads, 54
Barrett, Arabella, 191
Battus, 47
Baudricourt, Robert de, 96

Index

Beachy, Hill, 193–94
Beasley, Master, 166, **167**
Beaulieu, Francis, 182
Beauregard, M., 12
Bedford, Duke of, 98
Bell, Sir Charles, 68
Bellingham, John, 207, **208**
Benedict XIV, Pope, 94
Benedict XV, Pope, 93
Bergson, Henri, 246
Bernard, St., 90, 91
Berndt-Hollsten, Herr, **192**
Berosus, 77–78
Beverley, Abbot of, 168
Bismarck (German warship), 178
Black Book of Carmarthen, The, 63
Blackburne, Archdeacon, 162
Blackwood's Magazine, 169
Blanket curse, 186–88
Boadicea, 57
Boeotia oracle, 50–52
Bone divining, 56
Book of the Dead, 173, 201
Borman, Walter, 106, 214–15
Boulain-Villiers, Perceval de, 96
Brahan Seer. *See* Fiossaiche, Coinneach Odhar
Brahe, Tycho, 157–58
Bremen, SS, 177, 178
Brewster, Sir David, 81
Bridget, St., 61
Brihtwold, Bishop, 149
Brinsley, John, 112
Broku, Colin, 182
Browning, Elizabeth Barrett, **191**
Browning, Robert, 191
Brune, Charles Prideaux, 207
Brunswick, Duke of, 185
Brunswick Blue Drop Diamond, curse of, 185
Brutus, Decimus, 26
Buddha, 69
Budge, Sir Ernest Wallis, 11, 78, 173, 200–1
Bulganin, Nikolai, 227
Burke, Sir Bernard, 141

Cadwallader, 64
Cadwallo, 64
Caesar, Julius, 25–27, 58, 59
Cagliostro, Alessandro di, 109–11
Calcer, 63
Calendars, 143–44
Caligula, Emperor, 32, 36, 60
Calpurnia, 26
Cambrensis, Giraldus, 151
Cambyses, 22, 79
Campbell, Matthew, 132
Carlotta, Queen, 180
Carnarvon, Lord, 173

Carrel, Alexis, **7**
Cassius, 26, 27
Cassius, Dio, 27, **33**
Catholicus, 91
Cayce, Edgar, 229–35, 238, **245**
Cayce, Gertrude, 231–32
Cayce, Hugh Lynn, 232
Cazotte, Jacques, 103–9, **111**
Celsus, Archbishop, 89
Celts, 55
Centiloquy (Ptolemy), 247
Centuries (Nostradamus), 117–18, 120, 121
Chabot de Jarnac, Guy, 119
Chaldaeans, 11, 77, 78, 84
Chamfort, Sébastien Roch Nicolas, 104, 106
Chapman, John, 198–200
Charles I, King, 100, 113, 153–54, 155, 168, 169
Charles II, King, 100, 154–55, 168
Charles IX, King, 122
Charles Edward, Prince, 188
Charlotte, Queen, 220
Chaucer, Geoffrey, 144
Chauvigny, 128
Chechepetresonbu, 15
Cheiro (Count Louis Hamon), 218–23
Cheops, 18–19
Chephron, 19
Chilon, 48
Ch'in Shih Huang-ti, 82–83
China, astrology in, 80–83
Chisholm of Chisholm, 137
Christian Fathers, 13, 43
Chueni, 81
Churchill, Sir Winston S., 186, **226**
Cicero, 40, 78
Ciparis, August, 191
Claudius, Emperor, 35–36
Clay, Cassius, 236
Clement XII, Pope, 94
Clement XIII, Pope, 92–93
Clement XIV, Pope, 93
Clement of Alexandria, 13, **54**
Clerc, Fernand, 191
Clifford, Thomas, 188
Collection of Mexico, 87
Columba, St., 61
Condorcet, Marquis de, 104, **106**
Confucius, 83
Congan, Abbot, 90
Conscious mind, 189
Constantine, Emperor, 30, **64**
Cope, Mrs. Harley, 224
Costaz, 12
Cotter, Sir James, 211
Cotter, Tommy, 210–11
Cowley, Abraham, 154–55
Crane, Bob, 236

Index

Crewe, Sir John, 100
Croesus, King of Lydia, 40, 43–45
Cromwell, Oliver, 114, 124–25, 158, 169
Crookes, Sir William, 172
Crowley, Aleister, 185
Cumberland, Duke of, 185
Cuneiform Inscriptions of Western Asia (Rawlinson), 201
Curses, fulfillment of, 171–88
Curthose, Robert, 65, 150
Curzon, Lord, 223
Cymry, 54, 63
Cyprian, St., 13
Cypros, 61
Cyrus the Persian, 45

Dalai Lama, 68, 69, 72
Dalgleish, Michael, 186
Danes, 64
Darcy, Lord, 166, 167
Darius, Emperor, 79
David of Scotland, King, 89–90
David-Neel, Alexandra, 72–74
Davidson, Duncan, 139
Davies, Joseph E., 226–27
Déchelette, Joseph, 55
Dedi, 18–19
Dee, Arthur, 147
Dee, John, 143, 144–49
Dee, Rowland, 144
Deleuze, Dr., 106
Delphic oracle, 28, 34, 36, 38, 39, 40–43, 44–49, 92
Demonologie (Home), 154
Demys, Kyril, 40
Derwentwater family, curse of, 187–88
Deveria, 13
Digby, Sir Everard, 147
Diocletian, Emperor, 58
Divination, 144, 154; in ancient Egypt, 11–24
Dixon, Jeane, 223–28
Dodecapylon, 37
Dodona oracle, 39, 49–50
Dolfuss, Engelbert, 245
Domitian, Emperor, 32–33, 34
Drake, Sir Francis, 146
Dreams, 189–208
Drepung, 70
Dressler, Marie, 224
Druids and Druidism, 27, 54–67
Dubthach, 61–62
Dudley, Robert, 145
Duncan, Isadora, 195
Dyneis, Jonka, 170

Eachtach, 62
Edric, 65

Edward, Prince of Wales, 221, 236
Edward I (the Confessor), 65, 100, 152
Edward VI, King, 144, 148, 156, 168
Edward VII, King, 219, 220
Egypt, divination in ancient, 11–24
Eisenhower, Dwight D., 226, 227
Eleanor of Aquitaine, Queen, 150–51
Eleusinian mysteries, 35
Elizabeth, Empress, 180
Elizabeth I, Queen, 125–26, 143, 145–46, 148
Elizabeth II, Queen, 221
Emerson, Ralph Waldo, 248
England, 63
Epigenes, 78
Erotomania (Ferrand), 154
Erskine of Mar, 142
Ethelred, King, 65
Ethnea, 62
Extrasensory perception (ESP), 239–48
Ezekiel, 22, 23

Fairfax, General, 113
Fairley, Peter, 190
Faldo, Goodwife, 147, 149
Falkland, Lord, 154
Fals, Willem, 182
Family curse, 186–88
Figulus, Nigidius, 27, 28
Fiossaiche, Coinneach Odhar (Brahan Seer), 130–40, 206, 212
Fisher, Thomas, 207
Flodden Field, Battle of, 153
Florinville, Seigneur de, 116
Fohi, 81
Forman, Simon, 113
Formigny, Battle of (1439), 98
Francis, James, 142
François II, King, 122
Frankel, Samuel, 182
Franz Ferdinand, Archduke, 174, 176, 181
Franz Josef, Emperor, 179, 181
Frederick II, 243
Frederick William, Duke, 185
Freeman, Sir Ralph, 155
French Revolution, 67, 100, 118, 122–24; prophecies of, 103–11
Friedland, Duchess of, 157
Frobisher, Martin, 146
Frosch, Karl, 212, 213, 214, 215
Frosch, Frau Karl, 212, 215
Fu Yue, 82

Galba, Emperor, 32, 34, 36, 37
Gandhi, Mahatma, 226, 236
Gauric, 118–19
Gebelin, Antoine Comte de, 109
Genedow, Bertrand, 66

Index 252

Genghis Khan, 79–80
Genlis, Comtesse de, 106
Geoffrey of Monmouth, 64
George, Prince of Wales, 221
George I, King, 187–88, 220
George III, King, 159–60, 220
George IV, King, 142, 220
George V, King, 220, 221
Gish, Lillian, 223
Giuliaro, Salvator, curse of, 178–79
Gladstone, William, 200
Gneisenau (German warship), 177
Godwin, Earl of, 65
Göring, Hermann, 177
Graham, Sir Robert, 153
Gramont, Duchess de, 103, 105, 106
Grant, Admiral, 209
Grant of Grant, 137
Grasdot, Jérôme, 122
Great Plague, 114–15, 122, 126, 157–58
Gregory XVI, Pope, 93
Gundavala, Shashikant, 193
Gunpowder Plot, 66
Gustavus Adolphus, King, 145, 158
Gwyddonaid, 54

Hadrian, Emperor, 37–38
Halfpenny, Eric, 186
Hall, Kay, 225
Hall, Samuel, 225
Hammarskjöld, Dag, 228
Hamon, Count Louis. *See* Cheiro
Hapsburg dynasty, curse of, 179–81
Har-dedef, Prince, 18
Hardicanute, 65
Hardy, Sir Alister C., 8
Harmachis-Chepera Re-Tenu, 16
Harold, King, 149
Hatshepsut, Queen, 20
Hawkins, John, 146
Hemming, James, 159–60
Henri of Navarre, 122
Henrietta Maria, Queen, 169
Henry II, King, 118, 119, 120, 121, 150–51
Henry III, King, 121
Henry IV, King, 152
Henry VII, King, 101–2
Henry VIII, King, 66, 144, 165
Heraclitus, 46
Herbert, Benson, 241
Hermes Trismegistus. *See* Thoth
Hermon, 11
Hermopolis, 22
Herod Agrippa, 60–61
Herodotus, 44
Hi, Prince, 81
Hidden Channels of the Mind (Rhine), 194, 242

Hilprecht, Hermann, 203–5
Himmler, Heinrich, 177
Hippolytus, 30, 54
Hirshfeld, Tibor, 176
History of the Church of Scotland (Spottiswood), 140
History of the Pacific States of America (Bancroft), 86
Hitler, Adolf, 127, 128, 177, 237
Ho, Prince, 81
Homer, 27, 39
Homer, Elizabeth, 162
Hoover, Herbert C., 225
Hope, Bob, 227
Hope, Lord Francis, 182
Hope, Thomas, 182
Hope Diamond, curse of, 181–84
Horoscope, The (Pearce), 80
Horoscopes, 11, 28, 36, 52–53, 86, 113, 128, 145, 157, 159, 220, 221, 243
Horus, 12
Howard, David, 193
Huang-ti, 82
Hubbard, David, 193
Humphreys, John, 113

I Ching, 82, 83
Iamblichus, 247
Imouthes (Imhotep), 21
India, astrology in, 11
Indian Monarchy (Torquemada), 85
Innocent, Pope, 89
Ireland, 63
Isis, 17

James I, King, 66, 147, 148–49, 152–53, 157, 168, 169
James II, King, 100, 101, 156
James IV, King, 153
James VI, King, 126
Jeans, Sir James, 8
Jellicoe, Lord, 226
Jerome, St., 13
Jerusalem, 37–38
Jesus Christ, 15–16, 29, 30, 79, 123
Jewish Encyclopaedia, 78
Joan of Arc, 95–99
John I, King, 151
John XXIII, Pope, 94
John Chrysostom, St., 13
John of Capistrano, 158
John of Tuscany, Archduke, 180
Johnson, Lyndon Baines, 225, 236
Joseph (husband of Mary), 13
Journey to Lhasa (David-Neel), 72
Julian, Emperor, 38
Junctinus, Franciscus, 243–44
Jung, Carl G., 83
Justin Martyr, 13

Index 253

Kanitovsky, Prince, 182–83
Karmashar oracle, 70, 71
Karnak, Egypt, 22
Karolyi, Countess, 179
Kelly, Edward, 146, 147–48
Kennedy, John F., 224–25, 236, 245
Kepler, Johannes, 145, 156–57
Khayyám, Omar, 243
Khrushchev, Nikita, 227
King, William S., 235–36
Kitchener, Lord, 219
Königsmark, Count Philipp Christoph von, 220
Krieger, Joseph, 212, 213, 214, 215
Kublai Khan, 80

La Harpe, Jean de, 103, 105, 106, 107
Laduc, Lorena, 183
Laing, Robert, 212–15
Lamballe, Princess de, 110–11, 182
Lampridius, 57
Lao-tse, 82
Lathyrus, Ptolemy, 22
Layne, Al, 231
Leiter, Mary, 223
Lenormant, François, 12, 14
Leo X, Pope, 118
Leo XIII, Pope, 93
Leo XIV, Pope, 94–95
Levitation, 148
Li, King, 82
Lilly, William, 112–15, 166
Lincoln, Abraham, 198
Lindsay, Colonel, 158
Liston, Sonny, 236
Lloyd George, David, 236
Lombard, Carole, 224
London Fire of 1666, 112, 114, 126
Long, Max Freedom, 245
Longworth, Alice, 225
Louis XIV, King, 105, 106, 109–10, 181, 182
Louis XV, King, 182
Louis XVI, King, 123, 124, 182
Louis the Fat, King, 67
Lowry, D. C., 193, 194
Ludwig of Bavaria, King, 180
Ludwig of Trani, Count, 180
Lullingstone, Mr., 134
Lumley, Henry, 187

Macaulay, Thomas Babington, 46
MacCuilenon, Cormac, 88
Macedonia, 24
Mackenzie, Caroline, 139
Mackenzie, Francis Humberston. *See* Seaforth, Lord
Mackenzie, Sir Hector, 137

Mackenzie, Mary Frederica Elizabeth (Lady Hood), 138–39
Mackineely, 62
Macklin, Cyril, 237–38
MacLeod of Ramsey, 138
Magi, and Magism, 34, 79, 109, 246
Magic and magicians, 13, 14, 15
Magruder, Lloyd, 193–94
Magus' formulas, curse of, 185–86
Maithgen, 61–62
Malenkov, Georgi, 227
Malesherbes, Chrétien Guillaume de Lamoignon de, 104, 105, 106
Mankind, Their Origin and Destiny (Hadrian), 37
Mannerheim, Carl Gustav Emil von, 215–18
Manuel, Pierre Louis, 110
Mar, Earl of, 141–42
Marcellinus, Ammianus, 38
March, Lord, 140
Maria Feodorovna, Grand Duchess, 107, 108
Marie Antoinette, Queen, 106, 110, 123, 182
Mary, Queen, 221
Mary Queen of Scots, 146
Mary Tudor, Queen, 145, 168
Matheson, Alexander, 134
Matilda, Archduchess, 180
Matthias, Emperor, 157
Maximilian, Emperor, 165, 180
Mayas, 84
McClelland, George B., 197–98
McLachlan, Captain, 209
McLean, Edward, 184
McLean, Vinson, 184
Medici, Lorenzo de', 118
Médicis, Catherine de, 109, 118, 119, 120, 122, 124
Mehitousket, 21
Mela, Pomponius, 55
Memoirs (Welwood), 154
Memoirs of Marshal Mannerheim, 215
Memphis, Egypt, 22, 23
Menes, 23
Menes, Tomás, 245
Mercator, Gerardus, 144
Merlin, 59, 63–67, 95, 143
Merlinus Anglicus Junior (Lilly), 113
Meskhent, 17, 19
Mexico, astrology in, 84–87
Milan, Duke of, 96
Milarepa, Jetsun, 74–76
Mind control, 74
Mohammed the Prophet, 79
Monarchy and No Monarchy (Lilly), 114
Monk of Padua, 94–95

Monroe, Marilyn, 228
Montbrison, Comte, 107
Montezuma, 85–87
Montgomery, Comte Gabriel de, 121–22
Montharides, 183
Mummy curse, 173–74
Muratori, Ludovico, 30
Mussolini, Benito, 127
Mycerinus, 19
Mysticism and mystics, 15, 71–76

Nachung oracle, 70–71
Napoleon I, Emperor, 93, 111, 126–27, 128
Napoleon III, Emperor, 180
Naville, Édouard, 12
Neanthes, 52
Nebuchadnezzar, 23
Nectanebo, 23–24
Nefer-Rohu, 19–20
Nehru, Jawaharlal, 226, 236
Nekhebet, 17
Nephthys, 17
Nero, Emperor, 31, 35, 36–37
Nerva, Emperor, 33
Newton, Bishop, 239
Nezahualcoyotl (Nazahualpilli), 85–86
Nicolai, M., 105
Nixon, Robert, 99–102
Northampton, Lord, 167
Nostradamus (Michel de Notredame), 95, 103, 112, 115–18, 212
Nuagat, Modha, 62
Nubia, 21
Numerology, 109
Nut-Amon, 17

Obara, Nobichiko, 234
Oberkirch, Baronne Henriette Louise, 106–7, 108
Octavian, 27–30
Ogham, 55
Old Babylonian Inscriptions (Hilprecht), 203
Olympias, 24
Omens, 208–11
O'Morgain, St. Malachy, 88–94, 95, 228
Opus Majus (Bacon), 144
Oracles, 13, 21, 27, 28–29, 35, 38, 39–52, 69–71, 82
Origen, 13, 247
Orléans, Duc d', 106
Oswald, Lee, 225
Otho, Emperor, 34, 37
Ovates, 55–56

Padmasambhava, 76
Paget, Lady Muriel, 215, 216, 217

Paranazin, 87
Parapsychology, 246
Pasquerel, Jean, 96, 97
Paul III, Pope, 119
Paul VI, Pope, 94
Pausanius, 50
Pearce, A. J., 80–81
Penthièvre, Duc de, 110
Perceval, Spencer, 207, 208
Percy, Lord, 166, 167
Persia, astrology in, 11; prophecy in, 79
Pétion de Villeneuve, Jérôme, 107, 108
Philip Augustus, King, 151
Pickford, Mary, 223
Piglheim, Bruno, 212, 213, 214, 215
Piglheim, Frau Bruno, 212, 213
Piscotta, Gaspare, 179
Pius VII, Pope, 93
Pius XII, Pope, 93
Plato, 12, 51, 52–53
Pliny, 54
Plotinus, 38
Plutarch, 40, 47, 52
Poemandre, 15
Polo, Marco, 81
Poltergeist, 174
Polycrates, 48
Polygnotus, 39
Porphyry, 38
Potiorek, Oskar, 175
Prayer wheels, 68
Precognition, 239–48
Prel, Baron Karl du, 214, 215
Premonitions, 190
Priests and priesthood: Druids, 54–67; Egyptian, 11, 14, 16
Princip, Gavrilo, 181
Prognostications, 143–44
Prophecy of the White King and Dreadful Deadman Explained, A (Lilly), 113
Prydan, 54
Ptolemy, 37, 157, 247–48
Ptolemy Philadelphus, 77
Punt, 20
Puységur, Marquis de, 108, 109
Pythagoras, 54, 55
Pythia, 36, 39, 40, 41–43, 44–45, 46

Quetzalcoatl, 84

Radcliffe, Charles, 188
Radcliffe, Charlotte, 188
Radcliffe, James, 188
Raman, Professor, 236–37
Rawlinson, Henry Creswicke, 201
Raynes, Mary, 192–93
Recherches sur les Poissons Fossiles (Agassiz), 202
Red touring car, curse of, 174–76

Index

Rehk-get-Amon, 13
Reinke, René, 212, 213, 214
Rhine, J. B., 194
Rhine, Louisa, 194, 242, 244, 246
Rich, Irene, 223
Richard I, King, 66, 151
Richter, Baron Charles de, 194–95
Riley, Russell, 226
Rimpoche, Pu-ton, 71–72
Riviere, Raymond Briton, 209
Riviere, William, 209
Robert the Devil, Duke, 206–7
Romaine, James, 193
Rome, augury in ancient, 25–38
Roosevelt, Franklin Delano, 225
Roucher, Jean Antoine, 105, 106
Rousset, Richard, 103
Rubáiyát (Khayyám), 243
Rudolf, Crown Prince, 180
Rudolph II, Emperor, 157

Sabir, Abu, 183, 184
St. Bartholomew's Day massacre, 121
Saint-Charles, M., 107
St. John, Anne, 101
St. John Montagu, Charles, 210
St. John Montagu, Nell, 209–11
St. Remy, Jean de, 116
Sayce, Archibald Henry, 200
Scapulimancy, 56
Scharnhorst (German warship), curse of, 176–78
Schopenhauer, Arthur, 172
Scot, Michael, 243
Scotland, 63
Seaforth, Countess of, 134–36, 137
Seaforth, Lord, 137, 138, 205–6
Selenus, 35
Seneca, 77
Sennacherib, 14
Sesostris II, 15
Severus, Septimius, 38
Shakespeare, William, 39
Shar-tse-Khampo, 70
Shastri, Lal Bahadur, 226, 236
Shearer, Norma, 223
Sherborne, Sir Edward, 156
Sheridan, Clare Frewen, 186, 187
Sheridan family, curse of, 186–87
Shipton, Tobias, 164
Shipton, Ursula (Mother Shipton), 163–70
Sibylline Books, 26–27
Siculus, Diodorus, 22, 54, 56, 78
Sion, Llewellyn, 54
Siphnians, 46
Sixth sense, 239–48
Sixtus V, Pope, 117
Snefru, 19, 20
Socrates, 51
Solon, 48
Sophie, Duchess d'Alençon, 180
Sophocles, 41
Sortes Praenestinae, 32, 34–35
Sortes Virgilianae, 154–55
Southill, Agatha, 163
Specious present, 241
Spirits, 13–14
Spottiswood, John, 140
Spring and Autumn Annals, 83
Spurinna, Vestricius, 25, 26
Sputnik I, 227
Srkis, Dr., 175
Stahlberg, Kaarlo Jubho, 218
Stanley, John Constantine, 53, 205
Stannville, Marshal de, 108–9
Stead, W. T., 218
Stevenson, Robert Louis, 201–2
Stock market crash of 1929, 234
Stonehenge, 59
Strabo, 22, 23, 55
Strange Case of Dr. Jekyll and Mr. Hyde, The (Stevenson), 202
Streeter, Edward, 185
Stroheim, Erich von, 223
Strype, John, 144
Subconscious mind, 189, 248
Suetonius, 25, 28, 37
Suffolk, Duke of, 166–67
Sujujin, 80
Suleiman the Magnificent, 124
Sung-Chyongma, Lhamo, 70

Tacitus, 60
Taharka, 16
Tajao, 80
Tanuat-Amon, 16–17
Tashi Lama, 72
Tashil-hunpo, Lama, 71
Tatian, 13
Tavernier, Jean Baptiste, 181
Tay Bridge catastrophe, 192
Teachings of Amenhotep, 201
Telepathy, 74
Tenhaeff, W. H. C., 245–46
Tersidas, 50–51
Tertullian, 13
Thalberg, Irving, 223
Thales, 48, 52
Thebes, Egypt, 14, 22
Theogenes, 28
Thomas the Rhymer, 140–42
Thoth (Hermes Trismegistus) 15, 18, 21–22, 30, 92, 246–47
Thracian oracle, 28
Thrasyllus, 31–32, 35
Thucydides, 46–47
Thutmose II, 20
Thutmose IV, 16, 21
Tiberius, Emperor, 31–32, 36

Tibet, prophecy in, 68–77
Tiburtine Sibyl, 29–30
Timagenes, 54
Timarchus, 51–52
Tirpitz (German warship), 178
Torquemada, Juan de, 85
Treatise on the Astrolabe, The (Chaucer), 144
Trogus, Pompeius, 55
Trophonius oracle, 39, 50
Truchon, M., 110
Truman, Harry S., 225
Tsaphuwa, 75–76
Tspia, Lama, 72
Tum-mo, 74
Turrel, 103
Twain, Mark, 223
Tying, 14, 172, 173
Typhon, 12

Uachat, 17
Ulster King at Arms: Family Romance (Burke), 141
Umberto, King, 219
United Nations, 237

Vedas, 83
Vercingetorix, 58–59
Vespasian, Emperor, 33, 34–35
Vetsera, Baroness Maria, 180
Vicq d'Azyr, Félix, 105, 106
Victoria, Queen, 142, 219, 220
Villiers, George, 155, 156
Vitellius, 37
Vitruvius, 30, 77
Vivonne de la Châtaignerie, François de, 119
Voltaire, 123
Voorschouw, De (Tenhaeff), 245
Vopiscus, 57
Vortigern, King, 59–60, 64

Waddell, L. A., 68, 71
Wade, Marshal, 239
Wales, 63, 67
Wallenstein, Albrecht W. E. von, 157
Walpole, Robert, 188
Walters, Lucy, 137
Waratah, SS, 191–92
Wilhelm Franz Karl, Archduke, 180
William IV, King, 221
William Charles Ferdinand, Duke, 185
William of Orange, 100, 159
William Rufus, 65–66, 150
William the Conqueror, 65, 149–50, 206–7
Williams, John, 207–8
Wilson, Secretary, 145
Wimmer, Dr., 214
Wings of Myrahi (Demys), 40
Witches, warnings of, 161–70
Wolsey, Thomas Cardinal, 166, 167
Wood Dragon War, 68
Woodhouse, John, 156
Woodruff, Maurice, 236
Woody (King), 236
World War, Second, 233, 237–38
Wotton, Sir Henry, 157
Wu Ting, 81–82

Xochiquetzal, 84

Yao, Emperor, 81
Yates, Roger, 192
Ye-lü Ch'u-ts'ai, 80
York, Duke of, 221
Yorke, Gerald, 185–86
Youngden, Mr., 73
Younghusband, Francis, 68

Zodiac, 80
Zubata, Salma, 183